Notebooks/memoirs/
archives

Notebooks/memoirs/ archives

Reading and Rereading Doris Lessing

Edited by
Jenny Taylor

Routledge & Kegan Paul
Boston, London, Melbourne and Henley

First published in 1982
by Routledge & Kegan Paul Ltd
9 Park Street, Boston, Mass. 02108, USA,
39 Store Street, London WC1E 7DD,
296 Beaconsfield Parade, Middle Park,
Melbourne, 3206, Australia, and
Broadway House, Newtown Road,
Henley-on-Thames, Oxon RG9 1EN
Photoset in 10 on 12 Bembo by
Kelly Typesetting Ltd, Bradford-on-Avon, Wiltshire
and printed in the United States of America

Library of Congress Cataloging in Publication Data

Reading and rereading Doris Lessing.
Bibliography: p.
Includes index.
1. Lessing, Doris May, 1919–   – Criticism
and interpretation – Addresses, essays,
lectures. I. Taylor, Jenny, 1949–   .
PR6023.E833Z86   823'.914   82–5476

ISBN 0–7100–9033–1   AACR2
ISBN 0–7100–9034–X (pbk)

We who write are survivors.

Tillie Olsen

Ex Africa comes something old and stubborn, whose essence remains the same despite the various literary forms it uses as mask. Ex white Africa that is, for I have not yet read work by a coloured writer from Africa which shows even a trace of a certain attitude towards the country itself, and which is the emotional impulse behind nearly all white writing.

It is a nostalgia, a hunger, a reaching out for something lost; hard to define but instantly recognisable . . . Guilt, is it? The unease of those forced to divide themselves between two cultures and pay allegiance to both? Whatever the cause, the result is there, and to be seen nowhere more clearly than in the work of Mr. Van der Post . . .

But this book . . . is mainly valuable because of its conscious crystalisation of the white man's malaise, an unappeasable hunger for what is out of reach. All white-African literature is the literature of exile: not from Europe, but from Africa.

Mr. Van der Post has fallen under the spell of persuasive Papa Jung . . . very easy for us exiles to succumb, bedeviled as we are by that 'nameless something' which ties our umbilical cords fast to the contingent . . . No accident that the Jungians have found so much grist in the literary mills of Africa; vast spaces, hinterlands and the nameless can so easily be archetyped into sympathetic symbols. And I could wish Mr. Van der Post treated the unconscious with a little more sceptical respect: it is at least possible that our nostalgias could have more simple causes than he believes . . . An African once said to me that beyond all the white man's more obvious crimes in Africa there was the unforgivable one that 'even the best of you use Africa as a peg to hang your egos on'. To this charge Mr. Van der Post is open. So are all the rest of us.

Doris Lessing

Contents

Biographical notes ix

Acknowledgments xii

1 Introduction: situating reading 1
 Jenny Taylor
2 Reading *The Golden Notebook* in 1962 43
 Jean McCrindle
3 Yesterday's heroines: on rereading Lessing
 and de Beauvoir 57
 Elizabeth Wilson
4 Of mud and other matter – *The Children of Violence* 75
 Nicole Ward Jouve
5 Towards a narrative analysis of *A Man and Two Women* 135
 Margaret Atack
6 The more recent writings: sufism, mysticism and
 politics 164
 Ann Scott
7 'If you mate a swan and a gander, who will ride?' 191
 Marsha Rowe
8 Doris Lessing: exile and exception 206
 Rebecca O'Rourke
9 *Memoirs* was made of this: an interview with
 David Gladwell, director of *Memoirs of a Survivor* 227
 Jenny Taylor

Select bibliography of Lessing criticism 241

Index 245

Biographical notes

Margaret Atack was born in 1948, and studied French at University College, London. She has held temporary posts in the Universities of London, Southampton and Cardiff and now lectures in the Department of French at Leeds University. Her other research interests include the study of the narrative structures of French Resistance fiction.

Jean McCrindle was born in Birmingham, in 1937, was educated in London and read history at St Andrew's University, Scotland. She was Tutor-Organiser for the Workers' Educational Association in Scotland and then taught in the Extra-Mural Department of the University of Ghana, West Africa. Her daughter Claire was born in 1967 and since then she has taught liberal studies in colleges of art and further education and now teaches history and politics at the trade union college, Northern College, in South Yorkshire. She has been an active socialist and involved in the feminist movement all her life and is the co-editor, with Sheila Rowbotham, of *Dutiful Daughters*.

Rebecca O'Rourke was born in 1955, in Manchester. She read English at Hull University and studied at the Centre for Contemporary Cultural Studies at Birmingham University for four years. She is currently working in the Adult Education Department at Leeds University, and is completing a PhD on contemporary women novelists. She has been involved in the Women's Liberation Movement for a number of years.

Marsha Rowe was born in 1944, in Sydney. She left Australia in

1969, lived in London from 1970 to 1975, and has lived in Leeds since 1977. She was a founder editor of *Spare Rib* and has edited an anthology of its first years, due to be published in 1982. She has a daughter, born in January 1980.

Ann Scott was born in London, in 1950, and read history at Girton College, Cambridge. She was secretary of *The Black Dwarf* in 1968–9, and later edited the news pages of *Spare Rib* for two years. In 1980 she published, with Ruth First, a full-length biography of the nineteenth-century South African feminist and novelist Olive Schreiner, and is now completing a PhD on psychoanalytic accounts of mysticism at Kings College, London. She also teaches a course on psychoanalysis and female identity for the Extra-Mural Department of London University.

Jenny Taylor was born in London, in 1949, and read English at York University. She taught Communications in colleges of further education for several years before embarking on post-graduate research at Warwick University. She has also taught in the Leeds University Extra-Mural Department and for the Open University, and currently teaches Cultural Studies at Bradford University. She is on the editorial board of *Formations*, a forth-coming journal of Marxist-feminist cultural theory and practice, and is writing a book about the sensation novel of the 1860s.

Nicole Ward Jouve was born in Marseilles and studied at the École Normale Supérieure de Sèvres, Paris, and the Sorbonne. She taught at Cambridge University from 1962 to 1963 and is currently a senior lecturer in the Department of English and Related Literature at York University. She has also been a visiting professor in the Department of Romance Languages, University of Alberta, Canada, and the Department of English, Paris III, Sorbonne Nouvelle. She is married to the writer Antony Ward and has three children. Her other publications include *Baudelaire, A Fire to Conquer Darkness* (Macmillan, 1980), 'The Prison-House of Language: *La Chartreuse de parme* and the *Heart of Midlothian*' in *Comparative Criticism*, ed E. Shaffer (Cambridge University Press, 1981), and two novels, *Le Spectre du gris* (Editions des Femmes, 1977) translated by herself as *Shades of Grey* (Virago, 1981), and *L'Entremise* (Editions des Femmes, 1980). She has also

published texts of fiction and essays in *Femmes en mouvement,
Sorcières, Bananas, Fountains*, and *Granta*, and co-edited the
Special Contemporary French issue of *Bananas*, December 1980.

Elizabeth Wilson teaches Social Work and Social Policy at the
Polytechnic of North London. She has published three books:
Women and the Welfare State (Tavistock Publications, 1977), *Only
Halfway to Paradise: Women in Britain 1945–68* (Tavistock Publi-
cations, 1980) and *Mirror Writing* (Virago, 1982). She has also
published a number of articles, including 'Women in the Community' in *Women in the Community*, ed. Marjorie Mayo (Routledge & Kegan Paul, 1977), 'The Political Economy of Welfare',
New Left Review, 122, July/August 1980, 'Psychoanalysis:
Psychic Law and Order', *Feminist Review*, 8, summer 1981. She is
active in the Women's Movement, is on the editorial collectives of
Feminist Review and *Critical Social Policy* and is at present writing a
book on Simone de Beauvoir.

Acknowledgments

Extracts from the following works are reprinted by permission which is gratefully acknowledged: *Going Home*, copyright © Doris Lessing 1957; reprinted by kind permission of Curtis Brown Ltd, on behalf of Doris Lessing and of Michael Joseph. *The Golden Notebook* copyright © Doris Lessing 1962; reprinted by permission of Michael Joseph and Simon & Schuster, a Division of Gulf and Western Corporation. *Martha Quest* copyright © Doris Lessing 1964; reprinted by permission of Granada Publishing Ltd and Simon & Schuster, a Division of Gulf and Western Corporation. *Landlocked* copyright © Doris Lessing 1966; reprinted by permission of Granada Publishing Ltd and Simon & Schuster, a Division of Gulf and Western Corporation. *The Four-Gated City* copyright © Doris Lessing 1969; reprinted by permission of Granada Publishing Ltd and Alfred A. Knopf, Inc., New York.

Above all, I would like to thank the contributors for their patient and good-humoured support, co-operation and criticism in producing this book, Philippa Brewster for advising and encouraging the project, and Vera Hawley and Beverley Toulson for typing much of the manuscript. Thanks also to Gina Bruce, John Goode, Dave Laing, Terry Lovell, Francis Mulhern, Griselda Pollock and Janet Wolff for reading and criticising the introduction, and to Sarah Benton, Joan Bourne, Tony Bryant, Steve Burniston, Margot Heinemann, Alan Lovell, Peter Sedgewick and E. P. Thompson for providing information. I am grateful for their help; the responsibility for any shortcomings is entirely my own.

Jenny Taylor

1 Introduction: situating reading

Jenny Taylor

I

This 'Chinese box' arrangement is similar to Brecht's 'alienation technique' on the stage. Miss Lessing is struggling towards complete honesty through a thicket of stock reactions and counter-reactions, political, emotional and artistic. Only by removing herself by more than the conventional step away from her source material has she any hope of seeing it clearly. This enables her, too, to embody within a coherent fictional framework the sort of elements that are normally inimical to form: a critique of literature (partly through parody): of society's reaction to literature and of the society that gave birth to it. In doing so she achieves precisely that 'intellectual and moral passion' that Anna named as the prerequisite of the only sort of fiction worth writing, and her fiction proves her to be, in my opinion, not only the best *woman* novelist we have, but one of the most serious and intelligent and honest writers of the whole post-war generation.

Here Jeremy Brooks, reviewing *The Golden Notebook* in the *Sunday Times* in April 1962,[1] hands laurels to Doris Lessing. This perceptive review draws out the different ways that *The Golden Notebook* confronted the situation of the post-war writer and the crisis of writing in Britain in the late 1950s and early 1960s. It suggests that the position of the novel – its production and its audience – was linked with the specific problems of realist writing at that moment. It connects this with the social position and political stance of the novelist herself and demonstrates how ideological questions about how and for whom one writes which face the committed writer cannot be separated from questions of form. It stresses that this involves a process of both personal and political self examination; that subjectivity is central to the novel's aesthetic and political significance.

However, Jeremy Brooks's review was not typical of critics' response to *The Golden Notebook* when it first appeared. Many could get no purchase on the book at all, some saw it as a muddled failure, a sign of premature decline, a castrating threat – even Brooks's favourable remarks suggest something about the author's position by placing her ambiguously within a certain cultural formation and in a particular critical canon. Lessing had already become established as both a popular and serious writer by the time *The Golden Notebook* came out. Her reputation rested primarily on her status as a radical white Rhodesian exile and a committed realist writer. Her African writing offered both a satire of the crumbling Empire's expatriate delusions and of the 'sickness of dissolution' of Rhodesian white supremacy to a liberal English readership. And it was seen to import into the decentred metropolitan cultural configuration of the 1950s a wild and exotic innocence and the experience of another world. It provided what Lessing herself ascribed to the Angry Young Men – 'an injection of vitality into the withered arm of British literature',[2] and though she was part of a wider movement from periphery to absent centre, promoted through a dominant realist tradition, she arrived by her own particular route.

Yet the critical establishment's response to Lessing's work was often uneasy – she was celebrated as a strong new talent, but with qualifications. *The Grass is Singing*, clearly a novel which typified the social relations of apartheid, was described as 'a serious study of a woman's moral disintegration set starkly down . . . a powerful and bitter book', in the *Times Literary Supplement*, in April 1950,[3] while the reception of *Five* in 1953 was more ambivalent. The *New Statesman* had Lessing clearly categorised as an anti-colonial colonial: 'When she is writing of the subject that has claimed her, that of race relations in Africa, Miss Lessing often gives the impression that she is practising to write a masterpiece'[4] – yet this was a state of becoming rather than being. But after a while, reviewers further to the right rather peevishly asked, didn't this harping on about racial inequality become rather a bore? *The Times* included a discussion of *Five* in a review of new colonial novels entitled 'Local Colour', the critic remarking:

> The market for books about the colour question is apparently still buoyant. Scarcely a month goes by without its account of life in the Caribbean or in various parts of Africa . . . Miss Doris Lessing still seems to prefer the drab fringes of squalor to the bright light which shone in *This Was the Old Chief's Country*. The delight which she . . . took in the topography and climate of her native country is giving place to a thoroughly competent reporting of social evils of all kinds which comes near to journalism.[5]

While the following day, in the *Sunday Times*, J. W. Lambert took exception to:

> Miss Lessing's exceptional fondness for piling on the agony. As her earlier African books have made plain, Miss Lessing is a powerful writer, her narrative flows with such impetus and colour that it is never dull or gloomy, yet after a while her inexorable concentration on oppression, failure and weakness builds up resistance in the reader.[6]

Committed colonial writing, particularly when explicitly political, was only acceptable within certain limits. The mythic and allegorical ramifications of Lessing's early work was recognised primarily as a form of defamiliarisation that revitalised realism.

Ambivalence over how to place Lessing's writing emerged even more strongly when she was read as a woman writer who wrote about women. Here critics' reactions were confused – often hostile. They cast around for points of reference: D. H. Lawrence being an 'exemplar' often invoked. C. P. Snow (a very prestigious reviewer) admired the implied author's critical distance from her protagonist in his review of *Martha Quest*, 'Frustrations on the Veldt', in the *Sunday Times*, November 1952:

> It is a truth of a young girl's temperament; a girl clever, passionate, suspicious, shot through with resentment . . . Miss Lessing often plays down any glimmer of charity or tenderness . . . the reader has to supply much for himself in order to find out what [Martha] is really like.[7]

While in the same paper, in September 1954, *A Proper Marriage* produced the opposite reading from J. W. Lambert:

> A rich crop of satirical sketches flower, but there is too much tea table gynaecology. . . The real failing of a book with so many excellent things in it lies at its centre . . . the episodic story is presented from Martha's point of view, so much so that it could be told in the first person. And with Martha Miss Lessing is noticeably lenient; true, ironic comedy arises from her discovery that life seldom ratifies the theories that she is accustomed to take from books, but chips on the shoulder make poor substitute for prolonged acquaintance, she remains only a disagreeable young woman.[8]

Martha's passage through the roles of young girl and mother produced the very attitudes in the critics here quoted that the narrative itself seemed to question; moreover, existential journeys didn't often involve childbirth in the 1950s. By the publication of *The Golden Notebook*, in 1962, this ambivalence had crystallised into Brooks's final clause – 'not only the best *woman* novelist we have, but one of the most serious and intelligent and honest writers of the whole post-war generation.' Here are two categories, defined by gender or generation; Lessing has transgressed the boundary between them but they remain differentiated. And Brooks made sense of the novel by placing it within an explicitly socialist aesthetic and political tradition. The alienation technique and the use of montage, the way in which the novel 'lays bare the device' of the conditions of its own production, recall not only the work of Brecht but the debates of the Russian Formalists, and the writings of Walter Benjamin. Yet at the same time the stress on 'coherence', the way that the novel works towards resolving contradictions, creating a totality out of juxtaposed and disjointed elements, places it within the Utopian humanist framework of Morris, of Belinsky, of Lukács. In the terms of this review, *The Golden Notebook*, paradoxically, both subverts its status as Literature while securing its author as Artist.

'Not only the best *woman* novelist we have, but one of the most serious and intelligent and honest writers of the whole post-war generation.' An ideal blurb for the back cover of a paperback edition. Lessing's bulky novels and volumes of short stories were widely promoted through the 1960s and 1970s; they have now been gathered together into an *oeuvre*, achieving both inter-national and classic status. With the so-called 'sexual revolution' of the 1960s and the re-emerging Women's Movement, a public, particularly of women, constituted itself around her work which was, and is, widely read and discussed. For women who found reading and discussing novels an important reference-point, often a crucial form of self-perception and analysis, Doris Lessing loomed up – wherever one looked, she seemed to be waiting. The first four volumes of *The Children of Violence*, structured around the homologous relation between individual and social identity, and uneasily combining critical realism (the historical relationship between the individual and the social collective), and allegory (the mythic relationship between the individual and the 'collective unconscious'), was not simply promoted as the epic, archetypal story of our time, but was read, often compulsively, as proto-typical. But what processes are explored? *The Children of Violence* sequence involves a range of fictional and ideological contradic-tions. The narrative clearly refers back to the conventions of nineteenth-century realism, a mode which Lessing herself linked both with political commitment and the 'world-view' of liberal humanism in the 1950s. Yet within those terms, the resources of those conventions cannot 'transcend' the experience of dissolu-tion, exile and displacement which they represent, despite the implied totalising sweep of the narrative. There is a gap, which grows wider, between the presentation of the protagonist's con-sciousness and the omniscient narrative persona speaking the 'truth' from the standpoint of wisdom. The concerns of critical realism are there: the individual moves through the social world, through prescribed roles, in the quest for an authentic self, for freedom and knowledge, and, in the process, particularly through the specific position of women, calls the power struc-tures of that world into question – yet without being able to offer a personal or a political solution. This process is ambiguous – the liberal myth of the naturally free individual is doubly undercut. Both by social-historical forces of violence and power: in the family, in the divided, racist, disintegrating community, in the distant European war, and by a transcendent impersonal Nature – in Martha's sexuality, in the landscape.

This tension is an extension of a familiar literary history. The motif of the marginal observer whose ambiguous and interstitial position foregrounds contradictions within both society and the self, and where power and desire are reinforced through absence, becoming transformed into mythic or transcendent forces, is certainly not unique to Lessing. The work of Charlotte Brontë, Thomas Hardy, and D. H. Lawrence, for example, in different ways suggest comparable concerns. And the *Children of Violence* sequence describes a process, though it's presented as a product. The narrative traces the history of Martha Quest's consciousness, and the progress of her soul, but within the sequence – published between 1952 and 1969 – the implied conceptions of history, consciousness and progress shift. It's difficult to locate a precise moment of rupture though, as it's bound up with the question of how to represent the 'fantastic realities' of the present. Increasingly, explicit forms of fabulation and manifestations of unreason and transgression – dreams, visions, a gamut of disturbed or violent psychic states – press up against the realistic narrative, but they never quite operate as a Gothic or uncanny subversion of it. The most obvious break in the sequence is between the first four volumes and *The Four-Gated City*, which follows Martha's move to England, her shock encounter with mass society and the accelerating contradictions of late capitalism, her decentring as individual agent. The narrative moves from the reconstruction of history, into extrapolation into the future and the 'destiny' of the culmination of both natural and social forces of violence in the nuclear holocaust, which signifies both apocalyptic metaphor leading to revelation, and material threat.

Yet this, and the more recent writings, *The Memoirs of a Survivor* and *Canopus in Argos – Archives*, still work at and within the boundaries of liberal humanism. The metaphors grow increasingly transcendental, cosmic or atavistic, yet the universe remains one of a sceptical moralist. All are fictional explorations within a loosely defined mode of speculative writing which can operate both as a dystopian satire on the trends of the present through a process of cognitive estrangement, and self-consciously as a sign of disengagement from the historical world of empirical sense-experience. They represent a continuing struggle to break with the realist canon, a way into new literariness and fictiveness, explorations of narrative and myth, projections of Utopian 'new wholes' from the standpoint of the present. But Lessing's recent fiction also follows fissures within the canon itself, demonstrating just how unstable the categories are. Paradoxically, the work draws on marginalised, subversive forms as they become the new centre of critical interest developing the mainstream tradition of the novel itself. As a well-established professional writer, Lessing has gained a space to write experimentally, and to speculate on the origins of creativity, traditions and individual talents. A brave leap into the unknown? Or a retreat to innocence? An exploration and subversion of mythology? Or a relapse into superstition, a search for a lost order?

That space has partly been created by the accumulating reputation of *The Golden Notebook*. The novel is the stage where the formal and ideological contradictions of both realism and liberal humanism are most explicitly acted out and the position of the self-conscious, angst-ridden, isolated woman artist debated. In examining the conditions of its own production and consumption, and, in the process, exploring the boundaries of fiction itself, it works complexly as a fictional, historical and discursive text. Yet while *The Golden Notebook* has subsequently been claimed by the critical establishment primarily for its formal convolutions as a post-war problematic novel, the occasion of its production and reception was more embroiled. 'Now and again there appears a novel which opens up a new world not by revealing what is strange but by revealing what is familiar,' George Orwell once wrote of *Ulysses*. He claimed Joyce's 'real achievement was to get the familiar onto paper. He dared – for it is a matter of daring as much as technique – to expose . . . the inner mind and in doing so discovered an America that was under everybody's nose.'[9] *The Golden Notebook* had a comparable effect – only the 'England' that was under everybody's nose, constructed from expatriate distance, was at home in the kitchen. The analogy with Joyce is a loose one, however. *The Golden Notebook* primarily addresses the question of realism – of how to assimilate 'reality' while 'telling it like it is', but not by radically subverting language itself, though constantly encountering its limit. Structurally, it is an enigmatic novel. The central protagonist, Anna Wulf, is in all senses a problematic heroine – a fiction written out of the notebooks that she writes, and an impossible figure since the 'reality' and time scale of the notebooks places them in an ambiguous relation to *Free Women*, the main novel within the novel. The text, paradoxically, both operates within and frustrates a consistent history based on the unilinear progression of narrative time in raising questions that it finally attempts to resolve in the golden notebook by fictionally constructing a kind of mid-Atlantic androgyny.

Yet it was the ideological contradictions of *The Golden Notebook*, rather than their final resolutions, that acted on its readers. Thirteen years before, in 1949, Simone de Beauvoir had both questioned and extended existential humanism by raising the problematic position of women within it, in *The Second Sex*. Her analysis of the cultural, mythic conventions through which Man is constructed as the absolute human type against which women are measured and defined through being constructed as Other, the bearers rather than the makers of meaning, was itself written from an implied position that seemed to bind women back into difference – into the place assigned them of relative roles on the margins of male society. *The Second Sex* concluded with a discussion of the double bind in which the 'independent woman' in particular was caught by focusing on the ontological problems of integrating work and an authentic subjectivity. 'The woman who is economically emancipated from man is not, for all that, in a moral, social and psychological universe identical to that of a man,' she argued. 'The way she carries on her profession and her devotion to it depends on the context provided by the total pattern of her life.'[10] Writing some time before the 'sexual revolution' of the 1960s, de Beauvoir located the problem in the structure of the family and the organisation of work and the conflicted way that 'independent women' experienced themselves against the two. Inasmuch as the only acceptable place for woman was the family, she went on, and sexuality subordinated to reproduction, the 'free woman' is exiled from both home and work and, as such, is a meaningless figure. And it is above all the exercise of her sexuality – its recognition by others and by herself – that becomes the site of conflict and difficulty. But for de Beauvoir this was a symptom of something else:

> The advantage man enjoys . . . is that his vocation as a human being in no way runs counter to his destiny as a male . . . He is not divided. Whereas it is required of woman that in order to realise her femininity, she must make herself object and prey,

which is to say that she must renounce her claim as sovereign subject. It is this conflict that especially marks the situation of the emancipated woman. She refuses to confine herself to her role as female, because she will not accept mutilation; but it would also be a mutilation to repudiate her sex. Man is a human being with sexuality; woman is a complete individual, equal to the male, only if she too is a human being with sexuality. To renounce her sexuality is to renounce part of her humanity.[11]

The Golden Notebook was first read within this context of a renascent feminism, and extended it. But it was also a move away from it – and in the context of the contemporary Women's Movement the novel certainly isn't an explicitly feminist text. Anna Wulf produces alternative selves through writing – yet finally loses individual female selfhood through the breakdown of individual subjectivity, and the acceptance of mythic archetypes. Yet Anna Wulf, the woman writer with money and a room of her own, is still subjected to her own subjectivity and to the forces of literary production – she cannot write.

Why were these different writings produced when they were? Why there, and why in that way? Doris Lessing's fiction demonstrates particularly sharply the intricate ways in which a writer is produced and reproduced within a cultural formation, often by drawing on forms apparently outside it. It emphasises not only the complex relation between author, text and reader, but also the different contexts and settings through which meaning is both constructed and made active by different readers' own subjectivity and social position. This process is fluid – there is no fixed author or reader. But neither is it arbitrary or infinite. And Lessing's own changing position and attitudes as writer and producer are part of this process and are situated within specific contexts.

In the 1950s (I shall return to this) Lessing's concept of the role of the committed writer, and of the relationship between writer and audience, seemed optimistic. In some respects it corresponded to the notion of the relative social position between writer and audience that Sartre had identified in the rise of liberal humanism in the first half of the nineteenth century – though the conditions were those of the post-war world and Lessing was writing from an explicitly socialist perspective. At that time, she saw the individual writer, 'the small personal voice', as not only morally privileged by her position as 'artist' – 'interpreter of dreams and nightmare', 'architect of the soul' – but also as speaking to a mass audience in a more direct and less mediated way than contemporary workers in the media. But *The Golden Notebook* breaks with this canon while mourning its loss. Paradoxically, it operates both as a critique and a reinforcement of the figure of the isolated artist and the aura of the individual text. Anna's colonial novel of inter-racial romance, *Frontiers of War*, is presented as constantly encroached upon by a predatory and corrupt literary institution and film and television industry – a particular variation on the familiar theme of the alienation of the artist in the face of cultural crisis and social collapse. The committed communist writer is fragmented by the breakdown of the novel and its public into different 'realisms' and different readerships, while attempting to break away from a socialist realism which obliterated subjectivity, on the one hand, and a nihilistic modernism that collapsed everything into subjectivity, on the other. 'Once a pressure or a current has started there is no way of avoiding it: there is no way of not being intensively subjective; it was, if you like, the author's task for that time,'[12] Lessing commented later, still firmly holding on to a particular authorial position. Yet she asserted also: 'But what was intolerable, what really could not be borne any longer, was this monstrously isolated, monstrously narcissistic pedestalled paragon.'[13]

Moreover, *The Golden Notebook* itself, when taken with Lessing's own response to its reception, suggests a more convoluted process. The novel itself is part of a wider sense of split between creation and criticism. With the expansion of the media and higher education, the position of the independent writer was eroded. In addition, the freelance intellectual was undercut by the academic, and the practice of criticism was increasingly centred in the universities. These developments were widely but ineffectually complained about from several political quarters in the post-war period. In *The Golden Notebook* the process of criticism becomes incorporated into the text itself, which loses its innocence. 'If it were shaped the right way it would make its own comment on the conventional novel,' Lessing stressed, 'the debate about the novel that has been going on since the novel was born and is not, as one would imagine from reading contemporary academics, something recent.'[14] And many of her own comments about the confused reception of the novel itself both challenge and reinforce the bohemian conception that success can only be explained by a misunderstanding. In an interview given soon after its publication, in 1964, she remarked:

> The further I'm removed from this area – reviews, the literary gossip shop, the better. I got angry over the reviews of *The Golden Notebook*. They thought it was personal – it was, in parts. But it was also a highly structured book, carefully planned. The point about that book was the relation of its parts to each other. But the book they wanted to turn it into was called *The Confessions of Doris Lessing*.[15]

While in the 1972 preface (written in 1971), she examined the questions raised by the novel both in the context of its immediate reception and in the light of changes in attitudes and normative values during the subsequent ten years, connecting this with ways in which different readers reacted to the novel. She considered its many interpretations and uses; read as indictment of women's oppression, as explication of the crisis of communist commitment, as description of mental breakdown. She asserted that the novel is not ambiguous, that its inner meaning is plain for all to see. Yet she concluded by acknowledging that there can be no single relation between author, text and reader:

> These incidents bring up again questions of what people see when they read a book, and why one person sees one pattern in it and nothing at all of another pattern, and how odd it is to have, as author, such a very clear picture of the book that is seen so very differently by its readers . . . [the novel] is alive and potent and fructifying and able to promote thought and discussion *only* when its plan and shape and intention are not understood, because that moment of seeing the shape and plan and intention is also the moment when there isn't anything more to be got out of it.[16]

Lessing acknowledged that there is an ambiguity between the work as product, gesturing towards 'wholeness' from an already established set of meanings and the text as process, involving the active work of the reader, who proceeds towards a meaning that is inevitably postponed. Yet the paradoxical position of the preface is taken further by its very existence; it tries to put the record straight with the message that there is no message, no straight record. The paradox is unresolved in the later fiction: the apparent openness of speculative forms – fable, myth, space fiction – combine uneasily with their didactic, rhetorical connotations. And it is reinforced by the way that the figure of Doris Lessing has come to be presented – as singular sybil, as oracular voice, as chronicler of past and future history. Consider the covers of the first edition of the *Canopus in Argos – Archives* series alone. The front cover is anonymous, a plain black and white design. The back cover is a full-portrait photo of author as Sage.

The purpose of this collection of essays is not primarily to interpret the 'plan and shape and intention' of Lessing's work, nor to present it as a unity based either on a point of origin or the progression to a known end. Collectively, the essays demonstrate how controversial Lessing's fiction remains, how it is culturally active in different historical and discursive contexts, which involves considering the processes at work in reading itself. All the essays are written by women, and some are specifically concerned with developing a feminist critical practice, others are written from standpoints outside literary criticism altogether. Individually, their aims are very different. In the second part of this introduction, I outline a cultural and political history, within and out of which Lessing's early work was written. The contributions by Jean McCrindle and Elizabeth Wilson are concerned in different ways with examining the changing effect that Lessing's early writing has had on their consciousness as women and as feminists. Jean McCrindle's discussion of reading *The Golden Notebook* in 1962 has been developed out of a talk given at a History Workshop conference. A piece of political and personal history, it examines the subjective effects of the political events of the late 1950s, and how *The Golden Notebook* retrospectively helped her to make sense of them as a woman and political militant. Elizabeth Wilson, on the other hand, looks back at the experience of early reading from a different standpoint in the present. Her essay compares Doris Lessing and Simone de Beauvoir – both seen as rebel heroines in the early 1960s – and she is interested also in how these particular writers became constructed as heroines and exemplars. Nicole Ward Jouve's fascinating and controversial study of the politics of language in *The Children of Violence* is itself an example of a kind of feminist writing that challenges the distinction between creative writing and criticism. Margaret Atack develops an intricate analysis of the narrative structure of the stories in the collection *A Man and Two Women*, looking at the different 'selves' produced within the linguistic structures of the texts. Ann Scott explores 'some of the many meanings encoded in the notion of a turn to mysticism in Lessing's more recent fiction' by analysing the use of explicitly religious language within its own terms from the standpoint of the philosophy of religion, as well as considering its function within the narratives themselves. Marsha Rowe discusses *The Marriages Between Zones Three, Four and Five*, the second volume of the *Canopus in Argos* series, looking at the implications of applying different interpretative frameworks to the text. Rebecca O'Rourke takes up some of the questions raised in this introduction about Lessing's position as a colonial writer within the cultural formation, but develops this in the context of a wider discussion of the determinants of post-war women's writing. Finally, an interview with David Gladwell, director of the film *Memoirs of a Survivor*, briefly explores some of the processes involved in translating a literary text into a film.

II

To lead into Jean McCrindle's discussion of reading *The Golden Notebook* in 1962, these introductory notes will briefly indicate the contradictory ways that Doris Lessing was positioned within a range of cultural and political debates within the Left in the 1950s. The publication of *The Golden Notebook* in 1962 is the cut-off point, and this survey will situate the novel, which partly develops out of the discursive framework of these debates. One of the ways that the novel must be read, and undoubtedly was read at the time, is as an explicitly political novel which contains within it a discussion of its own position and status as a cultural object. It refers to and intervenes in the political and cultural impasse of the communist movement in the immediate post-war period, which had been developing through the 1940s and of which *The Golden Notebook* itself is one, very specific, symptom. Lessing's own strictures about reading the novel as a set of political and personal confessions must be taken seriously – but the various preconditions that prompted the novel both to be read and, in part, to be written as a confession, need to be considered: the ways in which that moment was represented are also the conventions through which Lessing wrote and transformed that history into allegory in *The Golden Notebook* itself. The novel isn't autobiographical in any straightforward way – its author's specific history and aspirations as a writer form a component in a range of aesthetic and political debates in the 1950s on the Left, converging around the question of the role and position of the writer and intellectual, on the relationship between political commitment and realist writing, and how both might be defined. In 1949, the year that Lessing arrived in Britain, Sartre argued in *What is Literature?* that the situation of the French writer was necessarily one of *engagement*, though its context and articulation remained problematic. For the British humanist intellectual in the 1950s, the situation and contradictions were very different, and Lessing, as a colonial woman writer, holds a specific place within them as well as a complex relation to them.

'Realism is an issue not only for literature: it is a major political issue and must be treated as such,'[17] Brecht wrote in the 1930s. The debates around realism, disputed throughout literary theory, have never been so embroiled as in Marxist circles, where they are closely linked to questions of the position of the writer in relation to party and class formations, of political commitment and viable intervention. 'Realism' has strong ideological connotations in all critical contexts, of course, but in overtly political *milieux* – most notably in the case of socialist realism – more than aesthetics is explicitly at stake. One of the reasons for the passion generated over realism is that it is both a descriptive and a prescriptive term, which simultaneously examines certain practices and assesses them, often by reference to different implied epistemologies and 'world views'. And although any realist practice need not necessarily presuppose a political position or epistemology, political views can certainly lead to the adoption of particular realist aesthetics. An important distinction (though one that is often blurred in practice) is between realism as a style – that is, a set of representational conventions, generally those of verisimilitude – and realism as an attitude – 'telling it like it is', derived from the non-literary sense of the word. They certainly overlap in the debates referred to here, which emerged out of an intricate political and cultural history, stretching back to the Romantics, to the Russian democratic critics, and beyond. But they had been developed within certain parameters, which begged specific questions about the formation of writers and intellectuals within dominant institutions as well as in oppositional groups and marginal cultural circles. The writer, both as artist, intellectual and political agent, was implicitly and profoundly encoded as male – not in any essential sense, but in the inextricable ways that political and cultural codes were articulated. These were also articulated within the framework of both a high cultural and a national literary heritage, which reinforced the figure of the artist as hero. This was premised on the notion of a possible viable symbiosis between the intellectual and class, usually via the party, but which generally assumed that the intellectual held a problematic relation to the class or the oppressed group. Through the 1950s these terms of class, of culture, of the state and of the role of the party shifted radically. And Lessing's position shifted in relation to them, involving varying perceptions of power, privilege and difference from different vantage-points. There are, however, three broad axes: the move from region to metropolis, the crisis of Stalinism and, the least visible, the position of the isolated woman intellectual.

Doris Lessing and her young son arrived in London from Southern Rhodesia, via Capetown, in 1949. It was four years after the end of the Second World War, the Nato alliance was established, the Cold War itself was escalating. It was a moment when a complex of economic, political and cultural forces were to have diverse effects on writers and intellectuals both inside and outside the communist movement. This included both those whose experiences had been formed primarily by the 1930s and the war, and the younger post-war generation. The 1945 Labour government, which had been swept into office on a wave of popular radicalism, had promised full-scale social changes. The Welfare State was developed and expanded, and there was a return to full employment; but women's ideological place in the home and family was stressed, despite their return into the labour market by the early 1950s. However, this immediate post-war radicalism was quickly defused; the Conservatives were re-elected in 1951 – they were to stay in power for the next thirteen years. By the mid-1950s the Tories had become securely established in their role as entrepreneurs of economic expansion, managers of the mixed economy and proclaimers of a new Britishness, uncontested by any coherent class opposition. The ideology of affluence and the myth of classlessness were nonetheless powerful for being myths; they were widely accepted. Domestic quiescence, colonial retraction, and the Cold War on an international level were accompanied by the retrenchment and depoliticisation of intellectual life in the immediate post-war period, and a prevailing apathy – the only approved extremes were either those of ultra-scepticism or passive acceptance. The intellectual reaction against communism that had occurred in the 1940s, the volte-faces of Spender, of Koestler, the confessions of *The God That Failed*,[18] and, though in a more contradictory way, the late writing of Orwell, were referred to as buttresses by both Right and Left.

By 1957 a reaction against this political malaise and the apparent sterility and incoherence of the British national culture itself had developed. It was most loudly proclaimed by the Angry Young Men – themselves a phenomenom displayed by the expanding media as a group, though politically they were heterogeneous. Different types of rhetorical statements were a part of this furore; two of its clearest manifestations were John Osborne's essay in *Declaration* (where Lessing's 'The Small Personal Voice' appeared), 'They Call it Cricket', and Kingsley Amis's Fabian Society pamphlet, 'Socialism and the Intellectuals'. Amis, for example, discussed the different positions and stances of various different categories of intellectuals in the immediate post-war period. He distinguished between academics – particularly those in provincial universities – who had traditionally veered towards the apolitical and the Right, on the one hand, and, on the other, 'the literary and arty man, the writer in the widest sense, the critic, the journalist, the self-employed intelligentsia if you like.'[19] These had formed the basis of the Marxist intelligentsia of the 1930s but, since the early 1940s, they had fallen into pessimism and passive acceptance. This was not only in the overt political response to Stalinism, but also because of structural transformations and ideological lacunae within English intellectual and political institutions. Amis's essay itself concluded with an equally confused reaction to the impasse of Labour Party politics as a viable alternative. It was partly in response to Amis's cynicism that the rising generation of radical intellectuals formulated the post-war impasse in the opening editorial of *Universities and Left Review* (1957):

> The post-war decade was one in which declining political orthodoxies held sway. Every political concept became a weapon in the Cold War of ideas, every idea had its label, every person had his place in the political spectrum, every form of political action appeared – in someone's eyes, a polite treason. Between the high citadel of Stalinist Russia and the 'welfare state – no further' jungle of the mixed economy, there seemed to be nothing but an arid waste.
>
> In these tight, compartmentalised worlds, buttressed by bans and proscriptions, suspicions and fears, supported by texts from Lenin and Stalin, mottoes from Burke and Bagehot, protected by massive armies with nuclear stockpiles and mutually exclusive military pacts, British socialism suffered moral and intellectual eclipse.[20]

Lessing cut across these 'tight, compartmentalised worlds' in Britain by arriving out of a place that was more tight and compartmentalised – Southern Rhodesia. Her position within both mainstream and marginal British cultural formations was, as has been seen, primarily as a colonial writer, revitalising, and contributing to, an already dominant set of realist literary conventions: 'Africa' signifying the exotic and the marvellous – a legitimate otherness. But the specifically political ramifications of her early literary identity are equally important. Lessing didn't arrive in England from an undifferentiated void, and it was both political necessity and literary ambition that drove her to London and an ambiguous place in both the Left and literary intelligentsia as an anti-colonial colonial woman and a self-employed writer, though this initially involved a difficult economic struggle. Her colonial identity also contributed to her passionate and explicit adherence to classic realism both as a style and as a attitude – that of radical liberal humanism – in the 1950s. Her commitment was expressed in 'The Small Personal Voice':

> For me the highest point of literature was the novel of the nineteenth century, the work of Tolstoy, Stendhal, Dostoevsky, Balzac, Turgenev, Chekhov; the work of the

great realists. I define realism as art which springs so naturally
from a strongly-held, though not necessarily intellectually-
defined, view of life, that it absorbs symbolism. I hold the view
that the realist novel, the realist story, is the highest form of
prose writing; higher than and out of reach of any comparison
with expressionism, impressionism, symbolism, naturalism,
or any other ism.[21]

It also meant that the developing cultural and formal contradictions of this position became increasingly urgent, finally to be
embodied and transformed in *The Golden Notebook*.

The directly autobiographical pieces – *Going Home* and *In
Pursuit of the English* – are very much products of the times in
which they were written, as well as of the pasts they represent.
They form part of Lessing's self-construction of a social identity
as a writer, and very different 'Doris Lessings' emerge from the
two accounts. But they are still important reference-points,
refracting and stressing the role that colonialism played in the
construction of a dominant British national identity, though in
the particular historical context of the ramified relations between
the British and Rhodesian states in the 1950s. And this is constantly
related to questions of writing and representation; as a radical
humanist writer, Lessing is formed through absent cultural traditions, yet this poses specific contradictions for an anti-racist white
writing about Africa – in England – and considering emergent
black writing – in Africa. Her reconstructions of her family
history stress the reverberations of British nationality within the
expatriate consciousness; the various myths of 'England' generated by her parents' interstitial position as unsuccessful first-
generation white settlers, as well as her own literary reference-
points and fantasies of metropolitan culture – myths reinforced
through absence and the physical isolation of her parents' farm. *In
Pursuit of the English* is a piece of light satire on Englishness, a
genre that was so fashionable in 1960 when it was published, and
it combined this mode with quasi-Orwellian down-and-out-in-
Capetown-and-London reportage of her early experiences as a
writer. It stressed the displaced sense of 'Englishness' in her early
formation: 'I did learn early on that while the word *English* is
tricky and elusive enough in England, this is nothing to the
variety of meanings it might bear in a colony, self governing or

otherwise.'[22] But earlier in the mid-1950s, the tone is different: England is primarily seen by the colonial as the citadel of radical liberalism – a myth dissipated on actual arrival, where marginality produces a critical distance from the dominant culture, which is then seen as disintegrating. This is the position of 'The Small Personal Voice':

> It is a country so profoundly parochial that people like myself coming in from outside never cease to marvel. Do the British people know that all over what is politely referred to as the Commonwealth, millions of people continually discuss and speculate about their probable reactions to this or that event? No, and if they did, they would not care. . . Does the Labour movement understand that hundreds of thousands of the more intelligent people in the Colonies, people whose awakening has very often been fed by the generous age of British literature – poets like Shelley and Byron and Burns, writers like Dickens – look to them for help and guidance? For the most part, socialists are not very interested in what is going on in the Colonies. . .
>
> Thinking internationally means choosing a particular shade of half-envious, half-patronising emotion to feel about the United States; or collecting money for Hungary, or taking little holidays in Europe, or liking French or Italian films.[23]

While in *Going Home* (1956), Lessing's report on the Federation of Southern and Northern Rhodesia and Nyasaland, sponsored by Tass, the Soviet News Agency, she described the series of 'psychological chances' in her family history which contributed to her increasing distance from the dominant white-settler culture and white Rhodesian nationalist identity founded on pioneer myths and the enforced difference of apartheid. This distance contributed to her rapid politicisation when she moved to Salisbury, at the end of the 1930s. What was important for her at that moment was the overlapping of communism and radical liberalism:

> When I became political, and communist, it was because they were the only people I had ever met who had fought the colour bar in their lives. Very few people did, – not the Labour Party, except for a few individuals – not the 'liberals', the word means

something different there than it does here – and not the members of the churches. But when you joined the communists, you met, for the first time, people of other races, and on equal terms. It was for that reason that the Communist Party had influence; not because of its theories.[24]

Going Home unequivocally poses the options open to the white radical in Southern Rhodesia by the early 1950s – breakdown, assimilation or exile. Moreover, with the banning of the Communist Party in South Africa and, later, the growth of the black nationalist and labour movements, the political validity and effectiveness of white communists was rapidly decimated, particularly during the time between Lessing's departure and her return visit in 1956. During the 1940s the impetus behind Marxist politics in Rhodesia undoubtedly came from outside, with the influx of RAF airmen shaped and sustained by the British communist movement in the 1930s, as well as European exiles (including Lessing's second husband) firmly committed to the official foreign policy of the Soviet Union. But despite its incongruous and marginal political position, the communist group did gain a limited purchase within Southern Rhodesian labour politics through the comparative respectability of the Soviet Union itself after 1941. And although, as a white Rhodesian, twice-divorced communist woman, campaigning for African rights, Lessing must have been an unusual, almost a unique figure, existing, by the late 1940s, in a situation that was politically and psychologically increasingly untenable, she did form part of a vocal minority – though its position could not be sustained. In *From Rhodesia to Zimbabwe*, for example, the black militant Lawrence Vambe recalls the political situation in Salisbury immediately after the Second World War, and the importance of radical white liberal intervention at that moment. It seems, though, to have been first formed during the war, earlier than the period that he stresses:

with such a great rush of new settlers into the country immediately after the War, white Rhodesian attitudes changed sufficiently to give rise to a sudden spurt of different political points of view. There emerged a very vocal liberal element, which derived its inspiration from the socialist movement in Britain. These people openly campaigned for a common front

between the working class Africans and Europeans in their
struggle for economic justice. The leading exponents of this
revolutionary school of thought were Mrs. Doris Lessing, the
well known British novelist, Nathan and Dorothy Zelter, as
well as J. B. Lister and Donald McIntyre, both MPs . . . these
men and women . . . made an impressive team . . .
Considering the forces of reaction that confronted them, I
thought they were a brave group of people . . . But the anti-
black elements in the Southern Rhodesian Labour Party and
white trade unions were formidable.[25]

Lessing thus came to England out of an extraordinary range of
displaced histories and mythologies, which reinforced a radical
liberal tradition and explicitly identified it with the communist
movement. Two of the reference-points of the communist
intelligentsia of the 1930s in Britain – Stalinism, and the Romantic
oppositional tradition traced from Blake, Godwin and Shelley
and including William Morris – were, in Southern Rhodesia,
paradoxically both necessary for survival and a sign of cultural
displacement. And as a white African feminist woman Lessing
had only one political, personal and literary reference-point – the
late-nineteenth-century feminist writer Olive Schreiner.

It was both necessity and desire – political marginality and the
absence of any viable literary institution to sustain her ambitions
as a writer – that drove Lessing to England. But what role could
the radical white writer play in England, given the ideological
context of the reception of her work? This problem is most clearly
raised as a question of language and representation in *The Golden
Notebook*, in Anna's brooding over both her own nostalgia for
Africa and the implicitly racist voyeurism surrounding the
success of her novel *Frontiers of War*. *The Grass is Singing* itself falls
within the category of the 'black peril' story structured round the
transgression of racial and sexual taboos.[26] And this problem is
also suggested by Lessing's own interest in, and transformation
of, Jungian psychoanalysis. This development of 'Jungian' conceptions of the collective unconscious, of individuation, of
mythic archetypes, of bad mothers, of seeking mythopoeic 'new
wholes' is a much discussed feature of Lessing's developing work
– but in the 1950s her ambivalence towards particular interpretations of Jungian conceptions of the unconscious are

foregrounded in their application to African mythology. Here she includes herself in the colonial cultural tradition of the internal emigré. In two *New Statesman* reviews of Laurens Van der Post's work – *The Lost World of the Kalahari* (quoted in the epigraph to this collection) and *The Heart of the Hunter* – she is particularly scathing about the white liberal heavy-handedly and nostalgically deploying Jungian conceptions of the unconscious by seeking a lost innocence and unity in the search for the 'real' Africa – as embodied in the Kalahari bushmen – an insidious form of colonial expropriation and voyeuristic fetishism. She remarked in the first review:

> An African once said to me that beyond the white man's more obvious crimes in Africa there was the unforgivable one that 'Even the best of you use Africa as a peg to hang your egos on.' To this crime Mr. Van der Post is open. So are all the rest of us.[27]

The second, written three years later, is similar:

> Mr. Van der Post projects his emotions into every animal, tree, bird or human that he sees, so that, identifying with the bushman in my own manner, I found I was in the middle of a fantasy where, hopping frantically on one leg in front of Mr. Van der Post, I was shouting 'Baas, baas, I'm not dead yet, please don't make me into an archetype until I am.'[28]

But in *Going Home*, this anxiety about the white observer's own position is embodied in the shifting and fractured perspective of the narrative itself. Lessing's self-consciousness is partly engendered by her own position as object of surveillance by the Rhodesian state: 'One feels the tight, suspicious watchfulness of the place everywhere,'[29] and she was pronounced a prohibited alien during the visit. This concern is extended to a consideration of emergent black writing, and to the question of whether the literary forms of a dominant culture can be adapted to the needs of a subordinate group or form the basis of an oppositional culture. She comments on how black African writing itself is colonised – while undercutting the white liberal fantasy of 'the mysterious African soul', it 'could all have been written in Britain in the late eighteenth and early nineteenth century.'[30] This is related to the limitations of the nineteenth-century realist tradition itself, established for the white writer addressing a European audience. It refers to a set of already encoded and familiarised perceptions:

> I long for the moment when the Africans can free themselves and express themselves in new forms, new ways of living. They are a free and vital people because they have been forced to take the jump from tribalism to industrialism in one generation. And yet – the stale patterns of white domination still exist. So because I was brought up with it I have a responsibility. And does that mean I have to go on writing about it?
>
> I have notebooks which are full of stories, plots, anecdotes, which at one time or another I was impelled to write. But the impulse died in a yawn. Even if I wrote them well, what then? It is always the colour bar; one cannot write truthfully about Africa without describing it. And if one has been at great pains to choose a theme that is more general, people are so struck by the enormity and ugliness that must be shown in it that what one has tried to say gets lost.
>
> When I am asked to recommend novels which will describe white settler Africa most accurately I always suggest a re-reading of those parts of *Anna Karenina* about landowners and peasants . . . In the person of Levin one finds the decent worried white liberal, who is drawn by the reserves of strength, the deep humanity of the African, yet does not trust him to govern himself . . . For the novelist based in Africa it is disconcerting that so much of what develops there is a repetition of the nineteenth century . . . trying to isolate what is specifically African, what is true of Africa at this time, one comes up against that complex of emotions, the colour bar . . . for the writer it is hard because the infinite complexities always narrow into a protest against that monstrous thing, the colour bar.[31]

By the mid-1950s, therefore, the specific contradictions of Lessing's position as a white colonial writer, increasingly cut off from Rhodesian political events, were clear, and they were specifically linked with the problems of realist writing. On the one hand, the absent tradition of nineteenth-century realism – sustained by colonial writing – retains a shaky dominance in the post-war English literary institution, and is a central reference-point for Lessing herself. On the other, this is itself untenable, 'false', both in the light of its own reception in Britain and in relation to any possible black writing. White realistic writing about Rhodesia can only represent dissolution and fragmentation as a gesture of protest.

In *The Golden Notebook*, Anna Wulf is ironically described as 'the first intellectual prepared to join the Party since the Cold War started,'[32] and this very approximately corresponds to Doris Lessing's own position on her arrival in England. Although her first few years in Britain were mainly occupied by the struggle for survival as a writer and single mother, and her precise relation to the party is not altogether clear, she visited the Soviet Union as a party member in 1952, and, during 1952–3, was involved with Margot Heinemann in editing *Daylight*, a supplement of *World News* (now *Comment*) set up to encourage working-class writing.[33] Her attempt to come to terms with orthodox Stalinism in the early 1950s is perhaps also suggested by an attempt at a socialist realist novel, *Retreat to Innocence* (1956), which, like Berger's *A Painter of our Time*, examines the concept of commit-ment, and the position of the exile, though there is a marked political shift between this and the 1957 postscript to *Going Home*, added after the Twentieth Party Congress (1956), which aligns her closely with the socialist humanist opposition to Stalinism within the British party. First, there were the increasing number of revelations of the effects of Stalinist policy, acknowledged officially at the Twentieth Party Congress. Linked to this, there was the Soviet Union's continuing repressive policies in the People's Democracies: the suppression of the strikes in East Berlin in 1953, and of the Polish workers' uprising earlier in 1956, as well as the actual invasion of Hungary in November. These far-reaching events themselves operated in the context of a growing disaffection of intellectuals within the Communist Party of Great Britain itself.[34]

The *Reasoner*, a duplicated internal party discussion document, edited by Edward Thompson and John Saville, was first circu-lated in the absence of any official acknowledgement of Khrushchev's Twentieth Congress speech by the British party. It first appeared in June 1956, four months before the Soviet invasion of Budapest, and in its first editorial stated that it aimed to 'provide a new forum for the far-reaching discussions going on

within and close to the Communist Party – questions of fundamental principle, aim, and strategy.'[35] It included specific discussion of inner party democracy, Soviet foreign and internal policy
and international politics, as well as more general debates on
socialist morality, commitment, and the re-creation of a British
socialist humanist tradition, which Thompson both related to,
and distinguished from, liberal humanism. The suppression of
the *Reasoner* within the party (Thompson and Saville were repri-
manded by the Central Committee in September 1956) under-
mined any hope of substantial party reform from within, and the
invasion of Budapest in November finally precipitated the break,
with an exodus of around 7,000, while many more left the following year, after the congress on inner party democracy. A grouping formed around the *New Reasoner*, which, in 1960, merged
with *Universities and Left Review* (set up in 1957) to form the *New
Left Review*, and published the collection of essays *Out of Apathy*.
The late 1950s also witnessed the development of a broadly based
anti-nuclear movement, CND. This focused on a sense of real
political urgency and promised to provide the basis of a loose
alliance between the emerging lower-middle- and working-class
youth cultures, more orthodox Marxists, members of the
churches; the tradition of nineteenth-century liberalism made one
of its final stands in the figureheads of Collins, Russell and
Priestley.

Lessing's involvements with these developments was primarily as an increasingly well-established, even celebrated, writer –
Five had won the Somerset Maugham Memorial Prize. In one
sense she was marked out as different from contemporary communist intellectuals, both as a woman and a literary figure, but
this needs qualifying – there was no coherent marginal cultural
group that she unproblematically related *to*. As a colonial woman
she had gained an authority to speak with both a 'public' and a
'personal' voice, which differentiated her within the dominant
discourse of femininity – that of passivity – in Britain in the 1950s.
Yet this was both as a 'free' and a 'real' woman, referring to
colonial codes of masculinity and femininity. As both a largely
self-taught writer, living almost entirely on the proceeds of her
writing rather than working freelance in television or journalism,
and existing completely outside any educational institution, she
was an unusual figure both in and outside the Left. Yet it was also

her connection with the communist movement and its aesthetic and political traditions via Rhodesia that gave her a position as an intellectual. She wrote a letter to the first number of the *Reasoner*, supporting the venture, though cautiously, and raised the question of the role of the intellectual both within the Communist Party and in relation to the Labour movement. She defended having 'kept silent' about Stalinist purges in the face of media vilification, and pointed out the dangers of self-righteous but impotent intellectual protest:

> Comrades, there is a danger in the form of your protest – for it is in fact a protest . . . Above all the Stalin era was deeply anti-intellectual in the sense that it suppressed emergence of ideas that were not of immediate service to the business of survival . . . There is no reason why we should do the same thing in reverse. Our job as intellectuals is to think . . . What we have to demand, I think, is not scapegoats, confessions and breast-beating; but a re-examination of our basic thinking, and this should be done at a full Party congress . . . you should do everything you can to prevent it from becoming something like 'a revolt of the intellectuals'.[36]

Lessing herself left the party at the same time as the *Reasoner* dissidents did. She signed a letter with E. P. Thompson, Rodney Hilton, Eric Hobsbaum, Christopher Hill and others, which appeared in *Tribune* and the *New Statesman*, condemning the Soviet intervention in Hungary and the attitude of the British party leadership. Two short stories – 'The Sun Between their Feet' and 'The Day Stalin Died' – first appeared in the *New Reasoner*,[37] and she was on both that editorial board and the first board of the *New Left Review*. She was active in the anti-nuclear movement, a member of the first Aldermaston March organising committee with John Berger, Wolf Mankowitz, Michael Tippett, Philip Toynbee, John Braine, George Melly, John Osborne and others, and was one of the platform speakers on the march itself. She appears to have been associated with almost every aspect of that complex cultural and political configuration, though always ambiguously. This emerges also in the range of her realist writings in the late 1950s: the continuing anti-colonial *Children of Violence* sequence, the committed communist novel *Retreat to Innocence, Each in His Own Wilderness* (very much an 'issue' play, concerned with youth and nuclear disarmament), performed at the Royal Court in 1958, the documentary account of working-class life, *In Pursuit of the English*, and her own version of the 'scholarship boy' story, 'England Versus England'.

Lessing's relation to the Left during the 1950s arose in part from her own very specific position and history as a successful colonial woman writer interested in psychoanalysis and subjectivity. But her situation was also bound up with the more general position of the committed writer within the relation of cultural production of the 1950s – those which became foregrounded in *The Golden Notebook* as questions of technique. The political and ideological isolation of the Communist Party in the early 1950s was one of the factors which led to its failure to develop a viable cultural strategy in the face of rapid developments in cultural production, though 'culture' itself became an increasingly contested term. The central predicament of the communist writer in the post-war period is summed up by the title of Jack Lindsay's *After the Thirties*, in the debates in the literary journal *Arena* which had mainly communist contributors, and in the cultural sections of *World News* in the early 1950s. They all take as their starting-point the need to develop a national popular cultural tradition, but one founded on a pre-war, literary notion of 'the British cultural heritage', which perceived post-war developments in the media in both Britain and America as both an encroachment and a threat. *After the Thirties* focused on the position of the novel, and related the political and aesthetic debates of the 1930s, including the sense of decay in the face of mass culture, to the post-war formation. A strongly idealist Utopian notion of realism is centrally instated here and linked with the Romantic tradition; Lindsay's analysis of the legacy of the 1930s took the form of tracing a British humanist tradition through the Romantic movement and Morris, on the one hand, and a critical examination of the tenets and practices of orthodox Soviet socialist realism, on the other. In particular, he stressed the role of English intellectuals – Ralph Fox, Christopher Caudwell, Alick West as critics, and Grassic Gibbon and Lewis Jones as writers – in creating a radical cultural strategy in the 1930s. Fox's *The Novel and the People* is a central reference-point in discussing post-war developments. Ralph Fox's conception of socialist realism closely resembled aspects of Lukács definition of critical realism in many respects – though his notion of realism was sometimes subtler than Lukács's. Like Lukács, Fox saw the development of the novel and the 'problematic hero' as corresponding with the rise of capitalism. He considered 'classic' realism a privileged form of knowledge, which is anti-naturalist – does not dwell on the 'surface forms of life', but penetrates to the 'essence of objects', thus revealing hidden contradictions and working through them to coherence. Unlike Lukács, he saw a role for the exploration of the consciousness and subjectivity:

> each man has, as it were, a dual history, since he is at the same time a type, a man with a social history, and an individual, a man with a personal history. The two, of course, even though they may be in glaring conflict, are also one, a unity, in so far as the latter is eventually conditioned by the former.
>
> The novelist cannot write his story of the individual fate unless he also has this steady vision of the whole.[38]

Fox, like Lukács, saw a decline of realism after 1848, and the split into 'subjective' and 'objective' realism in which the novel loses its epic character, manifesting instead the 'intellectual's isolation from the real human struggle of the age'.[39] He argued that the new (but not orthodox Soviet) socialist realism must be epic and heroic rather than merely typical; both 'close to the people', tendentious, and upholding a tradition based on the canonised work of nineteenth-century realism, while transforming it. This meant breaking with a realism that implied the passive observance of an already given world; Fox pinpointed the paradoxes:

> Art is one of the means by which man grapples with and assimilates reality. On the forge of his own inner consciousness the writer takes the white-hot metal of reality and hammers it out, re-fashions it to his own purpose, beats it out madly by the violences of thought . . . The whole process of creation, the whole agony of the artist, is in this violent conflict with reality in the effort to fashion a truthful picture of the world.[40]

Lindsay's analysis develops from here.

In his account of the post-war world, Lindsay draws close connections between cultural crisis and power relationships. In certain respects his position resembles Lessing's in 'The Small Personal Voice', seeing the realist novel as agent of cultural and social change and the artist as 'architect of the soul' by creating a

vision of 'new wholes' in the face of cultural and social disintegration. They both stress the threat of nuclear war as the material
manifestation of an unknowable power, using a similar language
and framework of reference. And though they are clearly speaking from different political positions – Lessing taking a more
strongly anti-Soviet socialist realist stand – their conception of the
individual artist who is both a privileged sage ('the traditional
interpreters of dreams and nightmares' and 'close to the people',
firmly opposed to the 'pleasurable luxury of despair' of contemporary nihilism) shares a common framework. Lindsay's descriptions of nuclear power as a material and transcendent force,
described through the language of revelation was virtually
ubiquitous. Here, he links this with a need to revitalise realism as
part of the humanist project of constructing a totality, transcending fragmentation while perceiving it, 'telling it like it is':

> It is the great moment when human unity becomes possible
> and necessary and man holds the universe in his hands . . .
> [nuclear power] necessitates the creation of a new kind of
> consciousness . . . for the first time there is a need for
> consciousness of unity of process, which is adequate to deal
> with all aspects of life, social, artistic, scientific, yet see each
> separate aspect in relation to the whole – and the whole is the
> whole of human life in its struggle, its unity with the whole of
> nature.[41]

Lindsay, like Fox and Lukács, stresses the problems of using
realism as a style to express modernist consciousness and
concerns: 'One aspect of the disintegration of culture under
imperialism is the way in which the components of art-forms
break up as things in themselves and fail to blend in the propor-
tions of great art.'[42] He cites Lessing's early African writing as
amongst post-war advances, and as an example of Fox's socialist
realism. Lessing herself had broken her political links with the
party by 1957, but her *Declaration* essay is one example of how
closely she shared the holistic rhetoric, as well as the socialist
humanist perceptions, of many of her contemporaries – particularly Lindsay and Thompson – though she stresses the limitations
of, as well as the need for, Utopian thought:

> We are living at one of the great turning points of history . . .

Yesterday we split the atom. We assaulted that colossal citadel
of power, the tiny unit of the substance of the universe. And
because of this the great dream and the great nightmare of
centuries of human thought have taken flesh and walk beside us
day and night . . .

What is the choice before us? It is not merely a question of
preventing an evil, but of strengthening a vision of a good
which may defeat the evil . . .

But to imagine free man, leisured man, is to step outside of
what we are. There is no one on earth who is not twisted by
insecurity and the compromises of thinking made inevitable by
want and fear . . . Those who say: 'You can't give man leisure,
he won't know how to use it' are as much victims of a
temporary phase of economic development as the coupon
fillers and the screen dreamers. Their imaginations are in bond
to their own necessities. Slaves can envy the free; slaves can
fight to free their children; but slaves suddenly set free are
marked by habits of submission; and slaves imaging freedom
see it through the eyes of slaves . . . It is because it is so hard to
think ourselves into the possibilities of the free man that the
nightmare is so strong . . . We think: the tiny units of my
hand, my flesh, are shared with walls, tables, pavements, trees,
flowers, soil, . . . and suddenly and at any moment, a madman
may throw a switch and flesh and soil and leaves may begin to
dance together in a flame of destruction. We are all of us made
kin with each other and with everything in the universe
because of this kinship of possible destruction.[43]

After the Thirties stands out as a landmark amongst Communist
Party criticism in the 1950s, but it falls back on the sustaining
memory of the Marxist literary intelligentsia and culture of the
1930s. The shift in the forces of cultural production and the
absence of such an intelligentsia in the 1950s, and, with this, the
party's failure to offer any alternative to the notion of a 'British
cultural heritage' based on canonised works, on the one hand, and
an often anachronistic, pre-war notion of the northern working
class, on the other, combined with the post-war eclipse of socialism, meant that it was unable to challenge the more sophisticated
cultural theory of *Scrutiny* and the Leavises – dominant influences
on intellectuals whose careers began after the war. *Arena*, the

communist literary journal, had put forward an ambiguous position *vis-à-vis* post-war cultural developments in its first editorial, in 1949, stating that it was:

> interested in *values* . . . our use of the term means *human values* and does not abstract value from activity . . . *Arena* neither seeks to label our culture as decadent nor acclaim it as securely progressive. We believe that the culture of our world is rent with intense conflicts, and for that very reason is full of the most violent potentialities for good or evil . . . *Arena* . . . aims at separating out and strengthening all that genuinely reveals the artist's prophetic function, his capacity to reach ahead into various aspects of the integration the world lacks but needs for its coherence.[44]

However, subsequent articles in the journal concentrated on the 'decadent' and apocalyptic rather than the 'progressive', simultaneously attacking Existentialism, Hollywood, and the passivity of the intelligentsia as undermining national cultural standards. 'The primary basis of our culture has been largely broken down,' Jack Lindsay commented in 'What is Happening to our Culture?', in 1950, '. . . there is a point where *angst* and Hollywood meet and shake hands . . . the last shreds of "innocence" have been torn from the intellectual in the post war world of atom bomb imperialism.'[45] *Arena* published pamphlets on *Britain's Cultural Heritage, Essays on Socialist Realism and the British Cultural Tradition*, and devoted an issue to the party's conference on 'The American Threat to British Culture',[46] and although socialist realism was defended with increasingly less conviction in the 1950s, it was still defended. Sam Aaronovitch, for example, argued, in 'The Capitalist Reaction Against Socialist Realism', that socialist realism – both national in form and socialist in content – is threatened by élitism and formalism, on the one hand, and mass culture, on the other.[47] Nevertheless, in *World News* the concept of 'culture' itself, and the differences between, 'high', 'popular' and 'working-class' culture were beginning to be debated more widely in the party by the mid-1950s. In 1954 it carried a series of articles on 'Politics and Culture'. Here, for example, in a continuing series of articles, Arnold Kettle posited 'culture' as a distinct sphere, separate from production, but defined as 'the way people live, their methods of tilling the fields, their marriage conventions, their art, their science, their religious rituals'.[48] However, Kettle's attempts to develop a broader cultural analysis within the party foreshadowed debates outside it – the developing work of Richard Hoggart, John Berger and Raymond Williams, and the focusing of the emerging New Left on the notion of cultural intervention.

> '. . . After all, you aren't someone who writes little novels about the emotions. You write about what's real.'
>
> Anna almost laughed again, and then said soberly.
>
> 'Do you realise how many of the things we say are just echoes? That remark you just made is an echo from Communist Party, criticism – at its worst moments moreover. God knows what that remark means, I don't. I never did. If Marxism means anything, it means that a little novel about the emotions should reflect "what's real" since the emotions are a function and product of a society . . . And there's something else. Fascinating if it wasn't so depressing. Here we are, 1957, waters under bridges etc. And suddenly in England we have a phenomenon in the arts that I'm damned if I'd foreseen – a whole lot of people, who've never had anything to do with the Party, suddenly standing up and exclaiming, just as if they'd just thought it out for themselves, that little novels about the emotions don't reflect reality.'[49]

By 1957, with the development of the Angry Young Men furore, the exodus of many writers and intellectuals from the party, and the emergence of the younger Left and the anti-nuclear movement, 'commitment' had re-emerged as a central and controversial term for the first time since the war. And, with it, the question of realism was reformulated outside the canons of Soviet socialist realism. Yet the debates about the role of the writer and the position of the intellectual were fraught ones, shifts within the cultural formation affected the position of different individuals and groupings at that moment in different ways. A complex of factors contributed to making it inevitable that 'commitment' would signify the self-conscious discussion of the concept of commitment; political action was subsumed into a cultural self-consciousness that spanned both sides of the commitment/apathy polarity and reinforced the opposition between them. Reverberations from the 1930s as well as the volte-faces of the 1940s remained a central reference-point, the figure of Orwell forming a lynchpin not only for ex-party members but for younger intellectuals. Defending discussion of the ideological position of literature and questions of committed writing, Stuart Hall's 'Inside the Whale Again', in *Universities and Left Review*, stressed:

> One had better say bluntly that this is no mere romantic recreation of the past, not a looking backwards in nostalgia. The question of the 'neutrality' of literature and the 'politics of culture' is not a form of political reversion. In spite of – because of? – John Osborne, we have tried to look back in order to take a proper perspective of the Thirties, because the problem of living and writing more fully now is related to the full, critical experience we have of the past . . . Orwell's theme was 'the position of the writer in an age of State control' – and we are not predisposed to simplify *that* problem. He was right to remind us of orthodoxies of the left as well as of the right, to question 'the subjective yielding of the writer to the Party machine', to draw sharp distinctions 'between our political and literary loyalties'. His comment that 'by being Marxised literature has moved no nearer to the masses' offers us, not merely a critical insight into the past, but a viewpoint on the future.[50]

Yet he closed romantically with a quotation from Lawrence's *Fantasia of the Unconscious*.

Three years later, Edward Thompson's essay 'Outside the Whale' charted a complex of literary forces as part of his explication of the lineaments of 'Natopolitian apathy' – from Wordsworth's later quietism, Eliot's hierarchical High Anglicanism, through Auden, Spender, Orwell and Koestler, to Golding, Amis, Osborne and Wain. 'It was an active cultural pattern, a logic which carried the mind down established grooves from one premise to the next, a drift of the sensibility,' he argued, and, in the process, regenerated the same dynamic between humanism and its demise: 'It remains the dominant ideology as we enter the sixties, and it tends towards the negation of man.'[51] A sense of the overwhelming power of the nuclear state is fictionally transformed in *The Golden Notebook*, yet develops from the same rhetoric and framework of reference. Anna Wulf charts the processes of her consciousness, and sees her own breakdown as symptomatic of internalised social fears. Structurally, this also functions as the culmination and resolution of the novel's constant negotiation of the commitment/apathy polarity:

> There was a kind of shifting in the balance of my brain, of the way I had been thinking, the same kind of realignment as when, a few days before, words like democracy, liberty, freedom, had faded under the pressure of a new sort of understanding of the real movement of the world towards dark, hardening power. I knew, but of course the word, written, cannot convey the quality of that knowing, that whatever already is has its logic and its force, that the great armouries of the world have their inner force, and that my terror, the real nerve terror of the nightmare, was part of the force.[52]

It was the articulation of economic, political and cultural developments that lead to the emergence of a radical intelligentsia around the New Left in the late 1950s, and contributed to its fragmentation and dispersal by the early 1960s. The grouping was always a loose one, formed primarily from the expanding professional middle class – it had no real purchase within working-class institutions. Politically, its development and effectiveness was bound up with the direction taken by CND, which formed the basis of a mass movement but offered no further political strategy, a vacuum which the Left itself was not able to fill. There was a very real sense in which CND was able to provide a crucial focus for moral protest against the Cold War, but not a more coherent explanation of it that could include an account both of its different manifestations and the ways in which they interacted. Such an explanation would, in many ways, have been a virtually impossible project. It would have involved a synthesis of a vast range of components: the economic and political struggle between Eastern and Western blocs, conflicts of colonialism and imperialism around and within nationalist ideologies, and the expansion and development of technical and military systems on both a national and international level. The broader political effectiveness of CND was also eventually weakened, in the 1960s, by the concentration of its energies into the Labour Party.

Within the New Left, therefore, the most coherent intellectual developments involved the analysis of cultural and literary tradi-

tions and of contemporary developments with media and communications systems – the work of Raymond Williams and the
early numbers of *New Left Review* being their clearest manifestations. But the position of the radical intelligentsia *within* these
apparatuses was more problematic – they saw a place to work in
the media, on the one hand, but on the other, viewed this in the
more traditional light as being an encroachment and a threat to
both high- and working-class culture. This dilemma was closely
linked to the debates about commitment of the late 1950s; and was
crucial both in broadly based collections such as *Declaration* and
Conviction and in more specific discussions, such as that on 'State
Patronage of the Arts' in the *New Reasoner*, or on 'Socialism and
the Intellectuals' and 'The Uses of Literacy' in *Universities and Left
Review*. In his *Declaration* essay, 'Get Out and Push', for example,
Lindsay Anderson had argued for committed intervention in the
media in a way that echoed Sartre's concept of *engagement* in *What
is Literature?*, but also in a manner that paradoxically both
extended and modified the conception of the privileged individual artist:

> Commitment . . . must mean a new kind of intellectual and
> artist who is not frightened or scornful of his fellows; who does
> not see himself as threatened by, and in natural opposition to,
> the philistine mass; who is ready to make his contribution and
> ready to use the mass-media to do so. By his nature, the artist
> will always be in conflict with the false, the narrow minded,
> the reactionary.[53]

Lessing shared many of these sentiments in her own *Declaration*
piece. She opened by stressing the importance of commitment,
but qualified the use of the term, stressing 'a current mood of
reaction against socialist art jargon, the words and phrases of
which become debased by parrot use to a point where many of us
suffer from a nervous reluctance to use them at all.'[54] And she
concluded by stressing the dependence of the novelist on a mass
audience and his/her relatively privileged individual position
compared to other media workers, who 'have to reach people
through a barrier of financiers, actors, producers, directors'[55] – a
position that is critically examined in *The Golden Notebook*.

By 1961, however, Lessing's growing ambivalence towards
the radical intelligentsia as an effective force is suggested by her

public critique of 'Smart Set Socialists' in the *New Statesman*.[56]
Taking as her starting-point an earlier criticism of one of John
Berger's weekly television arts programmes that she had made in
a letter to the periodical, she asserted that the radical intelligentsia's easy assimilation into the media was itself a sign of
socialist intellectuals' incorporation into a bland, hegemonic,
social democracy. She contrasted the soft options open to British
socialists with the conditions of those living under coercive
regimes, in Eastern Europe, in McCarthyite America, in colonial
Africa: 'Should we not even ask why so many people are Socialist
now, when one glance round the world shows that there was
never a time harder to think, live or act like a Socialist, or, for that
matter, to define what Socialism is?' And, in perhaps a hopelessly
Utopian gesture, she stressed both the weakness and the inherent
possibilities in British socialist humanism, and, more generally,
in prefigurative thought, again in contrast with the international
situation:

> They see us, not only able to challenge our own government
> with a form of Socialism highly developed in its possibilities
> for freedom and individuality, but free to speculate in a way
> that might throw a new Socialist light on the witches cauldron
> of good and evil possibilities that the world is in now. British
> Socialists could have shown (had we the will to understand our
> unique position, instead of enjoyably posturing around in out
> of date or self-indulgent attitudes) an example of what Socialist
> intellectual responsibility should be.
>
> I think the time is coming when we shall look back and kick
> ourselves for the opportunity which we have lost . . . No, I
> don't think that a brutal dictatorship is on the cards, but I can
> see all too clearly a darkening fog of urbane authoritarianism
> under which we caper and prance, getting our kicks from
> shouting insults at the police, thumbing our noses at wicked
> capitalists from the Royal Court stage, using irrelevant
> shibboleths like: Socialists must not criticise one another
> publicly. Shadow boxing with imaginary enemies, we fail to
> see the real pressures on us all.[57]

The pressures are strongest where least visible, she continued;
those of consent, not conspiracy: 'They work in ways to emascu-
late and soften, beguiling us into being bland, charming or witty,

or – if temperaments don't run this way – encouraging us to be *enfants terribles* or licensed clowns.' Almost Orwellian scorn is applied to academics as much as celebrities:

> The reaction to my saying this will probably be a 50,000 word monograph which will suggest, in words of 12 syllables, that the reason why Socialists are now riven into cliques and distrusting groups is that capitalist society has an inner drive to fragmentation. If we are not gadflies we are pedants . . . For months and months, we have been reading, in a dozen Socialist journals, interminable dreary polemics, about something called 'Communication'. This was mostly about television. But I can't remember anything being said that might help to answer the question: why does someone like John Berger, who has combined for years a unique artistic sensibility with an acute intelligence in an attempt to rescue from the philistines the idea that art must not be for a minority – how does it happen that he should now, and from the highest possible motives, be content to turn himself into a kind of Wilfred Pickles of the National Gallery?

Her closing note is apocalyptic; it is the 'sad, erratically inspired, prophetic dervishes like Norman Mailer, John Osborne, Hlasko, Donleavy, Pinter', who 'send off crazy showers of sparks to light the sordid anarchy that we have made ourselves impotent to change.'[58]

Here I've looked briefly at the diverse ways that Lessing was positioned as a white anti-colonial woman writer in Britain. Jean McCrindle and Rebecca O'Rourke develop some of the points raised from other perspectives. I've stressed the complexity of Lessing's response to the England she encountered as a committed realist writer, and how she was both connected with, and marked out as different from, a range of intellectual and political groupings. However, it is worth concluding with one example of how, independently of Lessing's intention, *The Golden Notebook* itself corresponded with a very specific aspect of the cultural criticism being developed within the New Left. In 1961, a year before *The Golden Notebook* was published, Raymond Williams stressed the historical roots and questions facing realism, in *The Long Revolution*:

The centenary of 'realism' as an English critical term occurred but was not celebrated in 1956. Its history, in this hundred years, has been so vast, so complex and so bitter that any celebration would in fact have turned into a brawl. Yet realism is not an object to be identified, pinned down and appropriated. It is, rather, a way of describing certain methods and attitudes and the descriptions, quite naturally, have varied.[59]

Williams opens by describing realism as a historically variable attitude, and while his essay and *The Golden Notebook* cannot be directly compared, being totally different objects of analysis themselves, they nevertheless each raise very similar questions about the definition and overdetermined practice of realist writing at the same moment. At least, if one reads *The Golden Notebook* as both a fictional and discursive text, as was suggested earlier, it certainly works over and embodies a directly comparable set of concerns with Williams, and their very compatibility in this respect is important in itself. Moreover, both exist within the broader discursive framework of the political problems facing realist writing on the Left in the 1950s that I have already outlined. Anna's own discussion with herself about the nature of the breakdown of contemporary realism and her sense that this is symptomatic both of contemporary social fragmentation and ontological insecurity is expressed in the sort of language and framework of reference that directly recalls Williams's formulation of the same problem – more specifically, I think, than the more general sharing of a humanist perspective. The implied definition of realism as an attitude is common to both, as is the conviction that, while a 'new realism' is necessary, this involves a development of, rather than a complete break from, the conventions of nineteenth-century realism. Conversely, *The Golden Notebook* can be read as fiction with the parameters that Williams set up, and the divisions that he then discerned between 'social' and 'personal', 'formula' and 'documentary', writing. The novel has certainly been interpreted as an allegorical 'formula' novel as well as a piece of documentary writing, and, as a feminist source text, it works as one example of the 'fiction of special pleading' that Williams identified. From a different perspective, the narrative resolutions arrived at – the breakdown both of individual authorship and subjectivity in the golden notebook and the ironically presented social assimilation of the two women in *Free Women* – correspond with the final point that Williams raises: that it is not always easy to distinguish between the exploration of breakdown and 'the simple, often rawly exciting exploitation of breakdown. Or else there is a turning away into known forms which remind us of previously learned realities, and seek, by that reminder, to establish possibility of a kind.'[60] The question of whether the novel *does* resolve those contradictions remains an open one.

Notes

1 Jeremy Brooks, 'Doris Lessing's Chinese Box', *Sunday Times*, 15 April 1962, p. 32.
2 Doris Lessing, 'The Small Personal Voice', in *Declaration*, ed. Tom Maschler, London, McGibbon & Kee, 1957, p. 22.
3 Anon., review of *The Grass is Singing, Times Literary Supplement*, 14 April 1950, p. 225.
4 J. D. Scott, *Five, New Statesman*, 11 July 1953, p. 55.
5 Anon., 'Local Colour', *The Times*, 11 July 1953, p. 8.
6 J. W. Lambert, *Five, Sunday Times* 12 July 1953, p. 5.
7 C. P. Snow, 'Frustrations on the Veld', *Sunday Times*, 2 November 1952, p. 5.
8 J. W. Lambert, 'Proper Marriage', *Sunday Times*, 25 September 1954, p. 5.
9 George Orwell, 'Inside the Whale', in *Collected Essays*, London, Secker & Warburg, 1961, p. 120.
10 Simone de Beauvoir, *The Second Sex*, Harmondsworth, Penguin, 1972, p. 691.
11 Ibid., p. 191.
12 Doris Lessing, preface to *The Golden Notebook*, London, Panther, 1972, p. 13.
13 Ibid., p. 12.
14 Ibid., p. 14.
15 Interview by Roy Newquist, in *Doris Lessing: A Small Personal Voice*, New York, Vintage Books, 1st edn, 1975, p. 51.
16 Lessing, preface to *The Golden Notebook*, p. 22.
17 B. Brecht, 'Against Georg Lukács', in *Aesthetics and Politics*, London, New Left Books, 1977, p. 82. For discussion of debates on realism, I am indebted to Francis Booth, whose unpublished dissertation, 'Realism and Materialism', provides an excellent discussion of the developments of these and other debates. I am above all grateful to Steve Burniston, whose thesis on *The Golden Notebook* provided a crucial reference-point.

18   *The God That Failed* was a collection of essays published in 1950, in which six European ex-communists outlined the reasons for their break with their former political convictions. For fuller discussion of this collection and its political implications in the 1950s, see 'The Ex-Communists Conscience' in Isaac Deutscher, *Heretics and Renegades and Other Essays*, London, Jonathan Cape, 1969.

19   Kingsley Amis, 'Socialism and the Intellectuals', in *Protest*, London, Panther, 1960, p. 257.

20   Editorial, *Universities and Left Review*, no. 1, spring 1957, p. 1.

21   Lessing, 'The Small Personal Voice', p. 24.

22   Doris Lessing, *In Pursuit of the English*, London, Panther, 1980, p. 6.

23   Lessing, 'The Small Personal Voice', p. 24.

24   Doris Lessing, *Going Home*, London, Panther, 1968, p. 311.

25   Lawrence Vambe, *From Rhodesia to Zimbabwe*, London, Heinemann, 1976, p. 160.

26   The explicitly sexual dimension of racism is widely discussed in documentary accounts of white supremacy in Africa. Vambe, for example, devotes a chapter of *From Rhodesia to Zimbabwe* to 'Sex the possible main root of the racial problem . . . relationships between employers and domestic servants; effect of sex on larger political questions', while Lessing herself describes in *Going Home* 'that anxious white myth, the potent and sexually heroic black man'. Other examples include Nadine Gordimer's *Burger's Daughter* (London, Penguin, 1980, p. 135):

Marisa is black; near, then, as well, to the white way of using blackness as a way of perceiving a sensual redemption, as romantics do, or of perceiving fears, as racialists do. In my father's house the one was seen as the obverse of the other, two sides of false consciousness – that I can add to anyone's notes.

27   Doris Lessing, 'Desert Child', *New Statesman*, 15 November 1958, p. 700.

28   Doris Lessing, 'African Interiors', *New Statesman*, 27 October 1961, p. 613.

29   Lessing, *Going Home*, p. 164.

30   Ibid., pp. 19–20.

31   Ibid., p. 164.

32   Doris Lessing, *The Golden Notebook*, p. 164.

33   *Daylight* was a short-lived venture, but it did not close down for lack of readers' interest – it sold over 7,000 copies. Montague Slater, Jack Beeching and Dave Wallis were part of the organising group, as well as Margot Heinemann and Doris Lessing herself.

34   One account of this process is given by Neal Wood, describing the increasing centralisation and bureaucratisation of party intellectual work in the late 1940s and 1950s, though his interpretation is open to question: 'Every effort of the intellectual must be geared to the

development of the Party line'. Neal Wood, *Communism and British Intellectuals*, London, Victor Gollancz, 1959, p. 179. Also Edward Upward, *The Rotten Elements*, London, Heinemann, 1969.

35 Editorial, the *Reasoner*, no. 1, September 1956, p. 2.

36 Doris Lessing, letter to the *Reasoner*, ibid., p. 11.

37 'The Day Stalin Died', the *New Reasoner*, no. 2, autumn 1957; 'The Sun Between Their Feet', the *New Reasoner*, no. 5, summer 1958. Lessing is also billed as speaking on 'Crisis in Africa' and 'The Water Today' for the Left Clubs in *Universities and Left Review*, no. 4, summer 1958.

38 Ralph Fox, *The Novel and the People*, London, Lawrence & Wishart, 1937, p. 34.

39 Ibid., p. 120.

40 Ibid., pp. 37–8.

41 Jack Lindsay, *After the Thirties*, London, Lawrence & Wishart, 1956, pp. 82–4.

42 Ibid., p. 187.

43 Lessing, 'The Small Personal Voice', pp. 16–17.

44 Editorial, *Arena*, vol. 1, 1949, p. 2.

45 Jack Lindsay, 'What is Happening to our Culture?', *Arena*, vol. 2, September/October 1950, p. 62.

46 *Arena*, vol. 8, June/July 1951.

47 Sam Aaronovitch, 'The Capitalist Reaction Against Socialist Realism', in *Essays on Socialist Realism and the British Cultural Tradition*, London, *Arena*, undated, probably 1953.

48 Arnold Kettle, 'Politics and Culture', *World News*, vol. 1, no. 41, 9 October 1954, p. 813.

49 Doris Lessing, *The Golden Notebook*, p. 61.

50 Stuart Hall, 'Inside the Whale Again', *Universities and Left Review*, no. 4, summer 1958, p. 14.

51 E. P. Thompson, 'Outside the Whale', in *Out of Apathy*, London, Stevens & Sons, 1960, p. 140.

52 Lessing, *The Golden Notebook*, p. 568.

53 Lindsay Anderson, 'Get Out and Push', in *Declaration*, pp. 177–8.

54 Lessing, in ibid., p. 13.

55 Ibid., p. 27.

56 Doris Lessing, 'Smart Set Socialists', *New Statesman*, 1 December 1961, pp. 822–4.

57 Ibid.

58 Ibid.

59 Raymond Williams, *The Long Revolution*, Harmondsworth, Penguin, 1975, p. 300.

60 Ibid., p. 315.

Additional references

Anderson, Perry, 'The Left in the Fifties', *New Left Review*, no. 26, January/February 1965.

Anderson, Perry, 'Components of the National Culture', *New Left Review*, no. 50, July/August 1968.

Arrighi, Giovanni, and John S. Saul, *Essays on the Political Economy of Africa*, London, Monthly Review Press, 1973.

Benjamin, Walter, *Understanding Brecht*, London, New Left Books, 1973.

Benjamin, Walter, *Illuminations*, London, Fontana, 1973.

Bennet, Tony, *Formalism and Marxism*, London, Methuen New Accents, 1979.

Blake, Robert, *A History of Rhodesia*, London, Eyre, Methuen, 1977.

Bowman, L. W., *Politics in Rhodesia*, Harvard University Press, 1973.

Bradbury, Malcolm, *The Social Context of Modern English Literature*, Oxford, Basil Blackwell, 1971.

Burniston, Steven, 'A Reading of *The Golden Notebook* by Doris Lessing', unpublished thesis, Centre for Contemporary Cultural Studies, Birmingham University, 1979.

Deutscher, Isaac, *Heretics and Renegades*, London, Jonathan Cape, 1955.

Deutscher, Isaac, *Russia, China and the West*, London, Oxford University Press, 1970.

Jackson, Rosemary, *Fantasy*, London, Methuen New Accents, 1981.

Lodge, David, *The Modes of Modern Writing*, London, E. Arnold, 1977.

Lodge, David, *The Novelist at the Crossroads*, London, Routledge & Kegan Paul, 1971.

McKensie, N. (ed.), *Conviction*, London, McGibbon & Kee, 1959.

Meyers, Jeffrey, *Fiction and the Colonial Experience*, Ipswich, The Boydell Press, 1973.

Mulhern, Francis, *The Moment of Scrutiny*, London, New Left Books, 1979.

Nuttall, Jeff, *Bomb Culture*, London, McGibbon & Kee, 1968.

Parrinder, Patrick, *Science Fiction, Its Teaching and Criticism*, London, Methuen New Accents, 1980.

Ranger, T. O., *The African Voice in Southern Africa, 1898–1930*, London, Heinemann, 1970.

Sartre, J. P., *What is Literature?*, London, Methuen, 1967.

Sartre, J. P., *The Ghost of Stalin*, New York, George Braziller, 1968.

Saville, J., and Milliband, R. (eds), *Socialist Register*, London, Merlin, 1976.

Spender, Stephen, *Forward From Liberalism*, London, Victor Gollancz, Left Book Club edition, 1937.

Widgery, David, *The Left in Britain, 1956–68*, Harmondsworth, Penguin, 1976.

Williams, Raymond, *Culture and Society*, Harmondsworth, Penguin, 1961.

Williams, Raymond, *Marxism and Literature*, Oxford University Press, 1977.

Williams, Raymond, *Politics and Letters*, London, New Left Books, 1979.

Zhadanov, A. *et al.*, *Soviet Writers Congress 1934*, London, Lawrence & Wishart, 1977.

2 Reading *The Golden Notebook* in 1962

Jean McCrindle

Jean McCrindle was interviewed by Jenny Taylor in the summer of 1980, and a substantially reworked version of that interview is presented here. The original paper on which it is based was given at the 1978 Ruskin History Workshop as a contribution to the theme 'In Our Time 1945–1978'.

The quotations from *The Golden Notebook* are from the 1973 Panther edition. I would like to thank Ursula Owen for useful criticism and Marsha Rowe for suggestions and encouragement.

> At last I understood that the way over or through this dilemma, the unease at writing about 'petty personal problems', was to recognise that nothing is personal in the sense that it is uniquely one's own. Writing about oneself, one is writing about others, since your problems, pains, pleasures, emotions – and your extraordinary and remarkable ideas – can't be yours alone.

I think the best thing is to start by saying why I decided to choose *The Golden Notebook* as a way of discussing the cluster of experiences which make up its subject-matter – the communist tradition and its crisis in 1956; the incipient but still unacknowledged advent of sexual politics; the theme of breakdown and chaos both personal and intellectual; political generations and their children; sexual life and motherhood and so on. Other books deal with some of these themes, but *The Golden Notebook* has them *all*, including detailed descriptions of things which I had never seen written down before, like the relationship between personal biographical time and the historical times in which you live – and how time exists differently when you have children, there's a different rhythm to your days.

Then I thought it was the most courageous book I had ever read – both in its structure – keeping the different parts separate and connected in order to express and avoid chaos – and in its honesty of content.

I felt very close to the subject-matter at that time. I was twenty-five when I read it. I had already been through many of the political experiences she describes in the *Red Notebook*: the impact of the 1956 Kruschev revelations about Stalin on the communist tradition, and the sense she has of the end of a particular historical tradition, its agonising effects of individuals. I felt very close to all that as did my friends and our parents.

Although I was not a writer and therefore not a member of the two journals which emerged from the post-1956 period – the *Universities and Left Review* and the *New Reasoner* – I thought of myself as an activist, and I agreed with the New Left's conception of politics.

My own background was very close to the politics of *The Golden Notebook*. My parents had been active communists in the 1930s – in Aid to Spain, the Left Theatre Movement, Friends of Russia, anti-Fascist struggles in London, the *Left Review*, and so on. So I grew up a child of that experience – with the *Daily Worker* for breakfast, Miners' Galas for entertainment, and marching down Oxford Street at the age of twelve shouting 'Go Home Ridgeway!' Many of the events Doris Lessing describes in *The Golden Notebook*, I can remember vividly. The electrocuting of the Rosenbergs for spying, the hysteria of the McCarthy anti-communist era, which affected my own father's life as a radio actor and many of his friends, the struggles against colonial rule in Africa – those were familiar household references when I was growing up. Doris Lessing was known as a successful writer who was also a communist, so we read her books with special interest and care.

Anyway, not surprisingly, I joined the Communist Party in the summer of 1955 when I was just about to go up to university, and I met and became friends with a group of party students who were active at Oxford – including Raphael Samuel and Peter Sedgwick, both of whom left the party at the same time as I did, and were founder editors of the *Universities and Left Review*, in 1957, and a lovely bloke whom Raphael and I recruited into the Communist Party only months before the 1956 crisis, called Denis Butt. He died in his early forties and was very important to a lot of people of that generation and time. He was an ex-wool sorter from Bradford and he'd won a scholarship through the WEA (Workers' Educational Association) to Balliol. We sat up night after night with him throughout the weeks after the crisis Party Congress, going over and over the details of all the horror – you can feel the atmosphere of that when you read *The Golden Notebook*.

I think I was always uneasy in the party, despite my background. I have terrible recollections of reading a Soviet journal called *For A Lasting Peace and a People's Democracy* and trying to understand why I found the language of it so offensive – phrases like 'laughing hyenas of Wall Street' and 'running dogs of Imperialism' to describe Tito or any critics of the Soviet Union. I still find 1930s' communist language hard to stomach, but perhaps people look back on the 1970s' jargon with just as much disbelief. There's a marvellous equivalent reaction in *The Golden Notebook* where a group of party members are discussing the language of one of Stalin's pamphlets, and this party education bloke says, to excuse its tone, that they have a different polemical tradition of debate in the Soviet Union and Anna thinks, 'This man has spent years in university studying philosophy; and I can't say to him: I know you're wrong because I feel you are.'

But it wasn't all negative, the experience of the party for me. There was a tremendous sense of belonging to a dedicated group of people, and most of them were working-class activists of great warmth and vitality, and you were taken into their lives and homes immediately wherever you went. Don't forget that we were terribly under attack throughout the late 1940s and early 1950s; you had to keep quiet about being a communist often, and you lived a strange double existence – you can see it in the descriptions of the party in Africa in *The Golden Notebook*. Doris Lessing captures the painful self-punishing humour that we indulged in to ward off the hatred around us. I can remember one party member who made it his business to know more than anyone else about the trials of the 1930s in the Soviet Union, the language of the prosecutor he could recite off by heart – it was grotesque really. I think it was a relief to be able to respond to that honestly after 1956.

So, after a troubled year in the Communist Party, I left in the exodus following the Hungarian Revolution, in October 1956; no, I actually stayed in to see if we could change the internal structure of the British Communist Party – something, we thought, ought to be done to rid it of the leadership who had clearly deliberately hushed up many of the facts now coming to light. We failed in the Spring Congress of 1957 and I sent in my party card then; my family were torn apart that year, but both my father and step-mother stayed in.

It was a pretty nightmarish time for many people. Doris Lessing has her Anna character decide to leave the party on the same day as she gets her period, and there's this amazing detailed description of how she feels on that day and whether her getting her period has affected her decision to leave – all that self-disgust and worries about smells and going off to the washroom – it's so near to experiences I've had, it makes me laugh with recognition.

That date 1956. I suppose it was the watershed because it was the Soviet Union itself giving its own acknowledgment of the crimes of Stalin and it meant we couldn't say any longer, 'Is there any doubt about this evidence?' During the Cold War there was always this possibility that the evidence of, for example, anti-semitism in the Soviet Union was tainted and that the CIA had produced it; that the *Daily Express* was the last source you could trust, and so on. *The Golden Notebook* has counter-balancing sections to the Communist Party scenes, where the corruption of bourgeois intellectuals, particularly media people, is seen as the appalling alternative to the distortions produced by having to defend Stalin.

The reason that Kruschev's revelations were so shattering was that nobody doubted that he had actually *given* that speech, or not many people! Even though it appeared in odd circumstances, I first read it in a special edition of the *Observer* one Sunday on a train going to Edinburgh, there was some quality about its reporting that made it clear that it was absolutely genuine. Of course, lots of people – and you can see this in *The Golden Notebook* – before 1956, had doubts and criticisms about many aspects of the Soviet Union and Eastern Europe – many of the communists I knew had fought against Fascism in Eastern Europe and knew that the campaigns against Tito and Trotskyists, etc., were fishy – but they kept quiet because what were the alternatives during the Cold War? So 1956 was a culmination of these doubts, not an isolated moment.

> It seems to me something like this – every so often, perhaps once in a century, there's a sort of act of faith. A well of faith fills up – and there's an enormous heave forward in one country or another and that's a forward movement for the whole world. Because it's an act of imagination of what is possible for the whole world. In our century it was 1917 in Russia. And in China. Then the well slowly fills up again. And then there's another painful lurch forward.

After 1956 and in the next few years, my closest friends and political comrades were people who had lived through that. I was working and living in Scotland, and became the Scottish secretary of the New Left Clubs which included the Fife Socialist League. It was founded by Lawrence Daly, a miner from Ballingry in West Fife – a traditional communist stronghold – and Lawrence left the Communist Party and joined up with the *New Reasoner* group. So there was our group of ex-students, this group of miners in Fife, and the older lot around the *New Reasoner*, and then the CND and Left Labour Party contingents – that was roughly the composition of the New Left in Scotland. We all helped to run Lawrence Daly's election campaign in the general election of 1959. He stood as an Independent Socialist against Labour and the Communist Party and did really well against the CP.

The Golden Notebook does try to deal with the post-1956 generation, but I think rather unsatisfactorily. The Tommy character who shoots himself and goes blind – he's a kind of symbol of the younger generation – it seemed to me that she mythologised younger people than herself, she sort of ideologised them, made them into constructs who were critical of her generation. She's not actually sensitive to what their make-up is, she can't understand it. That's part of her enormous ego I suppose. A sense of the world all being connected with herself. I think that it is a problem with her as a writer, why a lot of men dislike her books. You are never very far away from Doris Lessing somehow; her authorial ego is absolutely amazing. And yet she writes beautifully as a parent, what it feels like to have a child who stops you from killing yourself, stops you from depression, makes life ordinary again, provides another centre to your life, and so on.

There's another theme in the book which was enormously important to me then, a kind of catharsis. In the late 1950s and early 1960s a lot of Socialists were desperately trying to rescue that part of the communist tradition that had seen men and women give their lives and energies to causes which *were*, despite Stalinism, right and good. Much of the preoccupations of the *New Reasoner* were about fighting against a total negative pessimism which was identified with the Cold War slippage into Orwellian despair and *The God That Failed* syndrome. And there was a lot of that despair around.

You can see the attempt to salvage the communist tradition most clearly in Edward Thompson's writing at this time especially the essay on Orwell in the book of New Left essays, *Out of Apathy* (London, 1960):

> Orwell's profound political pessimism tended in the same direction as Auden's spiritual pessimism and once again, at a certain point the problem was simply given up (p. 159).

> It has happened before that the revolutionary, disenchanted or tamed in youth, has become in middle age the apologist of reaction. His arguments are the more persuasive, since they arise not from self-interest but from despair. They pollute the forces of change at their very source, casting a blight upon hope (p. 170).

There was a strong moral imperative to be optimistic, and it's very characteristic of the communist 'humanist' tradition – it's Darwinian progressivist tendency which still dominates Soviet official ideology. Now Doris Lessing dared have her characters say in *The Golden Notebook* what none of us dared say out loud – that it might have been futile after all, that the socialist dream had become too corrupted by the experience of the twentieth century to survive it. 'For our time at least a dream would be dead.'

I suppose what I'm trying to say is that *The Golden Notebook*, unlike anything or anyone else at the time, was saying maybe this optimism doesn't actually help us, maybe we ought to look at the dark sides of our movement and admit the possibility of failure. I locate the word optimism in a very prevalent oppression really – it meant you couldn't sit down and admit that there was no more possibility of relating to that part of the socialist tradition, no more posibility of relating to that kind of past, that corrupted dream. I think Doris Lessing somehow allowed me the possibility of pessimism – allowed the possibility of failure and still surviving, because you could emerge somehow with a kind of bedrock of truth. So, for me, her pessimism was a kind of renewal of politics, that they could be more open and honest.

I linked this with the madness theme at the end of *The Golden Notebook*, which many people at the time couldn't take. It seemed to me that to resist going down into what psychiatry was saying about irrationality and madness and chaos, by denying its significance, we were blocking something important in ourselves and our politics. It resulted in a false optimism, to deny the darker psychological moments.

It's hard to explain really. If you were in the Communist Party in the 1950s, you were haunted by an incredible fear that somehow if you walked away from the party, despite all its complicating tragedy, if you left it you would become this isolated, non-political person, hopelessly enmeshed in petty bourgeois pessimism. People who had left the party were looked on as totally broken, neurotic, retreating into personal concerns. And being pessimistic could lead you down that road. So any realistic appraisal of the party's position was impossible. Edward Thompson tried to sustain the optimism, to break with the impasse of the Cold War and to argue for a renewal of what was best in the communist tradition. I think Doris Lessing in *The Golden Notebook* was denying *that* route through, and I responded to her courage in saying it and I still do. There's almost nothing else I'd be critical of Thompson about – he was then, and is still, a huge influence on our generation, and rightly.

> Why do our lot never admit failure? Never. It might be better for us if we did. And it's not only love and men. Why can't we say something like this? – we are people, because of the accident of how we are situated in history who were so powerfully part – but only in our imagination and that's the point – of the great dream, that now we have to admit that the great dream has faded and the truth is something else – that we'll never be any use.

As you can see, I certainly didn't read *The Golden Notebook* as a rarified literary text. I read books as a way of finding out about the world and who I was and where we stood in the world and what love and emotions were all about.

There was no way in which I lived in an atmosphere of discussing literature in an academic way, or of relating politics to some sort of academic world. All the people I knew, the socialists anyhow, even though some were teaching in Universities, consciously worked against the academic world, were at odds with it, disliked it and had either been refused jobs there or refused promotion because they were Marxists. It was still not acceptable to employ known communist scholars. That's a huge difference from the 1960s and 1970s and the growth of academic Marxism, not to mention academic Feminism. There wasn't a milieu then of different journals on the Left where you could discuss your work and ideas about literature. It just didn't exist to nearly the same extent as now. In fact, there was a lot of anti-intellectualism in the party – 'bloody intellectuals' – and you made sure you licked stamps and sold the *Daily Worker* and mucked in with the daily grind of the party to avoid being thought of like that. The good side of that is that none of us would have conceived of a political movement which didn't have this close connection to working-class people. So, Doris Lessing's determined auto-didacticism also appealed to me.

> Why don't you read what I have written and make up your own mind about what you think, testing it against your own life, your own experience.

Apart from the politics, the whole area of love, sexuality, men, emotional life were what impressed me about the book. I admired her outspokenness about sexual activity and love and her analysis of women's position. Well, analysis is the wrong word, how she describes women's feelings and thoughts. I don't think there's a sense of women's oppression in *The Golden Notebook*, she doesn't blame men for women's frustration – women are misunderstood, confused, ambiguous, resentful and in struggle against something – but she doesn't locate that as 'men'. And I didn't then either.

> I laugh and kiss him although the resentment is suddenly so strong I clench my teeth against it. I control it as always, by thinking: If I were a man I'd be the same. The control and

discipline of being a mother came so hard to me, that I can't delude myself that if I'd been a man and not forced into self control, I'd have been any different.

The honesty of her sexual writing was new, for a woman to write about sex was unusual. Obviously men did, and I greatly admired D. H. Lawrence's ability to write about sexual emotion – but no one before *The Golden Notebook* had so accurately captured the different moods and ambiguity of women's sexual feelings. And then there's all the tension about the need for 'real' men, and women's nostalgia for them, and the fear that men are somehow disappearing, 'real' men. They seemed to be men who had experienced the war and the great struggles associated with it. She's really scathing about homosexual men, and I think even then, I found that rather strange, even though I assented to the stuff about 'real' men and I thought I knew what they were. But my own experience of gay men had been completely different from her descriptions. I can remember the gay men I met then were friends of my parents and were considered to be men of extreme sensitivity and thoughtfulness towards women, liking them a great deal. The gay couple in Anna's flat in the novel dislike women intensely and are very misogynistic. I think I thought that that was just an individual way of seeing those two people rather than a statement about being gay. She's not really interested in why they might be gay and what kind of life they lead, she's more interested in 'real' men and why they are dying out; the gay blokes are simply symptoms of that. I would love to get down to a detailed analysis of what real men are to her, though.

> I am always amazed, in myself and in other women at the strength of our need to bolster men up. This is ironical living as we do in a time of men's criticising us for being 'castrating' – for the truth is, women have this deep instinctive need to build a man up as a man . . . I suppose this is because real men become fewer and fewer and we are frightened, trying to create men.

I think my generation and Doris Lessing's carried around an awful lot of romantic notions about love which *The Golden Notebook* deals with and demystifies at the same time – she really does seem to understand the contradictions so well. My own love affairs at that time were diffused with this romanticism, but also an unease, a search for something more realistic, something that didn't objectify me, make me into a mysterious person – mysterious to myself, I mean. Don't forget, it was a much more repressive and deferential society, England in the 1950s, than it is now. Sexuality and its language was terribly limited and secretive. There were actually lots of problems that couldn't be talked about. And in a way, I see now, after the Women's Movement, that the kind of romanticism I am talking about was escapist, a way of avoiding real live women and men and, of course, it left the emotional work to women. My passions and my male friends' passions were clothed in the language of poetry. The Freudian dimension just wasn't discussed. Love was something that extended human experience beyond its normal boundaries, love was an assertion against bourgeois fidelity, meanness, calculation – Lawrence, Blake, Yeats all that. Of course, that was middle-class romanticism – there were other less literary kinds connected with the love lyrics of Sinatra and Peggy Lee.

Doris Lessing demystified all that for me; she wrote about more prosaic feelings and difficulties, illusions, projections. She described struggling within relationships and finding tensions and knots that won't go away – discovering truths about people you love that completely knock you sideways and you have no explanation for rationally. She described contradictions in your feelings.

> I am left with no more than some banal commonplaces that everyone knows: in this case that women's emotions are still fitted for the kind of society that no longer exists . . . I ought to live like a man, caring more for my work than for people; I ought to put my work first and take men as they come.

And then there were the material constraints on relationships in those days. You couldn't get safe birth-control easily if you were single; there were no legal abortions and so there was this constant fear of pregnancy. Sexual problems weren't much discussed, so you kept quiet between yourselves and your friends. A good marriage was the norm and it was assumed that most people

wanted that for life, even if divorce was an unfortunate possibility. I don't think socialists were critical of it really.

That was why *The Golden Notebook* opened up such a Pandora's
Box. She described all these people believing in their marriages
and yet practising, like every other generation of people, amazing
degrees of dishonesty and deception, and yet not really able to talk
about it openly, acknowledge it freely. I suppose that was part of
the neo-Victorianism of the post-1945 period. The desire to stop
all the agonies of separation and death and single living and create
some kind of 'normality' again. I think that was felt by men and
women – it wasn't just a cynical trick by the capitalist class to send
reluctant women back into the home to provide jobs for the
demobbed soldiers.

But the consequences were heavy with boredom and frustration for women, and with guilt for many men. *The Golden
Notebook* was the first time anyone acknowledged that cost. She
has women all over the place who are getting quietly drunk and
going mad all by themselves. 'The disease of our time' she calls it.
She also registers the sense of unease that men began to feel with
all these dissatisfied wives on their hands. Men seemed much
more dedicated to work than to thinking through the consequences of their relationships with women, or their own
behaviour towards them. Somehow they seemed to be avoiding
the problem. They were very romantic and that was a private
emotion and what really mattered was work, work, politics,
work. An obsession. I guess I moved in rather rarified cricles, but
it was unusual to find a man who would discuss his emotional life
seriously.

> Sex is essentially emotional for women. How many times
> has that been written? And yet there's always a point even
> with the most perceptive and intelligent man, when a
> woman looks at him across a gulf: he hasn't understood; she
> suddenly feels alone; hastens to forget the moment.

I find it almost impossible to read the current literature on
clitoral versus vaginal orgasm for the very reason that Doris
Lessing locates in *The Golden Notebook* – I find myself resistant to
thinking about sexuality in that instrumental way. I find it
offensive and it speaks nothing to me at all, just nothing. So I
think that the Women's Movement still hasn't actually come to

terms with the problem of the construction of a sexuality and its relationship to lived experience. It seems to me that a lot of what's been written about the so-called myth of the vaginal orgasm is actually ideology, a kind of reading back, a supposed false consciousness that we all had, and that there's a much more enlightened and liberated sexuality now available.

Of course, a lot of people who had admired her books until *The Golden Notebook* were very put off by the theme of breakdown and madness. To them it somehow 'proved' that if you left the party you did end up just talking about yourself and your personal problems. We knew that by then she had left the party. And no one that I knew saw what she was trying to do with that 'chaos' ending – it took the link-up with Laing and Cooper in the late 1960s to make sense of that whole area for me. And the Mother Sugar episodes, with Anna trying to use psychoanalysis as a substitute for writing and refusing to accept Mother Sugar's prescriptions – I don't think I had the foggiest notion of what all that was about when I read it first. I had had no experience then of psychoanalysis, and I thought it was something rich Americans went in for, paying someone to talk about yourself, self-indulgence!

I can't imagine what I made of it. I probably skipped a lot of it or just read it without understanding, and it was only years later, when I had reached the age that Anna is in *The Golden Notebook*, the thirties, when all sorts of crises in my life began to hit me, that I returned to read it and found so much I had just missed. That period, the late thirties, seems anyway a time when all sorts of biographical history catches up with you. It's a time when you begin to remember in a very conscious way what it was like to be a teenager, and you can feel what it was like to be your mother at that stage of her life, especially if you have children yourself. But in 1962, I think those parts just frightened me and puzzled.

It's similar to the problem of whether Doris Lessing prefigures the Women's Movement, and how we responded to that then. I suppose in a way by the time I had read *The Golden Notebook*, I was already calling myself a feminist, although very privately and only to a few close friends. That happened because someone gave me de Beauvoir's *The Second Sex* and her novel *The Mandarins*, both available in the 1950s in English. I was completely bowled over by them – as if I'd been looking for something that would make sense to me as a woman. Before that, I used to read anything I could lay my hands on by or about women – Florence Nightingale, Mother Jones, Beatrice Webb, Vera Brittain, Alva Myrdal, Margaret Mead, the Brontës, and so on – lots more. There wasn't an awful lot of encouragement from looking at women's actual lives in the 1950s. And all the women I knew in the Communist Party denied very hostilely that they wanted to be thought of as women – and 'feminism' was about 'bourgeois' women, utterly scorned. You were a comrade and wanted to be treated exactly as men were. The trouble was that you weren't, it seemed to me. *The Golden Notebook* describes very brilliantly the kind of women who stayed active in the party and they were often bitter, hard, and certainly didn't identify with the quiet wives sitting in the corner making tea while 'the comrades' discussed politics.

So the positive images of female friendship in *The Golden Notebook* were a life-line for me and I can remember consciously developing my relationships with women in that period – friendship networks – which enabled me as a single, independent woman to survive. I was a WEA tutor-organiser from 1960 and we started up women's afternoon classes at which we read de Beauvoir and Lessing and everything else I could lay my hands on, and the consciousness went up just like that – it was a spark, and women sat up and started talking. It was really exciting, as if everybody was waiting for something to happen. And then came Betty Friedan's book, *The Feminine Mystique*, naming the 'problem that has no name' and criticising exactly that dedication to 'family above all else' which made women feel so swamped. But in 1962, Doris Lessing isn't really saying that quite. Just hinting at it. And I think I just knew something was wrong and we couldn't just sit behind the kitchen table and moan about it.

Trying to conceive of another form of politics which would take women's lives as the centre was really hard and we had to wait for the first news from America of consciousness-raising groups. But that was after the early 1960s. Most men that I talked to about feminism were very sympathetic and interested, but they hadn't yet been confronted in their domestic personal lives and were anyway in favour of a more liberated sexuality!

So the book was prophetic. It does prefigure all sorts of things that were actually to happen in the next ten years – to me personally, and in the external world. I think I even felt that I wouldn't fully understand it until I had actually lived another ten years of my life. I can still pick it up now and say, 'God, *now* I know what she is saying about that.' I suppose that isn't legitimate literary criticism, but it's what makes the book important to me. I think it's a rich book in that sense – she talks about fragmenting and getting beyond it, something which we could pick years later in *Beyond the Fragments*. That may not be something that can be experienced by people who read it twenty years later; I don't know, certainly it was very powerful then.

3 Yesterday's heroines: on rereading Lessing and de Beauvoir

Elizabeth Wilson

Who are these women we admired so much? In the strange cultural landscape of 1960 they loomed up, Cassandras of women's experience, an experience that was everywhere silenced, concealed and denied.

They were, it is true, famous, fêted, ambivalently, as writers. But this almost seemed to be on condition that their 'testimony' was wilfully misunderstood. A generation of women – and men – ransacked their work for 'truths' about the human condition, and, especially, for the truth about women. Yet their work aroused anger and hatred at the same time as they were idealized. As Doris Lessing has said, they were 'reacted to' instead of being 'read'. So it is not simply a question of what they wrote, it is also a question of how their audience received it. How was their testimony read? To whom did they speak, secretly and silently? The statements of these women, each isolated in the spotlight of her gift, must have had a slow-release effect on their audience of millions of women, equally isolated, scattered across the globe. To these women they spoke as unique individuals, and yet they raised Woman's voice.

In writing of these exemplary women, I write as two readers. My impressions of them are blurred by the double vision of having read them as a very young woman and again now. This has modified my view of them, and I have also seen 'myself' (whatever that is) anew. For this reason I confine my discussion largely to the works I read 'then', and I have ignored the most recent works, especially of Doris Lessing. This is partly because I am not approaching their work as a 'feminist critic', but simply as a feminist, trying to chart my reactions to them then and now, and to gauge their political impact. I am not first and foremost concerned to interpret any given literary text within its own terms. I am less interested in the texts than in the writers and what they have come to stand for as feminists.

If I start from the idea of 'heroine' that is because I saw them as heroines twenty or so years ago. Nor was I alone in this. Margaret Walters writes:

> When I first read *The Second Sex* – about fifteen years ago, before the present women's movement – it struck me with the force of a genuine revelation. It helped me make some sense of my confused and isolated depression. Since the book appeared in 1949, de Beauvoir has received thousands of letters from women all over the world, grateful for the way her book helped them to see their personal frustrations in terms of the general condition of women.[1]

Margaret Walters insists, too, that: 'there is a very real sense in which [de Beauvoir] presents herself as an *exemplary* figure.' It is true that she was often seen, popularly, as a malignant rather than as an inspiring example. In *La Verité*, a French film of the period around 1960 (directed by Henri Georges Clouzot), the heroine, played by Brigitte Bardot, is a juvenile delinquent. In court, the judge is persuaded of the girl's moral turpitude when he hears that she had read *The Second Sex*. In Britain, journalists associated Doris Lessing (and Iris Murdoch) for a short time with the Angry Young Men. They were seen, that is, as rebels and social critics, which other young women novelists of the period from the mid-1950s to the early 1960s – say Edna O'Brien or Margaret Drabble – were not. Both Lessing and de Beauvoir were therefore seen as subversive and as, in some sense, political. But 'political' in those days never meant feminist, and their lives and writings raise questions about the relationship of the isolated woman to political movements.

In contrasting the lives and work of these two women, one sees immediately the similarities. Yet what two women – given that both were educated, politically conscious intellectuals who lived within Western capitalism – could be more different?

Both Doris Lessing and Simone de Beauvoir recount their youthful experiences as 'escape' – escape from stifling environments that would destroy them. Doris Lessing was brought up in what was then Southern Rhodesia and had to struggle to free herself from a backward, racist, philistine community. There was a jarring contrast between the vastness of Africa and the blinkered narrowness of imperialism. Her escape was a physical as well as a moral and intellectual escape. Yet it brought her only to the Cold War Britain of the post-1945 period. And in Britain she was always an exile. Simone de Beauvoir, on the contrary, grew up as an archetypal Parisian intellectual, firmly centred within a cultural tradition rich in art, literature and philosophy – the height of 'civilization'. A decade older than Doris Lessing, she also nonetheless felt stifled by the bourgeoisie as represented by her family, by the dusty pieties of Catholicism, and the philistinism of the middle class. Both of these families, also, were downwardly mobile.

Simone de Beauvoir's parents had once been financially secure but as she grew up they slipped down towards genteel poverty, although they made every effort to keep up appearances and did maintain some kind of 'normal' bourgeois life. Doris Lessing's parents, on the contrary, experienced a far wider gap between self-presentation and 'reality'. And that is the gap through which madness can leak into daily life. Her parents, foundering on a run-down farm, the very roof collapsing, exist, at least as she portrays them, largely in fantasies from the past. Her father harks back to his days in the trenches during the First World War. Her mother attempts to live out a dream of imperial grandeur based on fantasies born in suburban England. In her autobiographical book, *In Pursuit of the English*, Doris Lessing constructs her father as verging on the mad, and (here an ambiguity between fiction and autobiography is very clear) *Martha Quest* contains a similar account of Martha's parents. These white settlers, becalmed on their farm in the vastness of the veld, have in a sense lost touch with the reality that should have anchored them to sanity. Theirs is a bourgeois life run into a crazy caricature of itself, based on nothing, not even comfortable.

The great fear of Lessing's Southern African heroines is to be somehow lost down that gap where reality, daily life itself, becomes first meaningless and then mad. They fear annihilation in the endless, dusty, empty spaces of the veld. This does open out into madness in *The Grass is Singing*.

For Simone de Beauvoir it is the claustrophobia of the *foyer* (the bourgeois home) that threatens the integrity of the self. The young 'self' of her autobiography, *The Prime of Life*, escapes *into* the solitude and even the dangers of the hills above Marseilles. Martha Quest recognizes not only her own insignificance in the midst of the veld, but the insignificance of our planet in the vast inconsequentiality of the universe:

> During that space of time (which was timeless) she understood quite finally her smallness, the unimportance of humanity. In her ears was an inchoate grinding, the great wheels of move-ment, and it was inhuman . . . and no part of that sound was Martha's voice . . . that is, what was futile was her own idea of herself and her place in the chaos of matter.[2]

For Simone de Beauvoir, by contrast, the encounter with Nature – when she learns to ski, or when she explores the Mediterranean hills – is a test of her own mastery of nature, of an ego that can never be swallowed up in infinity:

> a sheer wall of rock blocked any further advance, and I had to retrace my steps, from one basin to the next. At last I came to a fault in the rock which I dared not jump across. There was no sound except for the rustle of snakes slithering among the dry stones. No living soul would ever pass through this defile: suppose I broke a leg or twisted an ankle; what would become of me? I shouted, but got no reply: I went on calling for a quarter of an hour. The silence was appalling. In the end I plucked up my courage and got down safe and sound . . .
>   In any case there were certain things, such as accidents, severe illnesses, or rape, which simply *could not happen* to me.[3]

Each of these young women has a strong sense of her own individual identity, even in the face of this huge, senseless universe. Each has also a strongly *political* sense of the gulf between individual pain and the difficulty experienced by the individual who tries to change or influence events. Simone de Beauvoir writes, in *Force of Circumstance*, of the horror of war in Algeria, the tortures and persecutions:

> Beauty, yes beauty remains . . . but often I loathe it too. The evening after a massacre, I was listening to a Beethoven andante and stopped the record halfway through in anger: all the pain of the world was there, but so magnificently

sublimated and controlled that it seemed justified. Almost all beautiful works have been created for the privileged and by privileged people . . . they are disguising the horror of misery in its nakedness. Another evening, after another massacre – there have been so many – I longed for all such lying beauty to be utterly destroyed.[4]

Doris Lessing's heroine Anna in *The Golden Notebook* is likewise obsessed with the senselessness and enormity of human suffering. She feels she is going mad as she surrounds herself with the 'senseless facts' from newspapers, pinning them up all over the walls, first of one room, soon a second. And – herself a writer – she finds it impossible to write, to assimilate artistically the horrors of the world.

Both Simone de Beauvoir and Doris Lessing assume, tacitly, in their way of talking about their sense of smallness and futility, that human life *ought* to be purposeful, rational and coherent. This is a feeling that permeates the literature of the post-war period – that Renaissance Man, centre of the universe, had somehow fallen from his pedestal, and had been decentred. The agony of man's smallness in the universe was a repeated theme of literature in those years. In Britain, certainly, the post-war literary atmosphere was one of romantic pessimism, tinged with a decadent religiosity. In France, Existentialism – of which Simone de Beauvoir and Jean-Paul Sartre were regarded as the 'high priests' in the late 1940s – represented in some ways a 'Left' version of this pessimism.

Many male writers of the post-Second World War period posed the individual creative man over against the senseless void of the universe – 'man's cosmic loneliness', as Bertrand Russell put it. *L'Homme revolté* by Albert Camus (once a close associate of de Beauvoir and Sartre, but far to the Right of them by the late 1940s) is an expression of this tragic humanism.

Doris Lessing and Simone de Beauvoir both rework these problems and move beyond them. Their bulky writings do partially fit into the 'great realist novel' tradition, and they have tried to retain at least that aspect of the nineteenth-century tradition which used the novel as a vehicle for moral and philosophical dilemmas. Yet as they use it, the capacious cupboard of the traditional novel – panorama of society that does not question the importance of our human concerns – bulges and bursts with the 'new consciousness' of these women.

Each appears to be offering a kind of testimony, the subjective voice of experience, catching the flux and flow of life, which pours like a river across the page, and for which the architectonic structure of, say, Proust, would be inappropriate. Each is at the same time explicitly committed to realism in the novel. Doris Lessing makes clear her commitment in her essay in *Declaration*, a collection of essays from the mid-1950s by authors who at that time were corralled under the label of the Angry Young Men. In Lessing's essay, 'The Small Personal Voice', she states:

> For me the highest point of literature was the novel of the nineteenth century . . . the work of the great realists . . . I hold the view that the realist novel, the realist story, is the highest form of prose writing.[5]

It is only through realism that she can get 'under the net' of all theorizations about life, and down to the thing itself. For Anna in *The Golden Notebook* Marxism and psychoanalysis – the theories she has used to try to make sense of her life – in the end mask the formless inner reality. To 'name' things, as she puts it there, is in the end to betray and diminish; so that when she looks round her analyst's carefully arranged consulting room – a room 'like an art gallery' – she feels that:

> Nothing in my life corresponds with anything in this room –̈ my life has always been crude, unfinished, raw, tentative; and so have the lives of the people I have known well. It occurred to me, looking at this room, that the raw unfinished quality in my life was precisely what was valuable in it and I should hold fast to it.[6]

Both art and theory in the end go against this feeling.

Simone de Beauvoir tells us that she and Sartre greatly admired the 'clipped realism' of the styles of American writers such as Dashiell Hammett and Ernest Hemingway, and in *Force of Circumstance* she criticizes the *nouveau roman* then fashionable in France:

> [Nathalie Sarraute] confuses truth and psychology, while [Alain Robbe Grillet] refuses to admit interiority: she reduces

exteriority to appearances, in other words, a false show; for him, appearances are everything, it is forbidden to go beyond them; in both cases the world of enterprises, struggles, need, work, the whole real world, disappears into thin air . . . On the whole, one of the constant factors of this whole school of writing is boredom; it takes all the savour, all the fire out of life, its impulse towards the future.[7]

Yet despite their commitment to a 'life' that shall be reflected in all its vividness in their work, neither of these women authors stays within the confines of classical realism as it's usually understood, since both also explore their subjectivity as women in the manner of the twentieth-century psychological novel. But they do not remain within what has been traditionally cast as the appropriate 'feminine' sphere of the woman writer. They are not like Edna O'Brien, Penelope Mortimer or Gillian Tindall who spend a lot of time exploring 'feminine' dilemmas. Neither do they take the road chosen by Iris Murdoch in her first novel, *Under the Net*. In this, she evaded the problem by making her first-person narrator a man, Jake (who consequently fits more easily into the British 1950s' mould of picaresque 'existential' hero).

Estelle Jelinek,[8] an American feminist critic, has suggested that the autobiographical form, the diary and the letter form are women's forms *par excellence*, reflecting the diffusion, the multiplicity of roles and the sense of a fractured consciousness experienced by women. She also points out that, contrary to a popular view, these forms are not necessarily confessional in the sense of representing always the exposure of intimate feelings and psychological truths about the 'self' that is portrayed.

These expectations, though, may account for the way in which the writings of Simone de Beauvoir and Doris Lessing have time and again been received – as the Voice of Woman. They are read as 'the truth'. As the blurb on the back of my (1964) Penguin edition of *The Golden Notebook* puts it: 'Doris Lessing scrutinizes the plight of the emancipated woman of today with an honesty and an intensity which most women will find as pitiless as a mirror on a Monday morning.' There is a kind of triple elision, between author, heroine and reader. The (woman) reader identifies with a heroine who is at once creator and protagonist. This is made all the easier because of the strongly autobiographical elements in the writings of both Lessing and de Beauvoir. For however strongly each may protest that her novels are not simply autobiographical records (and that is clearly the case) the similarities are often so striking that the reader, in a strange double effect, is able to identify simultaneously with the heroine and with the creator (woman writer–real, living woman) who has shaped the heroine who is also 'herself'. This curious effect gives a potency to the voice of the woman writer, so that, however passive and victimized womanhood is sometimes seen to be in the writings, the identification is not with woman as passive victim or martyr.

Both writers set up multiple mirrors that reflect a variety of identities or possibly comment upon the fragmentation of identity for a woman who refuses to be bounded by what have been the traditional identities for women. Looked at in another way, the work of each of these writers may be read as an exposition of the production of a 'self'. Each attempts repeatedly to construct a self outside the roles of 'wife' and/or 'mother'. ('Mistress' is frequently alluded to, especially in *The Golden Notebook* and *The Second Sex*, and in Doris Lessing's short story 'Between Men' (1965) as a third possible, and mutilating, identity for women.)

In writing so extensively in the autobiographical vein, Simone de Beauvoir does of course make a much less equivocal claim to 'truth' and 'realism' than we would expect from a work of fiction. Yet there is a rigorous limitation to her self-revelations, as Margaret Walters, in her fine article, demonstrates:

> The suberb consistency of her life and work is also its limitation. In order to keep it up, she has to reject great areas of experience . . . I am always bothered by a shadow behind the clear outlines of her self-portrait, feelings denied or kept strenuously at bay. Her rigorous self-examination can be a kind of self-evasion.[9]

Indeed, her autobiographical volumes display just that 'shaping' and imposition of a pattern on events that writers on autobiography[10] have traditionally held to be characteristic of this form, but which Jelinek suggested did not hold good in many cases for women autobiographers. And what Margaret Walters condemns as a form of self-evasion has to do in part, I believe, with the project that shapes de Beauvoir's autobiographies: her determination to prove that the unconventional life of an emancipated woman can be emotionally rewarding as well as a success in worldly and in intellectual terms. So we might turn the ambiguity of the relationship between fiction and biography on its head, and instead of seeing fiction as reflection of reality, might prefer to see autobiography as equally an ordering of the 'tentative, unfinished' raw material of the 'real' in a metaphoric and symbolic creation of 'self'.

Amongst other things these famous writers, stereotypes of 'liberated' womanhood, are famous for writing frankly about women's sexuality. Yet, curiously, sexuality is implicated with madness for them both, on account of its irrational force.

Doris Lessing's heroine Martha is confident of her sexual attractiveness, and it represents one possible escape from the prison of the wide open veld. Her sexuality, and that of Ella/Anna in *The Golden Notebook*, is part of that spontaneous core of self that Doris Lessing values so much, and which men are so greatly to damage as they take 'her' further and further into its depths.

Simone de Beauvoir depicts the youthful 'self' of her first volume of autobiography, *Memoirs of a Dutiful Daughter*, as far less sexually assured than the young Martha Quest. Her first love affair is with a cousin who seems to be seen as much, almost, as an ideal self as a lover – and the 'twin' aspects of her relationship with Sartre also suggests a kind of narcissistic identification with the masculine. Simone de Beauvoir's father disparaged her looks, but praised her brain which was 'like a man's'. She can learn to find herself pretty as she teaches herself to dress well – epitome of that very 'French' phenomenon, the *jolie laide*. Sexuality remains, however, an irrational, and therefore at some level a resented force. Teaching in Marseilles, and therefore often separated from Sartre, she complains of her frustrated sexual desire as a shirt of Nessus, a hideous torment which has grown into her skin, while she not only mocks but is repelled by the advances made to her by a female colleague, whom she cruelly caricatures.

The sexuality of both Doris Lessing and Simone de Beauvoir is resolutely embedded in heterosexuality. Each rejects lesbianism and masturbation as alike pathetic substitutes which bring only disgust and self-hatred. Their sexuality is a response to a man. It must also be a response to love. Ella/Anna bitterly laments the fact that men do not 'really love' women, and cannot therefore give them the 'true' vaginal orgasm. She longs only to be swept away by such a love:

> When she loved a man again, she would return to normal: a woman, that is, whose sexuality would ebb and flow in response to his. A woman's sexuality is, so to speak, contained by a man, if he is a real man; she is, in a sense, put to sleep by him, she does not think about sex.[11]

Menstruating, she washes her body compulsively, hating her own smell, and when she is aroused by a man who means nothing to her emotionally, she catalogues with disgust the physical manifestations of her arousal.

When, in *Les Mandarins*,[12] the heroine's American lover abruptly rejects her, she, too, loses all desire, her body loses all feeling. In general, Simone de Beauvoir retains a considerable reticence about her own sexual feelings, although it may be of relevance to recall Sartre's own loathing of passive femininity. (This is elaborated upon in a celebrated section of *Being and Nothingness*,[13] in which he likens femininity to the horrible, clinging gapingness of the 'slimy' – *le visqueux* – matter that is neither liquid nor solid.) Where Simone de Beauvoir speaks most frankly of sex and the ecstasies of love, in *The Second Sex*, she speaks through the voices of other women, their diaries, their memoirs, their autobiographical novels; not for nothing have her novels and novellas been described as 'clinical', as 'case studies' – as if this almost medical distancing could sterilize sexual experience of its viscous, cloying horror.

The dominant theme in many of Simone de Beauvoir's books is the theme of men's betrayal and desertion of the women who became dependent on them, partly because of their children and their economic dependence, but also through sexual surrender itself. In her old age, Simone de Beauvoir has indeed said that the 'cult of the orgasm' has made matters worse for women, and forged only a new link in the chain of their dependency on men. *The Second Sex* is full of stories of the wives and mistresses of great, or at least successful, men – women who sacrificed their freedom and often their talents to the genius or ambition of men, to reap only ingratitude. Simone de Beauvoir portrays her own life differently. She is the woman who has escaped enslavement.

She has managed to create a relationship of equality with a man. Yet she is haunted by those others, the women who were not so lucky. Indeed – and it is sinister – *Memoirs of a Dutiful Daughter* reaches its conclusion with the death of her great childhood and adolescent friend, Zaza. Zaza, as Simone de Beauvoir describes it, died, to all intents and purposes, from love, and from excessive devotion to her parents. Unlike Simone, she was not determined enough to break away. She was trapped, and therefore doomed. She is Simone's dark alter ego:

> The doctors called it meningitis, encephalitis; no one was quite sure. Had it been a contagious disease, or an accident? Or had Zaza succumbed to exhaustion and anxiety? She has often appeared to me at night, her face all yellow under a pink sun-bonnet, and seeming to gaze reproachfully at me. We had fought together against the revolting fate that had lain ahead of us, and for a long time I believed that I had paid for my own freedom with her death.[14]

Simone de Beauvoir's heroines are frequently marked, haunted by such ghosts, mad women who have been undone by love. There is Paule, in *Les Mandarins*, whose aggression turns against Ann. There is also an American woman who visits Ann's American lover, and conceives an insane jealousy towards Ann. To be sane, to love successfully, brings, it would seem, an enormous danger of retribution.

Strangely, given that both Simone de Beauvoir and Doris Lessing are seen and see themselves as exceptional women, their attitudes to sexuality reproduce attitudes current in a contemporary literature of sexuality which constructed female heterosexuality in a particular way. It was a major preoccupation of the period to construct a contradictory amalgam of femininity as highly sexual and yet as wholly anchored within heterosexual marriage. This tied female sexuality and eroticism more securely to reproduction just at the moment when contraception was enabling women for the first time reliably to control their fertility.[15]

Both Lessing and de Beauvoir do insist on a female sexuality that is divorced from reproduction and they refuse the identity of mother (Simone de Beauvoir does this quite explicitly; Doris Lessing simply marginalizes motherhood for her heroines, which in the end may be more subversive – they have children but do not make motherhood the centre of their lives). On the other hand, they aspire to 'true marriages' – Doris Lessing in a very Lawrentian way. (The Lawrentian ideal of relationships between men and women was influential in Britain in radical circles in the late 1950s and early 1960s.[16] The sexual relationship was seen as, in the words of Raymond Williams, being the 'quick of life', while the idea that sexuality was a 'throwing off of repression' gave it a privileged relationship to 'truth' and the reality 'under the net'.)

This 'return of the repressed' is what gives sexuality its power and its danger. Sexual surrender is repeatedly depicted as a threat to woman's identity. The final, and even more devastating threat, in which sexuality is implicated, is the threat of madness. In the work of these writers, the great beast of the unconscious lurks in its dark hinterland always ready to spring.

Simone de Beauvoir's deadpan prose style cannot stifle the demons trying to escape. Political and personal betrayal, genocide and madness burst forth more horribly for being so ordinarily described. Her reactions are the reactions of the 'ordinary', sane person, and, despite what she witnesses, she represents, defiantly almost, the clear and transparent gaze of reason. However horrible the atrocities, they do also represent acute *political* problems for herself, and for the French Left.

For Simone de Beauvoir (and for Sartre), madness is the ultimate representation of 'bad faith', and there are many examples in their work of women who abdicate 'authenticity' because they cannot confront the realities of their failing sexual attractiveness and their servile dependence on their men. Marcelle, in Sartre's *L'Age de Raison*, is a case in point; Sartre uses the ploys of such a woman as an example to illustrate bad faith in *Being and Nothingness*. *The Second Sex* has many examples of women who allowed their dependency on men to betray them in this way, and de Beauvoir more than once describes characters for whom this led to madness. There is Paule, in *Les Mandarins*, who goes mad because she cannot bear to admit that she is growing older, losing her looks, that her lover has wearied of her. There is Camille, once the mistress of the theatrical producer Dullin, whom, in *All Said and Done*, Simone de Beauvoir describes in her sordid and crazy old age, seeing her as yet another example of this 'feminine' failure of women to 'face the truth'. Madness is a state of self-deception, and delusions are a hideous game that women play with themselves. Simone de Beauvoir retains a highly intellectual attitude to madness. Not only that, but in her avid pursuit of happiness and worldly joy she often seems to be frantically denying the existence of the madness and cruelty of which, in fact, she is acutely aware. Significantly, she and Sartre did refer to her optimism and relentless search for experience and sensation as her *schizophrenie*. By this they meant, I imagine, what a psychoanalyst would call a hysterical splitting, the denial of unwelcome aspects of life rather than the schizophrenic dissociation of thought which is more akin to a misrecognition of the meaning of things. For a schizophrenic, the world contains too much meaning: the rays of the sun convey a special message; the neighbours are sending thoughts through the wall. For the hysteric, on the other hand, whole tracts of feeling and even consciousness may be simply blocked out or blocked off; in acute cases leading to loss of memory or hysterical paralysis. So, for a long time, Simone de Beauvoir refused to admit that there was going to be a world war; at the age of forty, she refused to admit that her love affair with Nelson Allgren was destined to end in despair, that he would not love her on her terms, because he wanted a woman who 'belonged' to him. So at times her determination to be happy seems almost itself to be verging on the mad.

Yet for Simone de Beauvoir madness is never the entry to another, more privileged, state of consciousness. For Doris Lessing, on the other hand, it is. Anna, in *The Golden Notebook*, temporarily driven insane by the horrors of the world, judges her madness as the truly sane response – it is the world that is mad. In this respect her work is close to that of R. D. Laing,[17] the radical psychiatrist who was so influential in the 1960s in Britain, and who tried to marry psychoanalysis to Existentialism.

Existentialism seems something quite different to Simone de Beauvoir. It is the philosophical expression of sane, rational *choice*. An individual can 'choose' liberty without descent into bad faith, provided that she/he recognizes the chance nature of life, and the absence of any supernatural plan for human life or the universe. As Sartre put it, 'Man is condemned to freedom.' Existentialism as interpreted by Laing and the other British radical psychiatrists, on the other hand, represented precisely a recognition of the supremacy of the irrational.

In *The Four Gated City*[18] Linda represents madness as a clearer than normal perception of the truth. When Linda is 'mad' she can get in touch with other worlds; her consciousness is not dulled but widened. In *Landlocked*,[19] Martha's former lover, Thomas, goes off to live in a native village, and, after his death from fever, a manuscript he had written comes into Martha's hands. This is the testament either of a madman ('He was nuts, wasn't he?' a friend comments) or of someone who had broken through some barrier of consciousness to get in touch with other times and other worlds and had begun to chronicle them.

So there they are, so alike yet so different – Simone de Beauvoir asserting the mastery of the will as her way of grasping experience, Doris Lessing valuing immersion in experience. This is why each has a very different attitude towards politics.

Both appear, and make their heroines appear, as politically conscious women, associated with Marxism, close to the communist parties of their countries. One important theme of the de Beauvoir autobiographies, and of *Les Mandarins*, is the evolution of the Sartre/de Beauvoir political position after the Second World War – close to, but never in, the French Communist Party, resolutely set against both anti-communism and mindless pro-Sovietism. Martha Quest, and Anna in *The Golden Notebook*, both traverse the Communist Party, finding in it an inevitable falsity and posturing. For Doris Lessing, the Communist Party is, in the end, ideas in the heads of individuals rather than a genuine lived relationship with the suffering of the black Africans in Rhodesia or of the poor women Anna meets when canvassing in north London. For Simone de Beauvoir, the taking up and working out of political positions is a wholly valid activity, but for Doris Lessing such manoeuvring necessarily distorts the truth of feeling for which she is always looking.

Both nonetheless saw themselves and their heroines as inevitably and inescapably political. Yet, as political women, they were distressingly isolated.

When I first read these heroine-authors, I was only eighteen – then twenty – then twenty-four. To reread them now that I am past forty is a strange experience – the double vision of seeing two of each of them and two of myself as well. How differently I now read these famous accounts of women's experience! And how sad, in one way, it is that I have lost my ability to identify with them as heroines and alternative selves.

Then, I was lost in admiration, so that I noticed neither their political isolation (as women), nor their contempt for lesbianism, nor their romanticism when it came to sexuality. Like many others, I took Simone de Beauvoir's 'bohemian' model of the liberated relationship with a Great Writer as *the* archetype of a desirable 'free' relationship. Now, in *The Prime of Life*, I encounter a young woman repeating frantically to herself: 'I'm happy – I'm so *happy*,' when actually she seems tense and lonely, introverted, obsessive, rude and contemptuous towards her spinsterly colleagues, and riddled with insecurity and terror lest Sartre leave her.

Now, in *The Golden Notebook* (which I first read as a manual of womanly experience), I discern attitudes towards both men and women whose ambivalence repels me. *Then* I looked up to Anna/Ella as an experienced 'older woman'. Now I judge her, looking back at her from a further, perhaps more cynical, possibly more stoical, landmark of experience, as one of *those* women – the ones who cry 'freedom' while hugging their chains.

This experience – of having read these books in my early twenties and then rereading them twenty-odd years later – has raised many questions for me about the act of reading and about the way in which the reader may identify with the 'heroine' or 'writer'. Many young women of today's feminist movement are very critical of Simone de Beauvoir, rejecting her as excessively male-identified and highly individualistic (which in many ways she is). Doris Lessing is, I think, more acceptable because she speaks so exhaustively of feeling, and particularly of painful feeling, and the contemporary Women's Movement tends to overvalue feeling, pain and subjectivity.

Of course, my angry rejection today of Doris Lessing's mystical vision of life is itself a kind of negative identification. For some reason, Lessing and de Beauvoir still invite these passion-ately felt responses.

Had there been a women's movement in the 1950s and early 1960s, women might not have needed to relate to them in the way they did, as heroines and exemplars, and they themselves might not have needed to present themselves – sometimes intentionally, sometimes not – in this way. It falsified their position. Yet when Doris Lessing claims (of *The Golden Notebook*):

> Some books are not read in the right way because they have skipped a stage of opinion, assume a crystallization of information in society which has not yet taken place. This book was written as if the attitudes that have been created by the women's liberation movement already existed . . . If it were coming out now for the first time it might be read and not merely reacted to[20]

we have to query this. For in some ways what Doris Lessing says is the antithesis of women's liberation. The situation and consciousness of her fractured heroine, Anna, is precisely the situation and consciousness the feminists of the late 1960s were in revolt *against*. They were trying *not* to feel bounded within masculine sexuality. They were trying to find a voice in politics, to live politics, to take women into the political arena instead of rejecting the political arena as an ultimate falsification.

Today, both Simone de Beauvoir and Doris Lessing seem stuck in one-sided representations of womanhood, caught in the impossible dilemma of being Artists at a period when the Artist represented the ultimate in individualism, and of having a representative Woman's voice at the same time. Exceptional women speaking as women, their audience assumes that they are speaking *for* women – hence the anger they arouse in many feminists today, since we have come to see our dilemmas differently.

This ambiguity between 'truth' and 'fiction', and between the unique and the representative voice, still haunts the consciously feminist writers of today. It is interesting – and deserves more analysis – that so many contemporary feminists have turned to imaginative writing in order to express their experience as feminists as well as women. The early works from women's liberation attempted to *theorize* woman's subordination, and, rightly, to make plain the collective nature of the isolated woman's pain.

In returning to individual lived experience, are today's feminists returning to a post-political or a-political consciousness? Or are they confronting the recognition that political theory in the 1970s still did not give women a new individualized identity, and that, although we need as much as ever our collective identity of 'feminist', each of us needs an individual identity as well?

Even if, today, we feel distanced from these pioneers, we should, however, salute two women who were brave enough to risk exposure and to court isolation for having outlined and explored the terrain on which feminists are still struggling: what they are talking about, and what we are still talking about today, is the relationship between political consciousness and individual consciousness. We may construct our experience differently today, but we are still engaged in the same project, which is to develop a literature of experience (which it should be called, perhaps, rather than either 'fiction' *or* 'autobiography') that both expresses and enlarges our understanding of the Janus-face of feminism – which faces both towards the personal and towards the political.

Notes

1 Margaret Walters, 'The Rights and Wrongs of Women: Mary Wollstonecraft, Harriet Martineau, Simone de Beauvoir', in Juliet Mitchell and Margaret Walters (eds), *The Rights and Wrongs of Women*, Harmondsworth, Penguin, 1976, p. 351.

2 Doris Lessing, *Martha Quest*, London, Panther, p. 62.

3 Simone de Beauvoir, *The Prime of Life*, Harmondsworth, Penguin, 1976, p. 93.

4 Simone de Beauvoir, *Force of Circumstance*, Harmondsworth, Penguin, 1968, pp. 669–70.

5 Doris Lessing, 'The Small Personal Voice', in Tom Maschler (ed.), *Declaration*, London, MacGibbon & Kee, 1968, p. 14.

6 Doris Lessing, *The Golden Notebook*, Harmondsworth, Penguin, 1964, p. 233.

7 Simone de Beauvoir, *Force of Circumstance*, Harmondsworth, Penguin, 1968, pp. 636–7.

8 Estelle C. Jelinek, 'Women's Autobiography and the Male Tradition', in Estelle C. Jelinek (ed.), *Women's Autobiography: Essays in Criticism*, Bloomington and London, Indiana University Press, 1980.

9 Margaret Walters, op. cit., p. 354.

10 For example, Roy Pascal, *Design and Truth in Autobiography*, London, Routledge & Kegan Paul, 1960.

11 Doris Lessing, *The Golden Notebook*, p. 447.

12 Simone de Beauvoir, *Les Mandarins*, Paris, Gallimard, 1954.

13 Jean-Paul Sartre, *Being and Nothingness*, London, Methuen 1969, pp. 607ff.

14 Simone de Beauvoir, *Memoirs of a Dutiful Daughter*, Harmondsworth, Penguin, 1963, p. 360.

15 Elizabeth Wilson. *Only Halfway to Britain: Women in Postwar Britain 1945–1968*, London, Tavistock, 1980.
16 Ibid.
17 R. D. Laing, *The Bird of Paradise and the Politics of Experience*, Harmondsworth, Penguin, 1967.
18 Doris Lessing, *The Four Gated City*, London, Panther, 1972.
19 Doris Lessing, *Landlocked*, London, Panther, 1967.
20 In Malcolm Bradbury (ed.), *The Novel Today: Contemporary Writers on Modern Fiction*, London, Fontana, p. 172.

4 Of mud and other matter – *The Children of Violence*

Nicole Ward Jouve

Note on abbreviations and sources

The following abbreviations are used to refer to Doris Lessing's books:

GS	*The Grass Is Singing*
MQ	*Martha Quest*
PM	*A Proper Marriage*
RS	*A Ripple from the Storm*
LL	*Landlocked*
FGC	*The Four-Gated City*
GN	*The Golden Notebook*
GH	*Going Home*
IPE	*In Pursuit of the English*
MS	*Memoirs of a Survivor*
SH	*Shikasta*

All quotations from these books were from the Panther editions, most currently available, except for *The Grass Is Singing* (Granada, 1980), *In Pursuit of the English* (Popular Library, 1960), *Memoirs of a Survivor* (Picador, 1974), and *Shikasta* (Jonathan Cape, 1979).

I say I. I am going to say I. I claim the right to say I. Since I, a woman using language, am going to say what I find wrong with the language of a woman I admire, I will not shelter behind the anonymous array of third-person modes 'crrrriticism', by tacit agreement, requires. I will be no puppeteer of my own sentences. No ghostly judge arraigning my betters in the name of some assumed (fatuous) moral right. If I 'pass' 'judgment' (rather, it suddenly occurs to me, as one passes water, or a motion), I will also lay my own head on the chopping block. Then (to go on with what's turning out to be in worse and worse taste) my judgment may appear due to fear.

For my own life.
My own language.

The logic of the sequence: from mud to the void

The Children of Violence: *what 'happens'*

	Martha, born in Rhodesia of first-generation, ineffective English settlers, leaves home (in the
MQ, 1952	1930s) and goes to live in the city – Salisbury (though neither Rhodesia nor the city are ever given their actual name). Proceeds to search for herself, search for truth, justice, freedom, racial and sexual and social harmony (the four-gated
PM, 1954	city), periodically allowing her bewilderment, good nature, liberal convictions or peculiar passiveness to snare her into unwanted situations (her two marriages, the birth of her daughter, Caroline), but always escaping in the end without doing too much damage: not
RS, 1958	remaining trapped in what for instance she sees as the unreality and paltriness of her friend
LL, 1965	Marjorie's marriage. Proceeds through communism, committee activities during the war, the odd affairs with RAF officers posted near Salisbury, a deep involvement with a radical Jewish/Pole settler, Thomas, more committee militancy for racial equality, till she finally leaves for England. Once there, goes at an
FGC, 1969 (time-span: from post- Second World War	accelerated pace through every struggle of the liberal intelligentsia from resistance to the Cold War witch-hunt to Aldermaston marches, caring for the drop-outs and the mentally sick, and surviving nuclear war. As she wends her

years to the year 2,000)	way through cause after cause, there is an increasing feeling of unreality. Martha realizes that she, and everyone else from youth to age spend their time stepping from one preordained role to another. A combination of breakdown and interest in mysticism finally delivers the vision that they all, not just the characters in the novel, everyone in England, in the world, are children of violence, acted upon by wave after wave of forces no one can control. Everyone is a succession of parts. Lives a partitioned, inauthentic existence. One can only escape from the violent impulses by plugging on to creative forces, developing new, mystical skills. Ceasing to play the game of violence. Withdrawing into a wise passiveness. The way for *MS* is open at the end of *FGC*.

The first thing to say about the sequence is that it is strongly autobiographical. In two ways: it is close to the 'events', the pattern, of Doris Lessing's own life; and the way Martha's vision of life evolves roughly corresponds to Lessing's own evolution. That it is so needs not be established by biographical research.[1] Strong evidence shows it: internal evidence – one feels the 'factual', the documentary quality of the novels despite the disguises, despite the (wavering) fictionalizing intention (at its strongest in the first two novels, where Martha tends to be entered into as a 'character'; at its weakest perhaps in *RS* and in most of *FGC*, where Martha, instead of functioning as a mirror of the self, is much more of a (near transparent) window to look out of). There is also corroborative evidence from the other books: the documentary (*IPE, GH*) where one recognizes the veld, the house on the veld, the parents (their quality, the father especially, as 'grail-seekers' strongly confirming the 'quest' element of Martha);[2] and the fictional: Anna Wulf's African experience, her German husband, and very similar to Martha's; the visions of Emily's childhood in *MS* spell out many things about Doris Lessing's family complex which are only half-expressed in *The Children of Violence*.[3]

There is nothing wrong nor even unusual of course about

novels being so strongly autobiographical. One could name
scores of great novels which are. But a question immediately
arises here, because of the *universal* significance which attaches to
the factualness, the documentary 'truths' which are being
presented: how does the 'fictional' form and the overall significance attached to it grow out of the 'documentary', the
'individual' 'truth'? And, in particular, how does the concluding
position, the late Martha's wisdom, tally with Martha's earlier
sense of life?

For she starts from mud. Warm African mud. Which is what at
the start 'signifies'.

> The bush lay quiet about her, a bare slope of sunset-tinted grass
> moving gently with a tiny rustling sound . . . her flesh was the
> earth, and suffered growth like a ferment (*MQ*, 61–2).

> This naked embrace of earth and sky, the sun hard and strong
> overhead, pulling up the moisture from foliage, from soil, so
> that the swimming glisten of heat is like a caress made visible
> . . . this frank embrace between the lifting breast of the land
> and the deep blue warmth of the sky is what exiles from Africa
> dream of (*MQ*, 252).

Mud. Sex. Mud is where Martha defends herself, her strong
body, against the inroads of convention – clothes, marriage:
propriety.

> he was agitatedly dancing on the steps, saying, 'Matty, Matty,
> do be careful'. There was something about that shrill and
> helpless exhortation which turned her mood into defiance. She
> looked calmly about her: there were six feet of muddy water
> between her and the gate. 'To hell with it', she [the text has 'he'
> – which must be a misprint] remarked; and fell all at once into
> her element. She lifted her crisp white skirts in a bunch around
> her waist, and composedly walked in her gold shoes, the water
> lapping cool around her ankles, to the sidewalk, saying,
> 'Oooh, it's lovely, it's lovely, Don', like a child paddling . . .
> She lifted her feet and examined them. The gold leather had
> dulled, and was crinkling; there was a faint brown tide-mark
> around her ankles. She could not help looking at them with
> satisfaction; the elegant, cool white dress seemed quite remote
> from her, a mere surface to her body, which continued

strongly upwards from those reckless strong ankles
(*MQ*, 165).

She began taking off her clothes, with rapid clumsy
movements. Martha did the same. They held the door half
open, for a last look for any possible invaders, and then
plunged across the road into the long grass on the other side
. . . [Martha] almost ran into a gulf that opened under her feet.
It was a pothole, gaping like a mouth, its red crumbling sides
swimming with red water. Above it the long heavy grass
almost met. Martha hesitated, then jumped straight in. A
moment of repugnance, then she loosened deliciously in the
warm rocking of the water. She stood to her knees in heavy
mud, the red thick water closed below her shoulders . . . In the
jelly spawn were tiny dark dots of life. She could see a large
snail tilting through the grass-stems . . . Then across the
white-frothed surface of the pool, she saw an uncoiling in the
wet mat of grass, and a lithe green snake moved its head this
way and that, its small tongue flickering. It slid down over the
red pulpy mud, and, clinging with its tail to a clutch of grass, it
allowed itself to lie on the surface, swaying its vivid head just
above the water (*PM*, 153–4).

Mud comes into its own – the strong, healthy body finds fulfilment ('Lawrentian' fulfilment, one cannot help but think, since in
a way and at this moment this seems to be very much where the
novels are going) in the brief affair with Thomas:

a young woman . . . lay face down on a rough bed, dipping her
arm in and out of the greenish sun-lanced light below her as if
into water . . . Martha turned on her back to stretch her body's
happiness in cool, leaf-smelling warmth (*LL*, 102).

Yet – yet, if one excepts this section of *LL*, it is as if mud
disappeared from Martha's universe after the end of *PM*.
Strangely, in *RS*, mud, grass, lush 'singing' African grass, is
given to a passing character, Jimmy, *not* Martha: and the 'tiny
dark dots of life' swarming in it are experienced as horrifying, not
beautiful:

The grass behind him was a solid wall, grown to its July
strength, the sap no longer running, each stem taut and

slippery as fine steel, massed together in a resilient antagonism [the text has 'antagonist' – which must be a misprint] to his back. He swung himself slightly; away from it and back again, and found himself laughing out loud out of a deep startled pleasure because of the toughness of the resisting grass . . . And again his nostrils filled with a sweet sharp breath of scent. His mouth fell open, his eyes stared and glazed a little, his body was tense, trying to absorb noises, scents . . . he had stared too long at the fine black outline, because it had clotted, on the delicate feather was a black knot. He blinked, hard and sharp, hearing, just above him, a sudden outburst of noise, as loud as machine-gun fire. And from behind his back, in the grass-stems, another. He shifted uneasily, his blood pounding, his nerves tight. He looked and waited. All of a sudden he realized that the *black* knot was an insect . . . My God, they were all over him, large, horny beetle-insects, clumsily moving their feelers and moving up over him. He let out a yell of fear, and brushed them off with frantic hands (*RS*, 150–1).

By the time of *FGC*, Africa's of course been left behind, there's no mud left anywhere. Anyhow. The disappearance of mud from the universe of the novels is bound up (runs parallel with) the disappearance of the home. The mud house. The childhood house. 'Roots'. They of course appear most strongly in the prose of the directly autobiographical *GH*:

the wall that faced my bed was not flat.

When the workmen had flung on the mud, naturally it was a little bumpy because no matter how you smooth on mud over poles, if there is a knot on the pole where a branch was chopped off, or if the pole had a bit of a bend in it, then the mud settled into the shape of bump and hollow . . .

I knew the geography of that wall as I knew the lines of my palm . . . The grain of the wall, like a skin, was illuminated by the clear light. There were areas of light, brisk graining where Tobias the painter had whisked his paint-brush from side to side; then a savage knot of whorls and smudged lines where he had twirled it around. What had he been thinking about when his paint-brush suddenly burst into such a fury of movements? . . .

A young tree used to shoot up under my bed every wet

season. There was a crack in the mud there; the linoleum began
to bulge upwards, and then split; and out came a pale, sickly,
whitey-yellowish shoot which immediately turned a healthy
green. We cut it off; but it sprouted up once or twice every wet
season . . .

It was the ants, of course, who finally conquered, for when
we left that house empty in the bush, it was only a season
before the ant-hills sprouted in the rooms themselves, among
the quick sprouting trees, and the red galleries must have
covered all the walls and the floor. The rains were heavy that
year, beating the house to its knees. And we heard that on the
kopje there was no house, just a mound of greyish, rotting
thatch, covered all over with red ant-galleries (*GH*, 51–5).

This is also Martha's house (the kind of connection that makes
one realize how deeply autobiographical *The Children of Violence*
novels are):

[The house] was built native style, with mud walls and
thatched roof, and had been meant to last for two seasons, for
the Quests had come to the colony after seeing an exhibition in
London which promised new settlers that they might become
rich on maize-growing almost from one year to the next. This
had not happened, and the temporary house was still in use . . .
The roof of the house too had sagged, and the walls had been
patched so often with fresh mud that they were all colours,
from dark rich red through dulling yellow to elephant
grey . . .

In the middle of the floor was a pole of tough thornwood, to
hold the end of the ridgepole. It had lain for weeks in a bath of
strong chemicals, to protect it from ants and insects; but now it
was riddled with tiny holes, and if one put one's ear to it there
could be heard a myriad tiny jaws at work (*MQ*, 20–1).

Martha is never described as being deeply attached to this
house. Yet, once mud is left behind by the novels, once the mud
house is lost, all sense of *home* is lost. I think that by that, I mean
the ability of things, people, to *signify*. Certainly, nothing has a
real *pull* upon Martha. Nothing is ever too much for her: no house
ever again has any weight of meaning:

The flat was bright, modern, compact . . . Coming into it was

a relief; one enters a strange place feeling, To what must I adapt
myself? But there was nothing individual here to claim one's
mood, there was no need to submit oneself. In this country, or
in England, or in any other country, one enters this flat, is at
home at once, with a feeling of peace. Thank God! There are
enough claims on us as it is, tugging us this way and that,
without considering fittings and furniture; who used them
before? What kind of people were they? What do they demand
of us? Ah, the blessed anonymity of the modern flat, that home
for nomads who, with no idea of where they are travelling,
must travel light, ready for anything (*MQ*, 178).

For me all houses will always be wrong; all bungalows,
cottages, mansions and villas will be uncomfortable and
incongruous and confining. I only like blocks of flats, the most
direct expression of crammed town-living. I did not
understand why this should be so for a long time, until I took
to dreaming nightly of the house I was brought up in; and then
at last I submitted myself to the knowledge that I am the victim
of a private mania that I must humour . . . In order to find a
place I live in tolerable, I have not to see it . . . If, in an
unguarded moment, I actually see it, all of it, what it is, then a
terrible feeling of insecurity and improbability comes over me.
The fact is, I don't live anywhere; I never have since I left that
first house on the kopje (*GH*, 36–7).

True, a new home is temporarily re-created for Martha by her
love for Thomas; it saves her from compartmentalization, that
curse of the four notebooks: from the separate rooms:

She had complained that her life had consisted of a dozen
rooms, each self-contained, that she was wearing into a frazzle
of shrill nerves in the effort of carrying herself, each time a
whole, from one 'room' to the other. But adding a new room
to her house had ended the division. From this centre she now
lived – a loft of aromatic wood from whose crooked window
could be seen only sky and the boughs of trees, above a brick
floor hissing sweetly from the slow drippings and wellings
from a hundred growing plants (*LL*, 103).

But soon that loft, what it signifies, collapses, while the old house
on the kopje falls to bits: an image of Europe in ruins two years

after the war; a warning of the future collapse of the city Martha is contemplating:

> Nearly a hundred miles away, in the red earth district, the old house had sunk to its knees under the blows of the first wet season after the Quests had left it, as if the shambling structure had been held upright only by the spirit of the family in it . . . It was wet and sultry on that hill, because of the heavy growth, although a thousand winds poured over it, and so walls and roof had rotted years ago in a fierce compost. The wet heat spawned, and the undersides of rafters sprouted fungus, and mosquitos bred in old shoes (*LL*, 196).

Thus, mud, home, are lost. Irretrievably lost it seems. Indeed, the apocalypse which closes *FGC* simply fulfils what has already happened to the mud house, what is 'envisioned' as happening to Salisbury: 'Yes, this city could be like the minute, brittle, transparent cases that have held insects and now lie blowing about on the sand. It would be like the carcass of a stick insect.' Mud is lost. Leaving the orphaned, the children of violence, a prey to violence, the 'forces' of two world wars, the splitting of the atom, the Cold War, madness. The empty anonymous shells of London tenement flats where they learn in their turn to shed their shells, the flats whose walls fall off or open in vision, the people who, limb after limb, lose their 'personality', their illusions of selfhood. For evidently what happens to 'home' – alias mud, alias significance – in these novels is also what happens to 'character'. The tree at the beginning of *FGC*, on a London bomb-site, has lost all 'tree-ness':

> This object had been a tree. For some days now Martha had been pausing by it, trying to make it out. Because it was hard to imagine it as a tree. Its surface was not smooth: if it had ever been planed, that smooth skin had been worn away long ago. Touching it was not touching wood, but nearer to water-eaten stone. It was almost spongy. Damp had swollen and filled every fibre. Wood had meant a hand on a trunk under which sap ran; wood had meant the smell of bark; wood had been the smell of oiled surfaces where grained showed patterns. Wood had never meant a great baulk of greyish-brown substance that smelled of wet, of damp, of rot, and of the gas which must

have soaked everything in this street since everything smelled of it (*FGC*, 19).

The people are exactly like the tree; they have lost all 'peopleness':

> There were very few people indeed, in, or near or associated with these columns of walking people whose lives did not have a great gulf in them into which all civilization had vanished, temporarily at least. There was probably not one here whose life had, or could, be [*sic*. proper syntax would have been: 'whose life had been, or could be . . .] remotely like that one once described by Thomas as 'being born under the elm tree, living, courting, marrying, dying, being buried under the elm tree.'
> These were people who had all been stripped (*FGC*, 428–9).

Martha's voyage has its own sullen, uncompromising logic. She goes from the complex mineral–vegetable–animal–and–human 'life' of the mud house on the kopje to the anonymous shell of London flats. From 'the individual to the collective, from the personal to the communal, from the female to the global, consciousness'.[4] The effort to make contact with world reality takes the form (among others) of having the space of one's room entirely plastered with 'world' information:

> In his study he had put up two enormous maps of the world . . . When Martha asked what they were for, he said: Well, he thought perhaps it might be an idea to see what was really happening – you know, *really* happening.
> One wall was soon devoted to atom bombs, hydrogen bombs, large bombs, small bombs (what one committee in the States had christened 'kitten bombs') and the establishments which developed them, made them, and sold them. Soon the wall was covered with little red flags . . . With black flags, on the same map, were marked the factories and laboratories which researched, made and sold, materials for germ warfare . . . With yellow flags, on this map, were marked areas of air, soil and water contaminated by bomb blasts, fall–out, the disposal of radio–active waste . . . Mark soon learned how very little indeed was known by the men who used these various techniques. For instance, the movement of the air around our globe, which might carry poisons of different

kinds into the lungs and flesh of humans and beasts, was not well understood. Therefore this map could never be anything more than approximate and rough (*FGC*, 308–9).

Whatever the complexities which the context of this passage creates,[5] Mark's (and Martha's) attempt to relate to a 'world' reality is part and parcel of, the means of furthering, Doris Lessing's own evolution towards a collective voice. It is a stage in that evolution equivalent to Anna's obsession with newspapers, except that it is presented as more systematic and less insane (the encounter with insanity is left to the Lynda of *FGC*):

> Anna found that she was spending her time in a curious way. She had always read newspapers, journals, magazines in large quantities; she suffered from the vice of her kind, that she *had* to know what was going on everywhere. But now, having woken late and drunk coffee, she would sit on the floor of the big room, surrounded by half a dozen daily newspapers, a dozen weekly journals, reading them, slowly, over and over again. She was trying to fit things together. Whereas, before, her reading had been to form a picture of what was taking place all over the world; now a form of order familiar to her had disappeared. It seemed as if her mind had become an area of differing balances, she was balancing facts, events, against each other. It was not a question of a sequence of events, with their probable consequences. It was as if she, Anna, were a central point of awareness, being attacked by a million unco-ordinated facts, and the central point would disappear if she proved unable to weigh and balance the facts, take them all into account (*GN*, 623).

Although the attempt nearly sends Anna mad it remains that it is in some way a necessary stage, that it corresponds to what Doris Lessing is trying to do herself, both in *GN* and in *FGC*, over the space of the novel. Anna's endeavours mystically to 'conceive', open herself up to, the world, are continuous with her creator's:

> something from my childhood. I used at night to sit up in bed and play what I called 'the game'. First I created the room I sat in, object by object, 'naming' everything, bed, chair, curtains, till it was whole in my mind, then move out of the room,

creating the house, then out of the house, slowly creating the
street, then rise into the air, looking down on London, at the
enormous sprawling wastes of London, but holding at the
same time the room, and the house and the street in my mind,
and then England . . . then, slowly, slowly, I would create the
world, continent by continent . . . until the point was reached
when I moved out into space . . . Then having reached that
point, with the stars around me, and the little earth turning
underneath me, I'd try to imagine at the same time, a drop of
water, swarming with life, or a green leaf. Sometimes I could
reach what I wanted, a simultaneous knowledge of vastness
and smallness (*GN*, 531).

In *FGC*, the attempt simultaneously to know vastness and smallness takes a different form, becomes a kind of 'atmospheric' or
'biological' mysticism.[6] It has to do with the lack of world knowledge Mark notices when pinning his little yellow flags: 'The
movement of the air around our globe . . . was not well understood.'

> . . . where do the ideas come from?'
> 'Oh', he said smiling, 'that's easy – I'll show you if you like.'
> 'Other space fiction', said Mark.
> 'Oh no', said Lynda, 'it's everywhere – all around you if you
> can look, from the Bible to poetry to every edition of every
> newspaper or if it comes to that how one is oneself . . .'
> . . . 'you assume that to think something is the end of that – a
> thought being self-contained, an end. Well, it isn't.'
> . . . 'The only way that would be of some use would be, not
> just throwing a pebble into a pool anyhow, so that ripples go
> out, but one doesn't know how, but knowing how to throw it
> so that the ripples go out exactly as one foresaw' (*FGC*, 457–8).

Of course, Lynda's idea is as old, if not perhaps as the Bible, at
least certainly as Romanticism.[7] But within the context of *The
Children of Violence*, it consecrates the breakdown of the personal.
The self is a permeable place where impulses upon the air reach
and in their turn pass out. The self is a void: no longer rooted,
feeling the need to burrow into warm mud. The Martha of the
early novels has disappeared, leaving room for the new Martha, a
transparency, a porous medium.

Ah, you could say. But there are links between the old and the new Martha. The 'old' – the young – Martha is presented from the word go as playing the 'role' of a young girl against two 'impersonal' 'matrons' – as she later, in *FGC*, will play the role of matron against two young girls. And think back to your first quotation from *MQ*. In her end is her beginning:

> The bush lay quiet about her, a bare slope of sunset-tinted grass
> moving gently with a tiny rustling sound . . . There was a
> slow integration, during which she, and the little animals, and
> the moving grasses, and the sunwarmed trees, and the slopes of
> shivering silvery mealies, and the great dome of blue light
> overhead, and the stones of earth under her feet, became one,
> shuddering together in a dissolution of dancing atoms. She felt
> the rivers under the ground forcing themselves painfully along
> her veins, swelling them out in an unbearable pressure; her
> flesh was the earth, and suffered growth like a ferment . . .
> during that space of time (which was timeless) she understood
> quite finally her smallness, the unimportance of humanity . . .
> it was as if something new was demanding conception, with
> her flesh as host; as if it were a necessity, which she must bring
> herself to accept, that she should allow herself to dissolve and
> be formed by that necessity (*MQ*, 61–2).

But the similarities are notional. For, in this passage, it is the strength of the contact with the earth which is the bearer of the mystical flight. In *FGC*, it is the completeness with which Martha, like everyone else, has been 'stripped', which brings about the possibility of plugging into universal forces. Martha the young girl is a fully-fledged being, richly-rooted in a particular location. The young girls of *FGC* barely exist as characters. A change occurs, not a growth. What strikes me about it, is how compulsive and repeated a change. One finds it spanning the whole of Doris Lessing's work, exemplary: her first novel, *GS*, is the most rooted in detailed loving knowledge of people and landscape and things and social relations. *MS*, and beyond it *SH*, the most detached, gutted. The 'transcendent' vision which is given to Mary before her death, in *GS*, literally springs from, has been earned by, the painstaking enquiry into the petty, the multifarious details of Mary's life:

The idea of herself, standing above the house, somewhere on an invisible mountain peak, looking down like a judge in his court, returned; but this time without a sense of release. It was a torment to her, in that momentarily pitiless clarity, to see herself . . . And time taking on the attributes of space, she stood balanced in mid-air, and while she saw Mary Turner rocking in the corner of the sofa, moaning, her fists in her eyes, she saw, too, Mary Turner as she had been, that foolish girl travelling unknowingly to this end. I don't understand, she said again. I understand nothing. The evil is there, but of what does it consist (*GS*, 207).

In a sense, Mary too is a child of violence: but the violence that has made her into a bitter, petty, frustrated and ultimately defeated and self-defeating racialist is the violence of white Rhodesian society and beyond that, of Western imperialism; our under-standing of Mary, of the 'impersonality' of her racialist hatred and violence and fear, are thoroughly informed by the novel. The 'transcendent' visions of the narrator in *MS* may be informed by Doris Lessing's own childhood, and if they work it is because we feel a pressure of untold things.[8] But in the explicit framework we are given, they spring from nothing, they are gratuitious.

And this change, from rootedness to the void, repeats itself inside *The Children of Violence*. Time and time again, not just from the first novels to the last, but inside the novels themselves, the texts seem to feel the need to root themselves again in Martha's body – then move, more and more, towards the void. In a sense, it's all perfectly logical – all of a piece: once you've lost mud (once you've moved from Africa to London?), all you can do is pursue the void. Make yourself the void. Burn through everything that promises significance, as Martha does in *FGC*, so as to be able to discard it. It's all perfectly logical – even though one thought at first, as perhaps Doris Lessing alias Martha Quest herself believed, that a 'Lawrentian' rather than a 'Sufi' fate awaited the strong healthy yearning girl.

My pole is full of ants. My mind is swarming. A myriad tiny noises.

'Is there really no mud left four years before 1984?' I think. Bitterly fighting it, the mud. Is there really no mud left in

London? Has Dickens's mud, the mud of *Bleak House* and *Our Mutual Friend*, all gone? The Thames, after all, is now clean. So clean, it seems, that all the 'matter' the London intelligentsia has got left to dream about, is the Apocalypse.

Darling, you may think there is mud left, because you live in some provincial backwater. But we do live in the age of the nuclear deterrent, black holes, and silicon chips, you know.

Has the prose which could be mud, which *knew* about matter, gone the way of all flesh? (and no grass singing).

What are you trying to say? This. The books that make up *The Children of Violence* go in one particular 'logical' direction: from 'mud' to the 'void'. Well, not quite so clearly as I have suggested: I have privileged 'mud' in my account; and there is no denying that Doris Lessing would not agree with my labelling Martha's wisdom, at the end of *FGC*, a choice of the 'void'. However, the general direction is evident. It is also evident that the experience conveyed through the agency of Martha is meant to be 'representative' in a most ambitious way. We feel it is 'typical', the only honest vision possible; not just the result of temperamental, nor even moral, options. Proof of this, if any were needed, is that all the other 'wise' or 'representative' characters Doris Lessing created in the period roughly corresponding to the long-drawn writing of the sequence, from Anna Wulf to Kate Brown, go the same way as Martha.

From 'I' to 'We'.

Lessing obviously believes that 'I' has gone rotten:

> Some sort of a divorce there has been somewhere along the path of this race of man between the 'I' and the 'We', some sort of a terrible falling-away, and I (who am not I but part of a whole composed of other human beings as they are of me . . . feel as if I am spinning back into a vortex of terror . . . and it is towards a catastrophe, yes, that was when the microbes, the little broth that is humanity, was knocked senseless, hit for six, knocked out of their true understanding, so that ever since most have said, I, I, I, I, I, I, I, and cannot, save for a few, say, We (*BDH*, 120).

The 'jelly spawn' full of 'tiny dark dots of life' where Martha 'loosened deliciously' has become ludicrous: a collection of 'microbes', 'the little broth that is humanity'. It can no longer be celebrated as 'life'; it's got to be saved. The ambition informing Lessing's work, and especially the last volumes of *The Children of Violence* is absolute. It is to evolve from 'I' to 'We', carrying into 'We' all the old 'I's of the *Bildungsroman*.

Supposing, for the sake of convenience, I made a ladder – not a neo-Platonic ladder, a ladder rising from the particular to the universal – and saw where *The Children of Violence* fitted. It would be a pretty shaky ladder, of course, with more holes than wood, like all ladders. But it should help me see what tradition stands behind Doris Lessing, and what kind of ambition was hers.

Martha, unlike, say, Colette's Claudine, does not have a 'particular' fate.[9] She is not 'just' a girl who grows up, becomes a 'free' woman, moves from one kind of exile to another. She is that, of course, but is meant to be much more.

The next 'step' is the 'progress' of a Rastignac, or a Moll Flanders. They are 'typical' in that they 'represent' a particular class ethos at a particular time in the development of capitalism or of French history. Other young men can identify with Rastignac, learn from him, etc. But, though Balzac's novels may exhale a 'terrible *moralité*',[10] Rastignac's fate is not meant in itself to be 'universally' valid in 'moral' or 'existential' terms. Martha's clearly is.

So are the fates of a Julien Sorel, a Jane Eyre or a Maggie Tulliver. They have the particularity, the 'class' and historical 'typicality' of a Balzac hero. But it is also implied that they are bearers of values, that the values their creators construct by means of them are, however modestly and particularly these values may be expressed, and whatever the individual failures of the characters themselves, absolute and universal. Yet Martha is meant to be more universal than that.

A further degree in generality could be found in *A La Recherche du temps perdu*. There, the narrative process, and the attempt to know, are the object and the agency, the end and the beginning, of the narrative itself. The contrast is extreme between the apparent 'means' and the 'end': between the obsessional, brilliant particularity of every piece of observation, every moment of time and turn of sentence, and the fact that a whole society and a considerable, continuous moment of history are actually being portrayed; between the eccentric, perverse, sickly, failed persona of the narrator and the universality his voice achieves.

And yet Martha is claimed to be more than that.

Resurrection could be regarded as going one better in that the wisdom achieved through – yet again – the particularity of Nikhlioudov's experience is more mystical, and more propagandist, than anything in the novels evoked so far. The insight into 'life' is more pantheistic, roots the author more firmly in the Russian soil, the peasant soul, has therefore more – fluid – extra sensory – implications than are to be found in Stendhal or George Eliot. Yet it still all remains mediated by the particularity of Nekhlioudov, his problems as land-owner versus peasants, etc.; there is no escaping from 'life' as 'we know it'. And that a certain kind of 'rootedness' should be implied anchors the novel in the specific. What, however, is striking about Martha Quest is that *she's been born uprooted*. That the metaphors that ultimately become significant for her are *weather* metaphors. 'A ripple from the storm'. The universality she is seeking, or her author through her, is one that wants *to get rid of the particular*.

By journeying through experiences and relationships (the sum total of her experience as woman, as lover, as political militant, etc.) Martha is meant to grow into a being who achieves a universal, absolute wisdom *through* access to the universal, not through development of the particular. It is through their *specificity* that Jane Eyre, Julien Sorel or Jude Fawley as individuals and members of a class, gain access to, or are the means of establishing, a particular but universally relevant, view of life. Martha, who seems to start with the 'particular' too, is presented more and more as a 'child of violence' like all the other 'children of violence'. And that comes to mean that all the particularity that the early novels have created comes more and more to be seen as irrelevant. It is implied for instance that the trouble in the affair with Thomas is 'determined' by mass forces – a ripple from the violence of Europe at war, racialism, etc., spreading to every consciousness. 'Usura steppeth between the bride and the bridegroom'.[11] The sequence is informed, or becomes informed, by a notion of the individual lost in the mass – as no more than an item in the series, basically. She/he achieves wisdom by coming to recognize this semi-scientific, semi-mystical, fact. By evolving from a 'mud' to a 'void' view of life. From fertile 'spawn' to a 'broth' of 'microbes'.

What I am trying to say is this. Not just that Doris Lessing wants to go 'one better' than the tradition of the *Bildungsroman* has done. But her subject-matter is 'modern' (or 'modernistic' – not everyone would agree to her view of consciousness) in that it becomes the discovery of twentieth-century 'mass' phenomena, and their interaction with the individual consciousness: world wars, totalitarian states, concentration camps, goulags, the cultural breakdown of relations between men and women, and the nuclear threat of universal holocaust.[12] *Yet* the novels are centred on the consciousness of a character which is largely portrayed like a nineteenth-century character. The social 'background', in Rhodesia as in London, at least at the start, is rock-solid. The adolescent Martha goes through fits of moodiness and rejection which are written about as if she were Emma, or Maggie Tulliver.[13] She's got all the baggage of the traditional fictional heroine. A distinct physique, a temperament, a very decided character, clothes, a family. She is located in all possible senses – socially, geographically, racially, historically – with the utmost precision. You name it, she's got it. She's got to have it all, because her author wants to 'do' it all – objects to all that Virginia Woolf leaves out.[14] The one thing she's got little of, but more about that later, is childhood.

Well, you could say. She's got it, and learns to shed it all, bit by bit, to arrive at wisdom. To actually understand what's been the matter with her. In *FGC*, Martha, dealing with a household of troublesome teenagers, and informed by a new realization of the forces of violence, comes to see her own adolescent throes (or the reader can choose to see them retrospectively) as, (a) produced by uncontrollable universal forces, and (b) the particular skin, role, every adolescent has to wear and shed.

Question is: can you use one mode to establish another? Can you *move* from the particular *to* the universal? (Rather than, as the nineteenth, etc., century had done, posit the universal *through* the particular.) Or move from the universal particular to the universal universal within one framework and equipped with the same language?

Can paddling in the mud – creating 'traditional' characters, using a prose that solidly establishes the 'existence' of a particular kind of social realist world – ever lead you convincingly to the void?

In other terms: I don't *believe* that the logic at work in those novels is right. And I think, if these texts created a truly *compelling* logic, I would be more inclined to believe them. And I think that all sorts of gaps and unresolved contradictions occur throughout.

Hold. What gave you in the first place the confidence to try and read *The Children of Violence* as a whole? To sum it up, in the first place, as if it were *one* novel?

Well: they follow from each other chronologically; in terms of recurring, 'realistically' presented characters; their time-span corresponds to 'historical' time (there is all the 'chronological' weight of world events to give authority to private events and individuals in them); and each novel is presented as yet another (a further) stage in the evolution of Martha. They have an overall title, *The Children of Violence*, which suggests they are moving towards, or informed by, an overall vision. That vision is being investigated through a central character whose surname is *Quest*. Furthermore, not only, as I have said, does the material of the experience of Martha Quest correspond roughly to Doris Lessing's own experience (geographical, emotional, political), but all the novels have been written quite some time after the event. By which I mean the author (like Proust) was not only in a position in which she could 'see it all' from a distance, but also decide (as she obviously did) that she was going to tell it all in the light of the wisdom gained after the event. Decide to narrate the search for, not so much 'temps perdu' as meaning, in the light if not of 'temps retrouvé', then time ahead. The experience that is presented in the first four novels was over and done with by the time Lessing started writing the sequence (by 1952 she had been in England already for some time). And most of the experience in the last volume, *FGC* (if one excepts the final year–2,000 section) was also quite some time 'behind' by 1969. She did decide to organize her experience into a sequence rather than try to present it through a series of different novels.

What this account of course excludes is that there might have been a change of heart, a change of vision, in between the writing of the first few volumes, and *LL*, and, even more, *FGC*. Perhaps even between the first two and *RS*. But then, there we are.

Precisely. How do you reconcile the existence of a claimed overall logic (manifested by all I have just said, the novels being written *as* a sequence) and the author changing her mind in the course of the writing?

One could go about it that way: show what the difference in the subject–matter and organization of each volume does to the overall logic (e.g. *RS* is much more concerned with general political issues, much more 'impersonal' than *MQ* or *PM*). But this is so obvious as to be hardly worth doing. Furthermore, in itself it would be no argument against the existence of an overall 'logic'. *La Prisonnière* is different, in all sorts of ways, from *Le Côté des Guermantes* or *Un Amour de Swann*;[15] yet each contributes to the 'logic' of the whole.

I could try another line of argument, which would be equally concerned with form. To a large extent, the 'vision' which Martha throughout is striving for, is an *existential* one. Indeed, the meditation on the tree on the London bomb–site which I quoted earlier reminded me, while I was writing it down, of Roquentin's own meditation on the root of a tree in Bouville public garden, in *La Nausée*.

But. From the word go, in *La Nausée*, all the 'realistic details', from pebble on the beach to Roquentin's contemplation of his own face and the Autodidacte's 'humanism', are suffused, made unstable by, the phenomenon of 'nausea'. So that the process of 'discovery' of the fundamental alienness of '*pour-soi*' and '*en-soi*', mind and nature, is continuously being catered for by the text. This is not so in *The Children of Violence*. The writing on the mud house is informed by a different sense of reality than the writing on the bomb–site. It is because experience has changed (Martha is older, she's left Africa, the war has occurred and destroyed parts of London) that the vision is different. Not because a more exact or deeper reading of reality has been arrived at; nor because life's caught up with itself. And yet that is what we are implicitly asked to believe.

Come on. All you've said is that *The Children of Violence* are not an 'existential' novel as you had thought (wrongly), or that if they are, they are so in the sense that they show the evolution, the capacity for change of the human being, the capacity to adapt to new circumstances, to be part and parcel of the great process of *surviving* (no mean art after all these days). And who says 'consistency' is a good thing? Who is the writer worth his salt who has not claimed the right to contradict himself? Take the nineteenth-century novel: it is full of the most strident, artistically unresolved, but *exciting* contradictions: from Scott to Anne Brontë to Mrs Gaskell to Dickens not to mention Balzac. There is a whole critical industry that thrives off theorizing on them. Doris Lessing's changes of heart, as you call them, are justifiable, praiseworthy even. All the more justifiable as the novels were written over such a long period: she herself must have changed very much. She did change: she owns as much in the preface to *GN* (1962), which was written in between *RS* (1958) and *LL* (1965):

> At last I understood that the way over, or through this
> dilemma (there was no way of *not* being intensely subjective),
> the unease at writing about 'petty personal problems' was to
> recognise that nothing is personal, in the sense that it is
> uniquely one's own . . . The way to deal with the problem of
> 'subjectivity' . . . is to see [the individual] as a microcosm and
> in this way to break through the personal, the subjective,
> making the personal general, as indeed life always does (*GN*,
> 13–14).

The fact that Lessing should have chosen to embody these changes in the same heroine – Martha Quest – makes a lot of sense, too. We're not just dealing with the tradition of the *Bildungsroman*, you know. Change – the picaresque – is ingrained in the very notion of questing. And Lessing did – does – believe in the necessity of a reconciliation between change and coherence.

> Literature must not capitulate and succumb to an inability or a
> refusal to fit conflicting things together to make a whole; so
> that one can live inside it, no matter how terrible: the refusal
> means one can neither change nor destroy; the refusal means
> ultimately either death or imprisonment.[16]

You haven't understood. I'm not saying that change is not a good thing. That age, sorrow, war after peace, do not change you. Nor am I saying necessarily that one should abandon the struggle for coherence, be it 'formal' or 'existential'. What I am saying is that you cannot have it both ways. You can't posit a structure in which everything follows from everything else and wisdom claims to be, as it were, logically deducible from the whole, and have actual *change* occur inside it. Or you only could if you did it. I mean, if the overall structure, the voice, had the capacity of integrating, the all-inclusive capacity it *says* it has, instead of proceeding as it does from hand to mouth. You can't make a compelling whole unless it is an actual whole. It is, I suppose, a question of *form*.

But who says the 'whole' is not there? Who says the end is not in the beginning? We've already had this one out, but you haven't convinced me. Elements of Martha's late 'mysticism', her under-standing of 'role-playing', are there from the start. There are signs of what is going to happen. In the same way, as at times, for instance when they enjoy solitude on heights, Stendhal's Julien Sorel or his Fabrice have intimations of the 'contemplative' state that will ultimately satisfy them, though when these states first occur, they are intent on Tartuffe-esque or Don Juan-esque ambitious careers. They have not got to the stage when they can catch up with themselves. Understand what they 'want'. In the same way, you could say, Martha's final discovery of the futility of the 'personal'; Doris Lessing's attempt, in her later novels, to show the shallowness of 'psychological realism', could be read in the tradition of the 'philosophical' novel. The self discovers itself to be elsewhere than it thought it was – and the discovery is all the more impressive as it has been achieved at the author's deeply felt cost, as well as at that of her heroine.

Sorry. That argument is not really tenable. It makes sense theoretically, but the texts don't bear it out. The *fact* that changes of heart are shown to occur in the course of the sequence means that they are not integrated. And they are not, cannot be, inte-grated, because the voice from the start claims to be inclusive. There is a totalizing intention written into every line of the prose. And it is because of this that one cannot allow the contradictions and lapses to go their own way. Or to signify in the way that, say, gaps would signify in a Balzac, or a Stendhal novel. In the famous passage in which Julien Sorel goes to kill Mme de Rênal and in which nothing whatever is recorded of his state of mind, the very absence of verbal matter acts as infinite wealth. Whichever way you choose to interpret it, you know that the truth of the character lies also in what cannot be made explicit – in the non-written as well as in the written. But then Stendhal's prose, his way of jumping from chapter to chapter, of moving across time, has made that kind of interaction between the written and the non-written, black and white (or red), possible. There is an abundance of absence, of 'more'. Nothing remotely like this occurs in Doris Lessing's prose. You are never given to understand that there is more to Martha than the text gives you – because whenever there is going to be more, or there has been more, the text is going to tell you. Reread any of the passages quoted so far: as you read them you know that the authorial consciousness, either through, or in default of, its characters, claims to be complete.

And this is why it cannot afford contradictions. The changes of heart flaw the coherence which the confidence of the tone and the progress forward parade. It cannot allow gaps to exist: they might pull the text some other way than it is intended to go. That is perhaps why all of Martha's dreams are so clear, readily and totally interpretable. Darkness, unintentionality, are not allowed in.

Yet they are there. The gaps, the contradictions, are everywhere.

Roots: childhood, Africa, the body

Childhood

> The baby was desperate with hunger. Need clawed in her belly . . . She yelled inside the thick smouldering warmth . . . She twisted and fought and screamed. And screamed – for time must pass before she was fed, the strict order of the regime said it must be so: nothing could move that obdurate woman there, who had set her own needs and her relation with her baby according to some timetable alien to them both . . .
>
> Perhaps I would have done better to have begun this chronicle with an attempt at a full description of 'it'. But is it possible to write an account of anything at all without 'it' – in some shape or another – being the main theme? Perhaps, indeed, 'it' is the secret theme of all literature and history, like writing in invisible ink between the lines, which spring up, sharply black, dimming the old print we knew so well (*MS*, 135–6).

Martha Quest, most bizarrely for a fictional heroine who is given five volumes over 2,000 pages – more, if one counts *SH*, etc. – has virtually no childhood. What there is of it is the passage on the mud house, which I have quoted earlier; and there are a few, very few, reminiscences, generally of clashes with the mother. Now there are all sorts of excellent extraneous reasons why this should be so. The best, which I can easily sympathize with,[17] is fear of offending one's parents or close relatives by writing about them, a taboo which for all sorts of reasons seems to be felt by women even more than men. It is surely no accident that Lessing's first *actual* foray into infancy and early childhood should be in *Memoirs* . . ., the work of a 'mature' woman, where one feels that perhaps through the deaths of loved ones she has left a great deal behind, has been somehow released. In any case, that's none of my business. But the absence of a childhood *signifies* in Martha Quest's progress in ways that the text, because it claims to be inclusive, does not cater for. There is no getting out of this: writing in invisible ink only functions successfully in a text if that text is prepared to allow absence, silence, to function.

As it is, there are two – related – areas where the 'gap' seems to me to show. The first is Martha's quite 'specific' temper; her combination of daring and passiveness, of generous courage, recklessness even, and bad temper; the contradictory ways she allows herself to be trapped – and yet never to be trapped; her strength of feeling and continuous cool observer's detachment: what makes her into a writer, of course, except that she's never allowed to become one.[18] It is all 'rooted' in a specific childhood and parentage, but we're never allowed to look far into that: our attention being instead concentrated on the fact it's all 'roles', impersonal. And it becomes more and more so, Martha finally having most of her 'character' ironed out of her in *FGC*. Yet there is an area which does not allow itself to be quite so easily ironed out. It's Mrs Quest, the awful, hopeless, exasperating Mrs Quest. For me, she is the most alive of the characters of *The Children of Violence*. And I think this is because the text somehow feels repeatedly compelled to give her passages of her own, passages which are rather unsuccessfully controlled by the author – and are presented as outside Martha's consciousness. It's as if the author wanted to be 'fair', to be 'sympathetic', but could not help showing Mrs Quest to be really as exasperating as Martha finds her. And the tension that is set up (which I, and probably many other readers, feel must be informed by Doris Lessing's own tussles with her mother, seething areas of frustration and resentment) comes to a pitch in *FGC* when news of her mother's threatened visit to England precipitates a breakdown in Martha. Mrs Quest's 'point of view', her inner world are presented there, her maiming youth and experience, her neurosis, her evolution towards 'wisdom': her own discovery of 'role-playing' (on lines parallel to Martha's own discovery of the same thing) which, it is suggested, makes it all the more ironic that Martha and she could not communicate, but that's yet another face of the 'violence' syndrome, the text goes on to suggest: evading its own neurosis in relation to the mother. For me, that neurosis makes it the most real 'relationship' of the whole sequence. But neither Martha nor her author are, of course, prepared to accept that that is where significance lies – more, perhaps, than in reading six daily newspapers and twelve weeklies at a go, or in watching Aldermaston marches. Marguerite Duras knew it, who felt Hiroshima on her own pulse, through a love story. And Virginia Woolf, of course, who explored the impending violence of war through a countryhouse play, in *Between the Acts*.

Politics aren't necessarily in the newsreel.

Africa

But perhaps Martha's lack of childhood represents the colonial situation. The white settler's point of view: the passing implantation of an English family in an African landscape. Martha is doomed to the nomad's flat because she's been *born* uprooted. Doris Lessing herself could only write about the childhood house once she'd left Africa, was settled in London, and briefly revisited her native country: in *GH*. The passages on the house in *GH* are much better realized, as I think should have been obvious when reading them, than the passages in, *MQ*. Peculiarly, it is only in *GH* that, through the passing figure of Tobias, the painter, an actual *labouring* African appears. The first four volumes of *The Children of Violence*, though they are preoccupied with racial issues, though the existence of the many white characters who appear is based on the *labour* of the black Africans, ignore that labour. Only the odd 'house-boy' or cook or nanny or waiter are shown, but hardly ever in a *working* situation. Even in *RS*, where the 'Marxists' go visiting black townships and distributing pamphlets, actual encounters with blacks are kept to a minimum. *Africans*, in the four novels that take place in Rhodesia, are there like children, who ought to be seen and not heard: worse, they are barely seen at all. Oh yes, they are occasionally perceived from the corner of the eye: a black driver, a child crossing a street, people crowding in at a meeting. They are crusaded for, with a wide-eyed realization of the futility of white liberal efforts. Racial prejudice is neatly caught on many occasions, all shades of it; from the landlady who lives in paranoiac terror of her house-boy murdering her, to Judge Maynard's infiltration of the leftist group by the only black member, who happens to be his spy. But if you reflect that the proportion of black people to white in Rhodesia is of more than 10 to 1, it becomes slightly surprising that the proportion is the reverse in the novels: surprising, not perhaps in itself (this must be how it was: blacks and whites just did not, could not, mix), but because of the 'totalizing' ambition of the texts, because you feel all along that it is some kind of all-inclusive statement that is being made. Also, the blacks in those novels are nearly always presented as ideas, as causes. Hardly any of them has any individuality at all. *Yet* in the period in which Doris Lessing was writing *The Children of Violence*, she was also producing the volumes of African short stories (to my mind, some of her finest work). Why did she thus have to partition the material? And how could she hope to represent an inclusive consciousness in the character of Martha when all the time she made her blind – I don't mean *ideologically* blind, I mean blind where it really matters. For instance, the whole 'sexual' dimension which haunts *GS* is totally ignored, bracketed, in *The Children of Violence*.

The partitioning is not simply between the African short stories (or *GS*) and *The Children of Violence* sequence: it is there in the novels themselves. Those extracts now about 'mud', and 'grass'. On reflection, it is no accident at all which gives Jimmy the only 'real' 'mud' experience after *PM*; which makes two *men*, Jimmy, then Thomas, take over what, until then, had been Martha's susceptibility to 'mud'. Jimmy's experience of course is *the* white man's experience of Africa: the drive to explore, to surrender, the sense of, yes, this is it, followed by terror, 'the horror', at the life that is discovered there; and rejection by the life that is there: soon after the discovery of the myriad beetle in the grass, there is the awfulness of the African township, the squalor; the poverty; and the exclusion of Jimmy. He is white, he is the enemy. Despite all his fraternal socialistic good-will, there is no way in which the Africans can accept him. Thomas goes to the extremes of that exclusion, he goes to die among Africans. But why did Doris Lessing keep this on the outskirts of her novels? Why did she have to give this central experience to one of her most peripheral characters, Jimmy, or make Thomas die in a way that is not shown, simply reported? Why give the experience to *men* rather than to Martha? Because women could not have it? Obviously they could: Mary Turner dies of it. Martha survives because Doris Lessing survived: left, *chose* something else. But then Martha should not be presented as having somehow exhausted the potential of the situation. Doris Lessing survived because she wanted to become a writer, because experience was for her a means to something else, and it is this unacknowledged and unwritten something else which is the only possible key to Martha's redirection. In fact, the African short stories and *The Children of Violence* are written from a position that is partitioned into rooms, notebooks – that very position which *GN* denounces.[19] Presumably the author is not herself aware of this particular partitioning, for if she were, how could it still affect *Landlocked*, published three years after *GN*?

In fact, choices are continuously being made, but they are not acknowledged as choices. For instance, if you think about it, you realize that Doris Lessing has two ways of writing about beetles: the way of the Jimmy passage, and the way of 'The Sun between their Feet'. Beetles can be the strange, horrifying creatures they are to Jimmy; or, as the dung-beetles in the African short story, beautiful, obstinate creatures, lovingly observed, battling on uphill, the shade of Sisyphus across their path, the very image of ongoing life. Maybe Jimmy is horrified because he is English, not used to this nature. But what about Martha? She's been born there. How comes, after her immersion in the red mud hole in *PM* it never occurs to her to wonder if there is no significance for her in this land? For instance, there could be two ways of looking at Marjorie. As Martha does – sympathetically, of course, and with an awareness of the futility of sympathy, as a fool who has allowed conventional pressures to trap her into a soul-destroying marriage. Or as the narrative voice of 'The Sun between their Feet' does – as the obscure heroine of everyday life, battling on with the mud she rolls uphill between her feet: the dung-beetle which is also a sun-beetle. But that contradiction is not allowed to appear. You know that if you want to think about Marjorie in other ways than Martha does, you're extrapolating. And yet I feel that the sense of life offered in 'The Sun between their Feet' ought to have been allowed to clash with the other, the sense that significance is elsewhere, in Europe, that you're getting near it by selling leaflets about the Red Army.

One must return to it – to Martha–Doris Lessing having been *born* uprooted, to her 'world view' springing directly from the white settler's situation. Among other things, he/she has no roots in Africa because his/her 'past' there is so small: he/she has little historical or cultural relation to the land and its people. Of course, the people themselves, the black Africans, have in a way no 'culture' either. They have no 'history' that could be 'written', and they, or at least those who are shown in the sequel, have lost touch with any tribal/oral traditions they might have had. One of the most interesting moments is when Johnny Lindsay attempts to record working-class experience in South Africa, by 'telling' it to people who *write it down* for him. Only, it is *white* working-class experience. There is nobody to tell (let alone write down) black experience, and when black Africans come to the whites for education, for 'culture', it is only white culture they can be given. *Sense*, therefore, necessarily, is *elsewhere* for the white: in Europe largely. It is also elsewhere for the blacks. Awareness of this is brought to the white people – to Martha and her 'liberal' friend – by the distrust and distance of the black people: but we are not shown the relation as 'happening'. There is no consciousness in the novels which is *shown* as *experiencing* estrangement, as Mary Turner is in *GS*. We are shown people – Martha, mainly – having an *awareness* of estrangement, of political impotency. But the core of Martha's experience is not what it *ought* to be, in the sense that it *is*: her *relation* to the Africa of her birth.

This 'white settler' position is also, of course, the source of Martha's – of Doris Lessing's – strength. Belonging, in terms of 'sense', nowhere, her relation to the world of sense, to language, is one of absolute freshness. People have often remarked on the extraordinary thing that happened when Olive Schreiner first used English words to convey the presence of an African land-scape. The words of a faraway culture were suddenly alighting upon a veld that had for thousands, perhaps millions of years, existed without them. This is also relevant to some extent to Doris Lessing writing about Rhodesia: the bush, the house on the kopje, even the towns, were also largely innocent of 'English' writing. But it is also true in relation to 'English' as a European 'culture' – medium of culture. She was (she still is?) outside it. She was born an exile from it, as much as from Africa. This has turned out to be a prodigious source of strength for her. It has given her the freshness of an outsider in relation to traditions of writing. She has come in particular to the language of 'realistic' writing without the weight of an inheritance. The nineteenth-century novel, as she discusses it in the preface to *GN*, is for her ageless. As if time were spatialised, the 'tradition' a panorama towards which she could reach out at will. Joyce and Kafka are no closer than Tolstoy. (Yes, there will be Musil later on, but for different reasons.)[20] Time has no depth[21] at least until *MS*, and she, Lessing, is in some strange way innocent of meaning. She is equal to anything. A natural nomad, she can take anything on, for she belongs nowhere, and sense is always elsewhere: she does not have to contend internally with it. Hence, perhaps, those crystal-clear dreams. She has chosen herself as a being without a subcon-scious. Estranged equally from the dark continents of childhood, of Africa and of an inherited *incorporated* culture.

But this is because a *choice* has been made. She could have chosen to belong. Perhaps, of course, that would have meant choosing to die, like Mary Turner or Thomas. Perhaps that would have made writing impossible. But there is no denying there was a choice. She chose to leave. The text of *The Children of Violence* chooses to ignore that it is informed by detachment rather than rootedness. It claims to be inclusive when it is exclusive. Like its heroine, it chooses exile, and claims there is only truth in exile. There is truth in exile. The *only* truth?

Martha chooses to become a grail-seeker. A Quest. She chooses the way of the father.

Of the body, the female body

I can smell you from a mile. Stinking to high male heaven. You're going to speak of the 'feminine sentence'. Virginia Woolf. Fluidity. Tradition passing on through the mother. Etc. Etc. Lord preserve us. All right. You've won. I won't. The way of the father, you say. Come come. Only of the father? *Both* parents are referred to as 'grail-seekers' in *IPE*.

Yes. But isn't the father's eccentricity so much more heart-warming than the mother's? Isn't the father, *not* the mother, recognizable as the source of the daughter's – I was going to say, 'eccentric' – centrality? And I don't think one can deny the point I've made earlier – that Mrs Quest pulls like unease, neurosis even, at the text. The mother is never chosen: she is avoided, rebelled against, fled from, even when she is actually closest.

'We relate to tradition through out mothers.'[22] This is not true of this particular daughter.

GN, because it was received by readers and critics as being essentially about 'women's liberation' and because the central character there is a *woman writer*, poses the question of femininity more directly than other works by Lessing: 'this attempt on my part assumed that that filter which is a woman's way of looking at life has the same validity as the filter which is a man's way.'[23] But the assumption is taken to be right. The preface, written over ten years later, in the full swing of the Women's Movement, is impatient of the attempts made to drive the novel into the 'women's' fold. Yes, dearies, it implies, I beat you to it by ten years and straightaway saw beyond it, how paltry it all really is. On to higher things.

Spite. Nasssty. OK. I'm sorry.

And yet. Are women writers altogether free to 'choose' between a 'feminine' style and a (presumably to be called so, since there are after all only two sexes) 'masculine', 'freer' one?

> [*The Trinket Box*] . . . – intense, careful, self-conscious,
> mannered – could have led to a style of writing usually
> described as 'feminine'. The style of *The Pig* is straight, broad,
> direct; is much less beguiling, but is the highway to the kind of
> writing that has the freedom to develop as it likes.[24]

I'm not trying to be prescriptive. I don't know any of the answers. And they're all necessarily dependent on what Luce Irigaray says: 'For in fact, we do not exactly know what "mascu-line" language is. As long as men claim to say everything and define everything, how could we know what the language of the male sex is?'[25] And all efforts to define a 'feminine voice' come up against the fact that the search for a *different* voice characterizes all 'modernist' or 'avant-garde' texts – which are being written by men as well as women: 'I do not find it easy to define a masculine or feminine speficity when I think of the great aesthetic experience of the decentering of identity,' Kristéva says. If that formidable theoretician can't, not many can.[26]

Yet women who want to write are, whether they know it or not, confronted by formidable taboos: I use this particular bit of Lacan as exemplary of all that Simone de Beauvoir sums up in *Le Deuxième Sexe* as well as of a great deal of what has come out of Freud and Structuralism:

> There is no woman but excluded by the nature of things which is the nature of words, and it has to be said that if there is one thing about which women themselves are complaining at the moment, it's well and precisely that – it's just that they don't know what they are saying, which is all the difference between them and me.[27]

Those women who – think they know what they are saying? – have taken stock of this:

> This is precisely what is at stake, always, in feminist action: to modify the 'imaginary' so as to be able then to act upon reality, to change the forms of language which through its structures or through history has been subjected to the patrilinear, therefore male, law.[28]

> through writing herself, woman will return to that body which has been, worse than confiscated, made into the disquieting stranger in the place, a sick or dead being . . .
>
> Write yourself: your body must make itself heard. Then the immense resources of the unconscious will spring . . . it will be an act which will signal the *Taking Word* of woman, therefore her deafening entry into *History* which has always been constituted *on her repression*.[29]

> Like millions of women, I want to inscribe my fighting body for something tells me – and it is not my man's science – that a great part of History, because it has neither been thought nor

written by us, has become fixed in the memory of the female body.[30]

Certainly, it would be over-simple to suggest that working to modify the 'imaginary', writing from inside the 'body' as the place where an identity can be created, a spring released, or where censorship, the law of the 'logos' can best be evaded, are specific-ally female procedures. It would also be wrong to claim that women *have to* start from there in that it would trap them inside yet another prescriptive circle.

I would, of course, not refrain from playing the devil's advocate: recalling that this is where *The Mill on the Floss* starts from: George Eliot's arms go numb on the arms of her chair, like the arms of the little girl on the stone bridge who is looking down into the water – the little girl who is both George Eliot as a child and the Maggie that's just been given birth to. I would also stress that *Jane Eyre* and *Villette* are anchored in the intensity of child-hood sensations – that Virginia Woolf's novels never allow narrative mastery to go outside a bodily hold upon the text – and that it is not for nothing that Joyce has put Molly Bloom in bed (though that particular remark invites trouble rather than brings water to my mill). Counter-arguments no doubt would sprout like the dragon's teeth. I would be reminded that *A La Recherche du temps perdu* also starts in bed, from inside the sleeping/walking body. That there are, as Woolf herself acknowledged, 'feminine' male writers as well as 'masculine' women writers. Indeed, that George Eliot herself is frequently described as one of the latter. It would further be said that if I had been about to say that Doris Lessing had 'bracketed' her 'femininity' because she writes such lucid, 'masterful', logical prose; deals with 'externals'; is pre-occupied with all that the world has to show from politics to racial issues to mysticism, I was going to speak nonsense, and it is just as well I have been stopped in time. That in any case the particular 'situation' or 'position' of women is continuously at stake in her novels. That that is why so many women identify with her heroines. Martha's wise passiveness at the end of the sequence, her 'Tolstoyan' acceptance of 'life forces', her finding more wisdom in the 'mad' Lynda than in all the supposed sages, are arrived at through specifically 'female' kinds of experience.

Yes. Yes. I'm not denying that that's what 'happens', what the narrative *tells* us. What I'm wondering about is, where do Martha's sentences come from?

And how come the text is haunted by the presence of Martha's *body*? Of her body as a source of *knowledge*? How come it keeps anchoring itself in that, touching it as if it were Anteus and Martha's body were the earth – and yet reneging on it, abandoning it, shedding it bit by bit as if that body were a series of skins (personality itself a set of chinese boxes), and, in its own favourite image, it was peeling it like an onion?

For it is very striking how again and again new chapters or sections start from Martha's *sensations*. There are, to return to them once again, the 'mud' passages I have quoted at the beginning of this essay. There are others, dying out virtually through *PM* and *RS*. In *PM* the 'body' passages are nearly all connected with child-bearing (like the time when Alice and Martha take a mud bath in a pot-hole) or being with a child. Yet she is – especially in the second passage – in a state of boredom and gloom:

> The two rooms at the top of the block of flats were filled with light from the sky as soon as the sun, splendid, enlarged and red, swelled up over the horizon of suburb-clotted hills, pulling behind it filaments of rose-and-gold cloud. By half-past five, fingers of warm yellow were reaching over the big bed, over Caroline's cot. Martha lay warm in the blankets, listening to Caroline wake (*PM*, 222).

> Above, trees: the glossy dark masses of the cedrelatoona, the sun-sculptured boughs of the jacarandas, and, between, those small stiff trees the bauhinias, with their pink-and-white blossoms perched on them like butterflies. It was October, and the jacarandas were purple and the streets were blue, as if they ran water or reflected the sky, which was unrelievedly blue and pulsing with heat.
>   Inside the gate was a large tree, under which Martha stood looking out. Behind her was a rough lawn, where Caroline was playing (*PM*, 273).

In *RS*, perhaps because Caroline has been left behind, and the focus is on 'politics', the 'sensations', the body-anchorage are all given to Jimmy. The only moment when Martha's body is used as a source of knowledge is her illness, in the early part of section II: but it is not really a knowledge of *place* that the body then registers: it is more a symptom of unease of self. Martha's body comes back very strongly in *LL*. From the opening of the book its resurgence as a medium of awareness of place seems to herald the affair with Thomas:

> The afternoon sun was hot on Martha's back, but not steadily so: she had become conscious of a pattern varying in impact some minutes ago . . .
> Areas of flesh glowed with chill, or tingled with it: behind heat, behind cold, was an interior glow, as if they were the same . . . And, since the patches and angles of sunlight fell into the office for half of its depth, and had been so falling for three hours, everything was warmed – floors, desks, filing cabinets, flung off heat; and Martha stood, not only directly branded by sunlight and by shadow, her flesh stinging precisely in patterns, but warmed through by a general irradiation (*LL*, 9–10).

> The heat of a stormy day had drained into the scarlet flush that still spread, westwards, under bright swollen stars only intermittently visible. Hailstones from the recent storm scattered the street and lay on the dirty windowsill . . . It would be winter soon, the ice seemed promise of it. Martha's calves sweated slipperily against the wood of the bench, and she sucked a bit of ice as an ally against heat (*LL*, 48).

Etc., etc. Obviously, the renewed frequency of such passages shows the return of Martha's sexuality. But they don't only serve that purpose, they bizarrely act as 'stills', a camera's fixed effect, that then allows movement – and what is the significance of this? What further contributes to making this problematic is that the very sensuality of the affair with Thomas is meant to be shot through with political implications: somehow rotten because of the evils in Europe, because also of the racialist evil in Rhodesia: but what relationship does the writing of the 'sensation' passage bear to that political rottenness?

> Perhaps, when Thomas and she touched each other, in that touch cried out the murdered flesh of the millions of Europe – the squandered flesh was having its revenge, it cried out

through the two little creatures who were fitted for much smaller loves . . . It was all much too painful, and they had to separate (*LL*, 167).

But what relationship does the writing of the 'sensations' passages bear to that *stated* political rottenness? Take the opening of Part II, from which I earlier on quoted in part, when discussing 'mud':

> Six inches of marred glass in a warped frame reflected beams of orange light into the loft, laid quivering green from the jacaranda outside over wooden planks and over the naked arm of a young woman who lay face down on a rough bed, dipping her arm in and out of the greenish sun-lanced light below her as if into water (*LL*, 102).

Now there recur here some of the elements of the other passages: the chequered heat – the sun-drenched African trees – the sunlight like water.[31] But what are we to make of 'marred' and 'warped'? Are the glass marred and the frame warped because Martha's and Thomas's love is already spoiled by the violence from Europe, or are they simply humble sources of the sensual bliss – 'Martha . . . [stretched] her body's happiness in cool, leaf-smelling warmth' – all the more touching, like the frail shed in which the two lovers meet, with its 'crooked' window, *because* they are humble and awry? I can't help but think that it's the latter: the first reading is hard to sustain. But isn't it rather *risqué* to allow words like 'warped' and 'marred' and 'crooked' to be present in a passage describing a love that's going to turn out to *be* marred if they are not *intended* to convey this?

The point I am trying to get at is this: there are two kinds of knowledge acting as sources for the text: the 'bodily' knowledge, which I shall with all the reservations and queries made earlier call 'feminine', and which is certainly feminine in the sense we have a woman writer using the closely autobiographical medium of a female character to convey her sense of place; and the 'abstract', political, knowledge of politics at large: manly, in that its simple sentence structure and the 'free' generalizing possibilities such a structure permits are regarded by Lessing herself, as her remarks about *The Pig* and *The Trinket Box* testify, as 'masculine'. It seems to me that Doris Lessing resorted to the first kind of knowledge when she returned to the writing of *The Children of Violence* after a gap in which *GN* and *GH* were produced. Now the positions reached in *GN* demanded that *LL*, itself looking forward to *FGC*, proceed in a 'trans-individual', 'abstract', ('male') direction, towards which in any case *RS* was fast going. I don't know whether the experience of returning to Rhodesia (*GH* was published in 1957, a year before *RS*, but seems, emotionally at least, not to have affected it at all) had anything to do with it. But it seems to me clear that what gets *LL* 'started' is what I described earlier as what gets *The Mill on the Floss* started: a 'Proustian', a bodily memory revived, at least imaginatively, by a return to place. The place of childhood and youth. Immersion within Martha's world of sensations is what makes the return to the place and theme possible.

But that bodily memory, although it permits the return of Martha's sexuality, is neither trusted nor made fully significant. The narrative voice does not really care about being 'there' since it wants to move on and wants Martha to move on, too. One of the reasons it wants to move on is that somebody there wants to 'write' about the experience: there is something analytical about those passages, showing Martha to be the 'detached observer'. But also, the pull of 'elsewhere', of Europe, is being felt. The pull of the 'trans–individual' consciousness that becomes prevalent in *FGC*:

> [Iris] knew everything about this area, half a dozen streets for about half a mile or a mile of their length; and she knew it all in such detail that when with her, Martha walked in a double vision, as if she were two people: herself and Iris, one eye stating, denying, warding off the total hideousness of the whole area, the other, with Iris, knowing it in love . . .
>
> Iris . . . had lived in this street since she was born. Put her brain, together with the other million brains, women's brains, that recorded in such tiny loving anxious detail the histories of window-sills, skins of paint, replaced curtains and salvaged balk of timber, there would be a recording instrument, a sort of six–dimensional map which included the histories and lives and loves of people, London – a section map in depth (*FGC*, 20).

Martha has got to where her author wants her: where her author is. Instead of 'living', of paying a bodily price for her own knowledge, of seeking for 'History' inside her own female body, she is ready to *use* the bodily knowledge of others – use Iris as her other eye, her source of knowledge: but for a wider quest. A bit like Scott who, having used, transcribed, 'written', 'oral' material, (a lot of it got out of *women*; see preface to the *Waverley Novels*) talked – playfully – about mechanizing the whole enterprise of *The Waverley Novels*, and of weaving them like damask,[32] Doris Lessing alias Martha seems poised here to computerize the whole process of female bodily knowledge of places. (A new age wants improved methods. We're on our way to the galactic files of *SH*.) Martha wants a section map in depth without having to pay the price Iris and the other million women have paid for depth: living.

Ah. Henry James & Co. But there we are. Precisely. If you're not going to 'pay the price' in 'living' you've got to pay it 'imaginatively'. In the relations you establish with your 'subject-matter'. In your readiness to be immersed inside it.

And that's where the gaps seem to me to be. In the passage from *LL* which we were considering, the fact that there is a tension between the bodily knowledge which has impelled and to a certain extent keeps impelling the text, and the 'general' knowledge the text is moving towards, means that the language does not control and organize sufficiently its range of significance – terms like 'warped' and 'marred' carry an uncertain load; the 'water out of sunlight' image appears equally in a gloomyish passage about suburban Salisbury in *PM* (p. 273, 'the streets were blue, as if they ran water or reflected the sky') and in a passage of sexual ecstasy ('dipping her arm in and out of the greenish sun-lanced light below her as if into water'). It is as if the text had no memory of itself at a deeper level – a metaphoric or unconscious level: and yet it is entirely concerned with continuity. It is as if it did not try to envisage on the level of language the questions it is posing on a theoretical level – what is the relation between sex and politics, between the feel of the body and the economical or political infra-structure at work, determining (or not) each individual life.

Language

It's all a question of how the text is imaginatively produced. Of the relations that exist between the authorial voice and the heroine who is devised as a mirror for authorial experience.

MQ, PM, and *RS* all start from *two* women – like *GN,* interestingly – before homing in on Martha (she is looking at the two
in *MQ;* she is one of the two, in the others). *LL,* as discussed
above, starts inside Martha's body. So does *FGC:*

> In front of Martha was grimed glass, its lower part covered
> with grimed muslin. The open door showed an oblong of
> browny-grey air swimming with globules of wet. The shop
> fronts opposite were no particular colour. The lettering on the
> shops, once black . . . was now shades of dull brown. The
> lettering on the upper part . . . said *Joe's Fish and Chips* in
> reverse and was flaking like stale chocolate.
> She sat by a rectangle . . . Her cup was thick . . .
> Across the room sat Joe's mother . . .
> For a few weeks she had been anonymous, unnoticed – free
> (*FGC,* 13–14).

Relentlessly, sentence after sentence, subject verb object with as
unique complements location ('In front of Martha', 'opposite') or
time ('once black', 'for a few weeks'). All the perceptions are
Martha's, the locations from Martha's own situation ('Across the
room sat . . . Joe's mother'); she is inside the cafe, so she sees the
lettering on the door in reverse. Yet the book is written in the
third person, which allows, among other things, the authorial
knowledge to be greater than that of the character: occasionally to
transcend it.[33] What is striking in this opening is the solidity and
unflinchingness of the knowledge that is being registered and
imparted: the author knows and tells us, without a shade of
doubt, who Martha is, what she sees, what the quality of what she
sees is (all rather dingy, dull colours that must be striking for
someone just come from Africa, fresh from the memory of
sunlight and jacarandas) where it is, what she feels, how long
she's been there, etc. Neither the author nor the character doubt
the descriptive power of language, nor the amenability of perception to order (first what's 'in front', next paragraph what's
she's sitting 'by', 'Across the room', then the characters being
gradually introduced with added information (that is, what
Martha knows from previous acquaintance with the characters is
slipped in to help the reader find out even more clearly where 'we'
are. God's in his heaven, all's right with the world. Subject verb
object, and precise, undoubtable locations in place and time.

Ah, you could say. But Martha here, in this last volume of the sequence, has fully developed her tendency of the 'detached observer'. That tendency has been there from the first – from the beginning of *MQ*:

> if she was often resentfully conscious that she was expected to carry a burden that young people of earlier times knew nothing about, then she was no less conscious that she was developing a weapon which would enable her to carry it. She was not only miserable, she could focus a dispassionate eye on that misery. This detached observer, felt perhaps as a clear-lit space situated just behind the forehead, was a gift of the Cohen boys at the station, who had been lending her books (*MQ*, 14).

Whether one thinks this 'detached observer' is a gift of the Cohen boys or the sign that Martha is a born writer (which the text does not envisage), it is seen as a specific product of the 'modern' world – a 'weapon' against 'violence'. Is it, in the opening of *FGC*, also meant to be a symptom of the modern disease? A disease in the eye, a split in the personality? Perhaps the very syntactical simplicity is a ruse: perhaps what's happening is that the kind of maniacal observing detachment that the narrator of *La Jalousie* shows is also at work here, demonstrating that all we can know are man-made dimensions, measure and number and place? But that's simply not tenable: how could such a stance be compatible with the fourth paragraph: 'For a few weeks she had been anonymous, unnoticed – free. Never before in her life had she known such freedom.' This is the free indirect speech, speaking of easy intimacy between author and character, the very reverse of the non-committal mode of Robbe-Grillet.

In Robbe-Grillet, all the certainty ultimately leaves you with is a state of absolute uncertainty. The opposite occurs here: everything is protectively, reassuringly, exhaustively significant. As you read (unless of course you're a fool, a hypothesis not to be excluded, since Doris Lessing often complains of the way her novels are being misread), you *understand* everything. You read, 'In front of Martha was grimed glass, its lower part covered with grimed muslin,' and you know that that's all there is to it. You know you can hang on to Martha, she won't let you down. You immediately picture to yourself that particular shop window with its half-way-up net curtain. You know that 'grimed' says a lot

about the dirt of the place, its working–class, end–of–the–war dereliction, soon confirmed of course by the other details. And no
more. No Mr Grimes hiding in the cupboard. You know the
character is in a bit of a trance, thus intent observing it all, but that
you've got nothing to fear, she isn't going to go mad, she'll move
from her bench within a suitably short number of paragraphs, you
won't get stuck, there'll be plenty more 'action' to keep you busy.
That kind of clarity is deeply comforting. Of course, that's got to
do with the A to Z principle, which requires the continued 'illusion'
of action. What's perhaps most comforting of all is the sense that
there is *no more* than what there is. The clarity, the subject–verb–
object routine, also ensure this. For instance, it's rather unlikely
that you should have to read 'flaking like stale chocolate' as *more*
than a precise visual indication. An ample one, certainly, London
of course *is* in a derelict state, and the dingy state of the fish shop
expresses, or partakes of, that dereliction; but you know that
things aren't going to become metamorphosed (as they might in
Marquez, where the chocolate might become literal, and escalate
into God knows what); you also know that they aren't metaphors
for Martha's state of mind: you know, because the language
operates in such determined grammatical ways, that nothing is
going to happen from *inside* the language; that the process of
writing itself is excluded, except as a tool, from the operation that
is taking place. Even if you take the most crisis-like passages,
Martha's breakdown towards the end of *FGC*, they are hemmed
in as an insurance against their running away with the text:

Here Martha succumbed again to the Devil.

*Hell (one of them?) is hot. It has a harsh light. There is a sticky
clinging feel to it. MOST IMPORTANT OF ALL it has a beat.
Both regular and irregular. Like a mad clock, like the way paraffin
lamps flare up before going out . . . Faces like embryos, half-formed.
A gallery of faces of people. Devils. Ordinary people . . . Hate,
envy, greed, fear, slide over people's faces so fast you can only just
catch them.*

It was at that stage that Martha was conducted through the
Stations of the Cross by the Devil. She knew nothing of this
ritual, had never been instructed in it, nor had known well
enough to affect her people who performed it. Yet it was as if
she knew it, knew its meaning (*FGC*, 566).

The very fact that the more broken-down syntax (which remains, however, perfectly intelligible and syntactically correct) should be italicized and bracketed between the comforting indications 'Here Martha . . .', 'It was at that stage that Martha . . .', takes the sting out of the breakdown. The prose never really confronts you with the *experience* of madness (any more than I think it does in *Briefing for a Descent into Hell*) unlike, say, the prose of Nerval or Poe or Artaud or Jeanne Hyvrard. It never fully actualizes the crises it is about. This is because Martha, as at the beginning of the sequel, has a 'weapon' against crises: she somehow knows it all in advance, perhaps one could say she is dual (hence perhaps those beginnings of books with *two* women together). The experience is only for the statement of it. Everything that happens serves one purpose, and one only: to contribute to the 'plot', which is the achievement of a certain wisdom about 'life'. The prose is interested in saying, *not* in doing. Less and less in doing as the 'detached observer' takes over in the later novels. The texts are, in more than a chronological sense, A to Z texts.

Are they? And are there no significant gaps between the narrator and her protagonist? Well, when I read more closely, I do feel there are. But I am not sure that they are *intended*.

This for instance:

> Martha turned her face away; her lids stung with tears; she felt
> the most rejected and desolate creature in the world. It
> occurred to her that the Cohen boys might have felt like this
> when she (or so it had appeared) rejected them; but she
> dismissed the thought at once. The possessors of this particular
> form of arrogance may know its underside is timidity; but they
> seldom go on to reflect that the timidity is based on the danger
> of thinking oneself important to others, which necessitates a
> return of feeling (*MQ*, 45).

This is a subtle 'psychological' remark, not infrequent, especially in the early novels of the sequence. It reminds one of Jane Austen, or George Eliot perhaps: the author in her superior wisdom stepping back from her character to comment in a 'general' way about the failings of that character or to draw a universally valid moral/wise lesson from the experience presented. Thus, when Sir James Chettam, at the end of chapter 6 of *Middlemarch*, hears that

Dorothea is going to marry Casaubon, he is bitterly disappointed but decides to put a good face upon it when he goes to see the Brookes:

> He really did not like it: giving up Dorothea was very painful to him; but there was something in the resolve to make this visit forthwith and conquer all show of feeling, which was a sort of file-biting and counter-irritant . . .
>
> We mortals, men and women, devour many a disappointment between breakfast and dinner-time; keep back the tears and look a little pale about the lips, and in answer to inquiries say, 'Oh, nothing!' Pride helps us; and pride is not a bad thing when it only urges us to hide our own hurts – not to hurt others.

Such comments – what would be called 'meta-language'[34] by Colin MacCabe – besides soaring above the immediate experience of the characters, being beyond what *they* are capable of thinking, weaves a relationship between author and reader. Often, too, when the remarks are made about the heroine or hero (as in *The Mill on the Floss* or *Pride and Prejudice* or *Daniel Deronda*) it is implied that the heroine/hero, though not yet or never quite capable of the kind of wisdom shown by the authorial voice, is still moving towards it throughout the novel in that she/he is 'learning' all the time. The novel is coaching him/her out of prejudice, selfishness or naivety. And we are being coached along too.

To this must be added that, be it in Jane Austen or George Eliot, the language of each text elaborately produces the mental operations it wants its readers to become involved in: Jane Austen being more concerned with 'judgment',[35] George Eliot, in *Middlemarch* at least, with knowledge: the concept of a meta-language is in fact too simple to represent the multiplicity of manoeuvres[36] and areas of language which are being resorted to; the novel is continually producing processes of knowledge, and staging them as processes.

Now, the remark about Martha makes the book seem to belong with 'classic realist texts', texts with a meta-language. But if one then begins to wonder whether the overall language of *The Children of Violence* is concerned with *processes* of knowing, the answer must be negative. The novels are interested in questing for sense, yes, but by means of what *happens* to the heroine. The remark about Martha is *odd*. The only reason I can see for its presence is that the author underwent a change of heart whilst writing the sequence (we're back where we were earlier). Martha was *intended* to have a different fate from the one she turned out to have.

Indeed, if I think of this remark in the light of what I have said earlier (that everything in the text contributes to Martha's progress towards 'wisdom'), I straightaway realize that this reflection does not. Martha is no Emma who would learn that you have to be kind to the Misses Bates, the Cohen boys, of this world. In fact, she never solves her bizarre conflict, attraction to/revulsion from Solly and Joss, though Joss turns out to be better than his brother: it is even suggested Martha could have had an affair with Joss; if the sequence built up into the novel it seems to set out to be at this point, she would. A *personal* commitment to others is not what Martha learns to make. We are never made to feel that Martha's *human* shortcomings matter, nor that she ever does anything she should feel guilty about (not even leaving her child). We are not in a *moral* world. We are not even in a world in which 'classical' psychological wisdom would help. Thus, when Martha watches Thomas come up a ladder, there is a sharpness to her perception of him which does not belong to the rest of what is happening: 'His face was thoughtful, held the moment's stillness that accompanies wonder – which in itself is not far off fear' (*LL*, 103).

Nathalie Sarraute's ironies about Camus's Meursault.[37] She argues that we are surprised as we read *L'Estranger* by some deep psychological remarks, which suggest that this estranged and distanced man has fished deep in 'human' waters. And that our unease at a wisdom which jars with Meursault's professed detachment, his implied claim that there is no sense, that there are no 'values' in life, is finally dispelled by Meursault's outburst at the end – his declaration of love for life. That outburst, she says, confirms that here indeed was a man who had a deep understanding of 'life'. It is a 'return' of the 'psychological'.

Well, the passing remark from *LL* has the reverse effect on me. It seems to belong to a *past* fiction, a fiction that might have been, rather than to the novel the sequence is becoming. It belongs to a world in which 'psychology' matters, in which observing other people acutely matters in itself, is a self-justifying activity even. But that world is, from *RS* onward, in the process of disappearing:

> She thought: and it was a moment of illumination, a flash of light: I don't know anything about anything yet. I must try and keep myself free and open, and try to think more, not to drift into things (*RS*, 186).

> She recognized Marjorie's dry and humorous tone, and thought: Why is it I listen for the echoes of other people in my voice and what I do all the time? The fact is, I'm not a person at all, I'm nothing yet – perhaps I never will be (*RS*, 279).

Sure enough that remark is followed up in the epigraph to the following volume, *LL* – the Sufi fable about the Mulla saying to the shopkeeper who thinks he has seen *him* walk into his shop, 'How do you know it [was] me?' We are on our way to the man – the woman – without qualities – to the Musil model that is used for one of the epigraphs of *FGC*. On our way to the 'children of violence' vision, a *plural* (therefore impersonal) vision arrived at through the single consciousness of Martha:

> Every fibre of Martha's body, everything she thought, every movement she made, everything she was, was because she had been born at the end of one world war, and had spent all her adolescence in the atmosphere of preparations for another . . .
> The soul of the human race, that part of the mind which has no name, is not called Thomas and Martha, which holds the human race as frogspawn is held in jelly – . . . was twisted and warped (*LL*, 202).

(See what I mean about 'warped'? It's as if she reused the word because it was 'there' but she, who yet knows everything, does not know this is why.) Impersonality – the discovery of it – is soon to prevail:

> She sat looking at the blank television screen. As far as she was concerned, the scene they had just played out was no more real than what they could see on that screen by turning a switch . . .
> Oneself, or Paul, had to be, for as long as it was necessary, screaming baby, sulking adolescent, then middle-aged woman, whose eighteen hours a day were filled with a million

details, fragments, reflected off the faceted mirror that was one's personality, that responded all the time, every second, to these past selves, past voices, temporary visitors (*FGC*, 369).

'Make love'. 'Make sex'. 'Orgasms'. 'Climaxes'. It was all nonsense, words, sounds invented by half-animals who understood nothing at all. Great forces as impersonal as thunder or lightning or sunlight or the movement of the oceans being contracted and heaped and rolled in their beds by the moon, swept through bodies (*FGC*, 510).

To sum up: the texts act (especially the first two volumes) as if the authorial voice had a knowledge and wisdom superior to Martha's. But in the end, they have no use for that knowledge and wisdom. They are in excess of what the writing can make 'signify'. Not simply in the 'psychological' remarks I have quoted: when Anton is first introduced, he is presented in much more merciful and sympathetic terms than when he gets to be known to Martha, and seen through Martha's eyes (*PM*, 326) – there is, of course, the Jimmy episode, the account given of Mrs Van, which shows that Martha doesn't understand her. Now these gaps between the author's knowledge and Martha's have different effects. Some – the piece about Anton – suggest that the author changed her mind about what to do with this character: why present him sympathetically if he was going to turn out to be so unattractive and limited? To show that 'from the outside' he could have sounded appealing to Martha, and justify her marrying him? But obviously, there is no need to justify the marriage, Martha is open-eyed and generous in marrying Anton (she wants to preserve him from expulsion), there is no need to justify that. To suggest there is more to Anton than Martha ever sees? Now that would be interesting, but again that is not tenable, since more and more we are asked to take the novels as Martha's, her vision is more and more the central, the acceptable vision – nowhere more so than in *FGC*. And yet, had the kind of remarks I underlined been given more scope, it could have been so. Mrs Van is a different case; she comes home to roost in *FGC*, in that Martha sees herself finally as turning into another Mrs Van, and this gives her retrospective understanding of the old woman. But I think the point has to be taken: despite the claimed smoothness of Martha's progress, there are gaps inside the text which are not all recuperable by the 'totalizing' intention. They reveal a change of heart in the writer, and perhaps more.

It all comes back again and again to the same question: Is Martha the author? To what extent is the narrative voice Martha in her 'superior' wisdom – later on in life – presenting Martha's experience 'live'? If so, in what way and to what extent does the later wisdom colour the present-day experience? There must be – there is – a gap between *how* it happened and how it is being 'totalized' when it is shown as happening this way or that. This is evident if, reading for instance the following passage from *LL*, one keeps wondering *who* knows what is being told. For it supposes previous or extraneous knowledge; it also implies overall knowledge, knowledge of what is going to happen, since the hotel which lies on top of massacred black bodies is going to be the place where Thomas will confront Sergeant Tressell, and consciousness of the opposition of black Africans will finally become intolerable to him – wrecking his relationship with Martha. Reading this, gaps also appear if one wonders who is seeing, and who is speaking from *where*:

So heavy with memories was this land that people building houses here had been known to run away from them. They were unable to forget the painted warriors who walked for all to see with assegais and shields through the dark hours. The hotel, Parkland Hotel, had been such a house . . .

Does Martha know this as she drives in? Did she (did Lessing) learn of it afterwards? Does Lessing choose to have the scene occur there on account of it or did such a scene just 'happen' there in 'real' life?

As usual there was a long line of about fifty cars, although it was mid-week. It was just as well the six had booked a table.

Who knows 'as usual' since the six have never been there? Does one of the six say this? Martha? General thoughtful remark?

Is Martha perceiving this? Or official description?

The hotel was half-way up a sharp hill. In front the ground fell away to a small river from which rose a wraith of white mist and a smell of stagnant water. The building was long and low, across the hill. All its front was glassed in to make a dining space. Behind this was a long, low-ceilinged room with a platform for an orchestra. Very different, this place, from those where Martha had danced, in another epoch, five years before. Then, the city's young people moved from place to place, as if they owned them all; everybody knew each other, and the managers knew them and greeted them by name. Now, as the six went through the dining tables, and then stood waiting for a moment to cross the dance floor, there was no face they knew . . .

. . . then came Martha and Thomas, not touching: it was enough to walk beside each other across the sprung wooden floor that sent up a smell of wood and fresh beeswax . . .

. . . Maisie held out a big white arm into the light of the flames to show – what of course they could not see in the shifting light – gooseflesh because of the frosty table. They sat exclaiming and enjoying the cold – one of the sharpest pleasures of living in hot countries is this – to savour the vivifying degrees of

Same precision (journalistic?) as in opening of *FGC*. Why? So we can visualize the scene?

Here we get back to Martha.

She is remembering, presumably – stream of consciousness, or is the author telling us?

No, it's not just Martha, it's the six. Except of course that it can't be, because at least Anton, Athen and Thomas, never participated in that life, and therefore cannot share in the memory.
Does Thomas feel this as well as Martha? Or does Martha assume this is what he is feeling? Or is she as author remembering the scent?

Who sees Maisie's arm as big? Not Maisie, certainly: Martha? everybody? Does Maisie say, look at my gooseflesh, which no one can see? What is the point of making everyone, reader included, look at gooseflesh no one can see? Obviously, to make the reader imaginatively participate in the pleasure of the cold. But the cold on a winter's night (*LL*, 141–2).

text pretends to exclude relationship with the reader.

The passage, confident as it looks, is full of uncertainties: you can't say who is seeing, nor what for. The only way in which you can make the whole thing cohere is if you give it to Martha, but in a near-Flaubert-like perspective: the author as *deus ex machina* is all over the option, moves in and out of one or several characters at will. Without of course having to pay the price Flaubert pays for his omniscience and omnipresence, the continuous undermining of the text by itself, the authorial solitude, the renunciation, to hope, to sense. But can that be?

One has a well-organized piece of 'realism' here, which convinces because of the speed with which it skates over the surface; also, because the 'tricks' are so recognizable, one thinks one knows where one is. In fact, the narrative is gliding over contradictions ingrained in the nature of the ground it is covering. Time has been ironed out, lived time, the relation between the time of writing and the time during which the events are made to occur. The text is informed by *retrospective* knowledge (the scene with Sergeant Tressell, the 'black Africa' issue; even knowing that feeling the cold is one of the pleasures of hot countries implies one should have left them to appreciate it: Martha has not been out of Rhodesia yet): but it nowhere acknowledges that it is; it uses that smooth preterite which is the assumed present of fiction. The *recherche du temps perdu* element, the actuality of the autobiographical process is erased. And the process of the writing itself is erased.

Yet time and time again, the text stumbles across a consciousness of the actuality of language: 'but these are words, and if she understood anything it was that words, here, were like the sound of a baby crying in the wind' (*MQ*, 62); 'It was as if she were afraid of the power of language used nakedly' (*PM*, 69).

Here, 'language used nakedly' is Mr Maynard being able to say with relief, in 'this country' (coming from the circumlocutions of the English), 'The blacks need firm treatment.' Before this, the more 'liberal' phase, he could even have said, 'The kaffirs are getting out of hand.' Now, if this is so, naked language is language that expresses economic/social and, in this case, racialist, positions. You would have thought that with this perception firmly in hand, Martha's next step would be to wonder what is her *own* 'naked' language, what sort of language, that is, could express her true position; and is there a place in language where one could achieve something better than 'naked' language – a place of 'values', where not only you wouldn't be a 'salaud' (which Mr Maynard, dislikeable as he is, is not), but would become positively – free. And yet the writing continually operates from a supposed position of 'innocence'. The solid concatenation of the texts is achieved at the cost of actual exploration, even when the apparatus for the insights is there. You never lose your moorings. The bird's eye view, the eye of God vision, even, since it sees in hearts as well as exhibits an unfailingly clear sense of location, is achieved at the expense of any actual immersion in reality.

There you are. Back in mud. You've been going round in circles. Try to get hold of it again. You've gone too far away from yourself.

My quandary: the same again and again when I read or reread Lessing. There is no doubt she is a great lady. No doubt that it is a blessing, in an age in which so much shit is being written and acclaimed, that for once a thoroughly serious, honourable and deeply concerned writer should be popular. There is no doubting either Lessing's prodigious flair for the topical, her energy, her power. Perhaps one should not doubt either that her vision of a dismal future and her belief in the need for a new humanity to evolve if humanity is going to survive may be right. Time may reveal her to have been a prophetess.

And there I am, carping about 'aesthetic' issues (am I?). Just being a petty and irresponsible lout.

SH: in her young girl's diary, Rachel meditates on the strange understanding of her brother George. George is in fact an 'incarnation' (literally) of Johor (the archangel Gabriel turned into a twentieth-century Christ who has had a 'special' relationship when he was seven with a Jewish woman called Miriam). Benjamin, the earthly brother, has refused the 'special contacts'. Rachel fears she has too:

I am thinking about it, and there is something so *awful* there I don't know what to do with myself, because of course I am

thinking, what have I refused? I have always been offered
everything too, but I always had some good reason not to. Like
loving Mrs. Jones and wanting to be in the kitchen cooking
with her and feeding the chickens (*SH*, 222).

Now that sentence hit me. I am like Rachel, I thought (which of
course was what I/the reader was supposed to think). We're all
capable of living our lives in this 'trans-individual' way Lessing
suggests, open to 'we' or 'cosmic' forces, and I choose not to. I
have chosen myself immersed, tied and gagged by the passionate
details of trivial daily living, of ordinary relationships. A thick
network of people and things which take up, joy or despair, most
of my consciousness. I have chosen myself loving Mrs Jones and
wanting to be in the kitchen. We're back to the dung-beetles.
Back to the mud issue yet again. The reason why I 'object' to
Doris Lessing's evolution to this detached trans-individual
vision, why I like her short stories, the African ones especially,
GS, the early novels of *The Children of Violence* (despite the
problems I find there), Rachel's journal (part of which – the best –
is written while the girl is, surprise surprise, living in a Moroccan
mud house) in *SH*, the anguished passages of *GN* rather than the
framework or the 'wisdom' which is mean to emerge, is that they
feed my own choice of life. Because being *submerged* and struggling seems to me to be where life is. Depth. Thickness.

My choice. I remember a story my father (my own 'voice of the
father'?) used to tell me when I was little, which always impressed
me. It's about St Louis de Gonzague, a child in a religious school.
The young boys are playing ball, there is a lull in the game, and
one of the boys says, 'What would we do if we knew that in one
hour's time it was going to be the end of the world?' One boy
says, 'I'd go to my room and kneel and pray.' Another, 'I'd try to
recall my past life and have it with me when I face God.' Another,
'I'd go to confession and repent my sins.' And St Louis de
Gonzague says, 'I'd go on playing ball.'

That's the point of dissent, I suppose. I'm not persuaded that
one cannot work towards 'sainthood' (meaning by that working
with the forces of 'peace' rather than 'violence', or writing so as to
make 'sense', writing towards 'truth', whatever that be) by
staying in the kitchen with Mrs Jones just as well as by conversing
with galactic forces. I'm not convinced that the way to trans-

individuality is in disregard of, or contempt for, individuality, rather than *through* individuality. That the fate of Mary Turner is not more 'universally' relevant *because* so narrow and precise in its unfolding than the fate of the late Martha, or the various people who flit across *SH* and can be catalogued as number 3 or number 8 terrorist. Evidently, Lessing is of the opposite opinion. So my criticisms only amount to a statement of my own difference or my own political and moral backwardness.

You have only devised these arguments, I was saying to myself, in order to give authority to your dissent – to your immaturity.

But – perhaps precisely because I was – am – immature and individualistic and petty bourgeois – I could not accept this. I did not accept it because, genuinely, I felt uneasy. Not just because I felt on the spot. It did seem to me that there were some genuine contradictions and impossibilities where I had tried to describe them. But I had not got to the core of the matter: which was, why can't such writing *do today*?

I was stuck.

Oh, of course, theoretically, I knew the answers. All the post-Joyce-Proust-Kafka, post-existentialism, post-*nouveau roman*, post-*Tel Quel*, post-Saussure, post-Freud, post-Marx, post-Barthes, post-etc., etc., arguments: 'We now know that language cannot pretend to "imitate" reality.' 'Language as production.' 'Language that pretends to be mimetic is ideological language.' But somehow that sort of talk got on my nerves. It did not click, where it matters. I had read hundreds of things that ought to have helped me formulate my difficulties, and if I were to try very hard for theory I could have formulated them, but I didn't want to. It would have been like giving *The Children of Violence* the kiss of death by means of the Establishment. A high-brow Establishment kiss of death. The tidy bundling and posting to no-man's-land of texts into which life and faith had gone. If I was going to come to terms with my dissatisfaction with these texts, it would have to be from the depths of what had meaning for *me*. The whole of me. In any case, I often felt that it was at the expense of the actuality, the dimensions of the so-called 'classic realist text' that the theories were arrived at.

While I was musing upon this, I found myself in front of

Saint-Sulpice. I had twenty minutes to spare before a rendezvous. I remembered the Delacroix, and went into the church.

As when I go to Saint-Sulpice I normally look at Jacob's fight with the angel, I concentrated for once on *Héliodore Chassé du Temple par les anges*.

How fantastically convenient, I thought. To have a subject-matter. A Biblical story behind it, that enables you to *read* the shapes in a particular way. An ordered world, heaven above earth, so that the upper part of the picture, the draught created by the descent of the angel, can be *read* as heaven; that some forms can be read as *super*-added forms, the flesh and draperies of the winged angel, the angelic horse and his rider, different, separated from, of another order than, the flesh of the humans. What a blessing for a painter, I thought, to have a framework of belief (or convention) that helps him organize his space, give it an up and a down and multiple levels of conflicting significance. Why can't we have it anymore, I thought. Of course we can. I can still look at this picture. I have my own way of believing in heaven.

Ah, but something whispered, do you believe that heaven is up?

Shut up, I said. I am sure it must be possible. I can understand 'imitative' writing. I like chronological stories. Just because people now like messing up the order of things just for the sake of seeming original I don't see why . . .

Ah, but something whispered. Are *you* chronological? Has *your* existence taken place in chronological *order*?

That evening I was having dinner with a friend, who is a painter. I spared him till after dessert. 'Louis', I said, 'why can't you paint figuratively?' *Il en resta assis.* 'You've got a way of asking questions,' he said. 'Why don't you ask me who made the world?'

He is a beautiful man. He actually took the trouble of answering. 'Because,' he said, 'on ne peut plus répercuter son moi à l'univers.' '*Grosso modo*,' he said. In Balzac's time, the world of an individual could be put into correspondence with, *represent*, the world. The vision an individual had of the world, the fate of an individual, could act as a *valid model* for what was happening at a universal level. But now, because of what's happened, you know just as well as I do, as everybody does, the sciences, the 'sciences humaines', the discovery of the unconscious, politic . . .

Yes yes yes. Everything gelled suddenly. Of course. No more polymath figures after the beginning of the nineteenth century. Cassirer describing how all the sciences begin to pull apart, arguing that Comte is the last man to have tried for a global, a cohesive theory of knowledge. Specialization. In factories, as in the sciences. End of the frontier. Relativity. Speed of communications. Break up of communications. The impotency of 'totalizing' reason. This book by Feyerabend I was reading.

> We must therefore conclude that even inside science, reason cannot, and must not, have a universal relevance; it must often be overstepped, or eliminated, and other principles resorted to. There is no one rule that remains valid in all circumstances, and not one principle to which one can always appeal.[38]

In other terms: there is no single organizing formal principle fiction can hope to rely on; there is no one syntactical mode that will do to account for contemporary reality.

In Balzac's time, Louis said, it was possible for an author to hold a privileged position. A position of authority. Both to know his characters, and to know better. To know how your characters fitted into the world; because you could know the world. Now, all we can do is what Lévi-Strauss says. Use a *sharp angle*. Work on it, get it to work, so that it releases the largest possible point of view. Construct models. Individual models. Hope our individual models will have some relevance.

A Hundred Years of Solitude, I was thinking. The 'model' of Macondo. The 'universal' reached there because the particular, the extraordinary too, rather than the 'average', the 'typical', are being sought. The 'model' with a modest dimension. Couldn't care less that he doesn't have the ultimate word to speak about universal wisdom, Hiroshima, or Marxism: he has the Flood in Macondo, or the strike of the banana plantation.

Van Gogh, Louis said. Van Gogh knew that the sky could be at the bottom of a picture. He knew that putting the sky only at the top of a picture was projecting onto the world an anthropomorphic ambition that had ceased to be tenable.

Chronological sequences, I thought. Chronological sequences the equivalent in fiction of up and down, or left and right, in pictures. The development of certain fictional sequences (the history of a private individual; born in such a time and such a place), stretching in chronological order, youth being regarded as the key-moment, the moment when real choices are made, corresponds in time, '*grosso modo*', to the Industrial Revolution, the development of the sciences. Why? Is it because that type of sequence makes possible a certain form of rationalized 'progress'? Or represents the conditions in which certain forms of (financial or mechanized) progress can occur? It would be interesting to find out. But then, how is it that people – Doris Lessing for one – can go on writing like this once those conditions have become altered, or have escalated into monumental and divisive complexities? Well, forms after all go on reproducing themselves long after they are *actually* dead. People went on writing imitations of *La Princesse de Clèves* late into the eighteenth century, when the fabric of power at the French court and in the aristocracy had changed. Even now, nearly two centuries after Scott, when conceptions of history have radically altered and the conditions which gave rise to the historical novel have largely disappeared, popular writers go on churning out historical fictions.

Claiming that human life, that consciousness, goes from A to Z and can at all times be both aware of all there is to it (including those transparent dreams that always tell Martha, in perfectly intelligible language, what her 'deeper' state is) as well as of all there is to the world, is like continuing to put the sky at the top of the picture. It perpetuates a fiction that we like, of course, and *recognize* because that is what we are used to, what we need to feel 'at home', but that is truly a fiction: that no longer relates to reality. Martha may at the end of *FGC* discover that her consciousness of reality had been false: but the manner in which she is led to make that discovery in itself perpetuates that falsity.

The time-span in *A Hundred Years of Solitude*, I was thinking. Perpetually taking off, speeding up, escalating, yet things endlessly repeating themselves (yet not repeating themselves): circular in the end; above all, the circularity containing the awareness, the fact, too, of the writing of the book. That book knows, among others, the relativity principle.

Martha's fate. In *fact*, what the books are really giving us is a portrait of the artist as a young woman. What other justification at bottom is there for Martha's 'observer' moods, her detachment, her will to freedom? What else *really* is she keeping herself free for? Yet Martha never writes a line. Never thinks about language, even. The autobiography goes far enough to include a great deal of personal experience, but the most important aspect of that experience, the one that is part and parcel of the *writing* of the books, that was part and parcel of the getting to the stage when the books could be written, is erased from them.

All that can happen to me, Louis said, is that I am haunted by figurativeness. 'Hanté par le figuratif.'

Martha, discovering emptiness with her customary painstaking honesty, discovers what is at the basis of the kind of writing which has been given to her. She also discovers the fundamental truth of her character. The truth: that the mud house, once gone, she ceased to belong. Rather, decided that she would not belong. The nomad's flat, anonymous, empty. Naked language.

Ah yes, but it is not really naked, as we have seen. It only pretends to be. It pretends, with colonial simplicity, that because you're not really 'involved', you are, you can be, 'objective', 'all-knowing'. Which is yet another, unrecognized fiction.

Nomads belong to nomadism. To movement. How many writers this century have been exiles, of one kind or another? James, Eliot, Pound, Joyce, Beckett, Jabès . . . Berger even claims that to be an artist is to be an exile.

Was the only language open to them 'naked' language? The language of the 'detached observer'? . . .

Nomads. The Scythians. Small transportable art forms. Gold handicraft. Carpets.

If you have to flee, you put your values into movables. Jewels, for instance – ingots.

The language of circulation.

The kabbala. Esoterism. You belong to a secret, a spiritual society.

'Rome n'est plus dans Rome, elle est toute où je suis.'

They did not think they had to plaster the world – nothing less – all over the walls of their tents.

Martha's mammoth ambition. For the ultimate.

If you want the ultimate and you want to be able to *transport* it you carve in gold.

It is Martha's refusal to relate to the Africa that is there, that could be there, as the African short stories show, that makes her into a spiritual globe-trotter.

That the authorial stance, the all-knowing, all-encompassing voice, the confident voice, is false. Unreal. Or represents exactly what it is, 'news'. What is good about it is precisely that: the social world that is being portrayed, in Africa above all, but in London, too. The truth those novels offer is documentary.

That Martha, because she is questing for some kind of truth or freedom or self or whatever it is, because she is *voyaging*, becomes a tourist of life; she discards more and more, needs more and more people, experiences, to burn through. So that what she grows to perceive as the ultimate truth – the unreality, the comedy, the 'roles' of it all, people being activated by impersonal forces – is in fact her understanding of what her choices have made her into, of what the prose has made her throughout. The novels as they proceed become aware of something false, a vacuity, which is the falsity of their own fictional mode. It is a mark of the profound honesty of their author that they do so. Except where all the 'heart' goes into the 'mud' of experience, or when that 'mud' catches up with Martha, in the form of Mrs Quest, Doris Lessing fails to give herself the means of a reality principle. Perhaps if it is purely freedom you are after, you deliver yourself into the void. Mud, or the void. Hence probably the unease the reader feels in relation to Martha. One admires her as a thoroughly esteemable person – courageous, honest, disinterested, uncompromising, strong, competent, even at times loving – yet one feels a sneaking dislike for her, as though one was being conned by means of her: the sense that she is neutral, bland, whatever it is: a consciousness that fails to spring into full life because it is not rooted in life.

The 'philosophical' truth the sequence of *The Children of Violence* unearths is simply the principle of its own articulation. All that Martha can discover in her efforts to come closer to herself and to reality, to 'conceive' the universe, to 'roll it into a ball', is the emptiness of the universalist fictions that have been used to mimic the relation of the individual consciousness to the world. There has not been enough language there, not enough 'body' as opacity, as presence, as a place, the only place, where a *model* of knowledge could have been born.

Notes

1 See Dee Seligman, 'The Autobiographical Fiction of Doris Lessing', PhD, Tufts University, 1975, and 'The Four-Faced Novelist', *Modern Fiction Studies*, vol. 26, no. 1, spring 1980.

2 'My parents were, now I come to think of it, grail-chasers of a very highly-developed sort. I cannot even imagine a country in which they would have been definitely ready to settle down without criticism . . . I would, of course, be the first to blame my parents for my own grail-seeking propensities.'

3 See Dee Seligman's paper, 'The Autobiography of a New Consciousness', p. 28 (unpublished).

4 Elaine Showalter, *A Literature of Their Own*, London, Virago, 1977, p. 309.

5 The context makes this a quite complex moment: more than can be discussed within the framework of this essay. Mark's fanatical 'mapping' concern, which sends Martha researching and filing rather as she had done in Africa for Mrs Van Der Bylt on an anti-racialist campaign, is regarded by his communist friends as 'reactionary'. It is no longer 'socialist realism' but a search for individual vision on a world-scale. Yet, for Doris Lessing alias Martha, the decision to transcend the personal springs from communist convictions. 'The personal is by definition a private possession and may represent for the former communist a form of selfishness, a capitalist hoarding of emotional territory' (Lynn Sukenick, 'Feeling and Reason in Doris Lessing's Fiction', in *Doris Lessing: Critical Studies*, eds Amis Pratt and L. S. Dembo, Madison, Wisconsin, 1974, p. 115). Anna, in *GN*, is convinced that the personal is political, that 'if Marxism means anything, it means that the little novel about the emotions reflects "what's real"', since the emotions are a function and a product of society' (p. 43). It would be interesting, therefore, to work out why the steps Mark and Martha and Anna take towards transcending the personal are so suspect to their communist friends.

6 The epigraphs, e.g pp. 11, 165, 301, make this abundantly clear.

7 Goethe, Poe, Gautier, Baudelaire among others:

> as no thought can perish, so no act is without infinite results. We moved our hands, for example, when we were dwellers on the earth, and, in so doing, we gave vibration to the atmosphere which engirdled it. This vibration was indefinitely extended, till it gave impulse to every particle on the earth's air . . . It is indeed demonstrable that every such impulse *given the air*, must, *in the end*, impress every individual thing that exists *within the universe* (Poe, *The Power of Words*).

On this, see Georges Poulet's article on Gautier in *Etudes sur le Temps Humain*, Plon, 1949, pp. 278–307, and Nicole Ward Jouve, *Baudelaire: a Fire to Conquer Darkness*, Macmillan, 1980, pp. 280–4.

8 As if Lessing, through the voice and persona of her narrator, and that narrator's relation to her/Emily's infancy and childhood, carried out her own analysis.

9 Of course, in a sense there in no 'particularity'. A great deal of Colette is invested in Claudine, and Claudine's whole sense of life of course carries its own 'universally relevant' value. Yet there is a modesty and irreverence in Colette's creation of her heroines that makes them less obvious candidates for 'universal' status than others.

10 Baudelaire said this of his own *Fleurs du mal*. But he says very similar things in a discussion of Balzac, 'Les Drames et les romans honnêtes', in *Oeuvres complètes*, vol. II, Pléiade, 1976, pp. 41–2.

11 After Pound's *Usura Canto*, of course.

12 Ultimately, in *SH* (in so far as one can call any recent work of such a prolific writer 'ultimate'), it's God's vision she is interested in through the medium of the archangels Gabriel *et al.* (Johor, etc.) and of Heaven's files.

13 The connection with Maggie Tulliver has been noticed before. See Walter Allen, as quoted in S. J. Kaplan, *Feminine Consciousness in the Modern British Novel*, Urbana, 1974, p. 153.

14 'I find [Virginia Woolf] too much of a lady . . . I feel that her experience must have been too limited, because there is always a point in her novels when I think, "Fine, but look at what you've left out".' Quoted in Nancy Joyner, 'The Underside of the Butterfly: Lessing's Debt to Woolf', *Journal of Narrative Technique*, vol. V, 1974, pp. 204–5.

15 See on this Malcolm Bowie's inaugural lecture for Queen Mary College, 'Proust, Jealousy, Knowledge', delivered 24 October 1978, published by Queen Mary College.

16 Preface to the African short stories.

17 See Elaine Showalter's discussion of contemporary (and Victorian) women novelists' fear of hurting their families or offending their friends, op. cit., pp. 302–3.

18 In *IPE*, there is a revealing incident. Rose, the narrator's young friend, cannot understand why the narrator continues to meet the 'spiv' after it's become quite clear that he *is* a 'spiv':

> 'He's like that', she commented. 'He was always like that. That's why he frightens me, see? So don't you have nothing to do with him.'
> 'He said he was going to take me to see a flat tonight.'
> She let her hands drop away from my arm. 'You didn't say you'd go?'
> 'Yes, I did.'
> She was silent. 'Why?' she asked at last timidly. 'You don't believe what he says. I know that.'
> 'Well, it's because I've never met anyone like him before.' When she didn't reply, I said: 'Why don't you like that?'
> She thought. Then she said: 'You talk like he's an animal in a zoo' (*IPE*, 72–3).

The narrator's reply – that she's interested because it's new to her – convinces neither Rose nor the reader – and is probably not meant to. Rose's suspicion is right: the narrator's interest *is* treacherous, *is* exploitative, *is* novelistic. She's fishing for material. Martha is fishing, too. But she is never acknowledged as doing so.

19 'The essence of the book the organization of it, everything in it, says implicitly and explicitly, that we must not divide things off, must not compartmentalize' (preface to *GN*, p. 10).

20 *The Man Without Qualities* is used for one of the epigraphs of *FGC*. But it is the combination of a stripped self and a sensitivity to 'biological' or 'atmospheric' pressures that makes the book attractive to Lessing: not the writing itself.

21 See Margaret Scanlan, 'Memory and Continuity in the Series Novel: The Example of *The Children of Violence*', *Modern Fiction Studies*, Doris Lessing number, vol. 26, no. 1, spring 1980.

22 'We think back through our mothers if we are women,' Virginia Woolf, *A Room of One's Own*, Panther, 1977, pp. 72–3.

23 *GN*, p. 11.

24 Lessing's own statement, quoted in Lynn Sukenick, 'Feeling and Reason', p. 99; see also Showalter, op. cit., p. 309.

25 Luce Irigaray, *Ce Sexe qui n'en est pas un*, Editions de Minuit, p. 127.

26 'It is becoming more and more difficult today, confronted by the experiments of modern art, not to question along with the identity of the subject the very principle of a sexual identity, which is nevertheless claimed by feminist movements. I do not find it easy to define . . .', etc. 'L'Autre du sexe', *Sorcières*, no. 10, p. 37, transl. Stephen Heath. Kristéva is actually full of contradictions in this respect. She had tried to define a specific 'femininity' in an article for the *Cahiers du grif* and moved towards it, both in *Des Chinoises* but above all in her location of the feminine as the 'pulsational' in texts: see *Polylogue*, Le Seuil, 1977, and *La Révolution du langage poétique*, where she argues that femininity can be located in the breaks and pulsions of the text; it acts as the limits, 'les bords', or the 'trans-symbolic' questioning of the text (see especially discussion of Mallarmé's 'Prose' and 'Coup de dés'). But when woman resorts to the making of a text so as to constitute her own identity (i.e. text as child-substitute – as penis-substitute) she participates in the 'general fetishism' (*La Révolution*, Le Seuil, 1973, p. 614). I'm not sure I follow this in that it seems to me that texts can always in some ways be seen as attempts by the writer to constitute his/her identity: is woman not to write then? or only those texts which are, *like* the texts of men like Mallarmé, Lautréamont, etc., 'pulsational'? Which lands one right back in the 'no-difference' area. For translations of Kristéva or discussions of her work, see *M/F* 5/6, 1981, pp. 149–57 and 158–63; also J. Kristéva, *Desire in Language*, Basil Blackwell, 1981, and Mary Jacobus, 'The Difference of View', in *Woman Writing and Writing about Woman*, Croom Helm, 1979.

27 Lacan of course, from *Encore, Séminaire XX*. Transalation borrowed
    from Stephen Heath, 'Difference', *Screen*, vol. XIX, 1978, p. 68.
28 Catherine Clément, 'Enclave Esclavep', *L'Arc*, 61, *Simone de Beauvoir
    et la Lutte des femmes*, Aix-en-Provence, pp. 13–19 (my translation).
29 Hélène Cixous, 'Le Rire de la Méduse', *L'Arc*, 61, *Simone de Beauvoir
    et la Lutte des femmes*, p. 43 (my translation).
30 Madeleine Gagnon, in Cixous Gagnon Clément, *La Venue à l'écriture*,
    10/18, 1977, p. 63 (my translation).
31 I wonder, given the *Waste Land* source of the epigraph and title for
    GS, whether there is a reminiscence here of the 'water out of sunlight'
    passage from 'Burnt Norton'?
32 See preface to *Chronicles of the Canongate*.
33 Of course, when it happens, it is 'significant' in more ways than are
    meant; but certainly the authorial voice never ceases to be analogous
    to Martha's.
34 Colin MacCabe, *James Joyce and the Revolution of the Word*, Macmillan,
    1978, esp. pp. 16–23.
35 Obviously these points ought to be fully argued: they are well put in
    David Lodge's *The Language of Fiction*, Routledge & Kegan Paul, and
    Columbia University Press, 1966.
36 Even the notion of 'free indirect style' (see Roy Pascal, *The Dual
    Voice*, Manchester University Press, 1977) fails adequately to
    represent the way the narrator in *Middlemarch* uses languages whose
    sources are in the personality and culture of the character concerned,
    but which are still in excess of the consciousness of the character and
    outside his/her range or readiness for self-knowledge.
37 *L'Ere du soupçon*, Gallimard, 1956, pp. 15–23.
38 P. Feyerabend, *Against Method*, New Left Books, 1975, end of
    chapter 15.

5   Towards a narrative analysis of *A Man and Two Women*

Margaret Atack

The observer and the observed: structures of the self and the other

> When he had first seen Barbara Coles, some years before, he
> only noticed her because someone said: 'That's Johnson's new
> girl.' He certainly had not used of her the private erotic
> formula: *Yes, that one.* He even wondered what Johnson saw in
> her. 'She won't last long,' he remembered thinking, as he
> watched Johnson, a handsome man, but rather flushed with
> drink, flirting with some unknown girl while Barbara stood by
> a wall looking on. He thought she had a sullen expression.

To see, to notice, to watch, to look on: in this, the opening
paragraph of 'One off the Short List', the first story in *A Man and
Two Women*,[1] the relations mediating the group are almost
entirely visual. It is a shifting network, where subjects and objects
of the verbs interchange in a visual chain, where he watches
Barbara who watches Johnson whose attention is all for the
unknown girl. The information about each is minimal – each
element is there to hold its position in the chain, and the information given is just enough to elucidate the nature of the chain. It is a
complex example of one of the basic units of Lessing's narrative
structure, that of the unreturned look – a dual structure where
reciprocity plays no part. It is a simple pattern allowing of many
variations:

> In my tiny bedroom I looked out on to a space of flat white
> sand . . . and there hurtled a mad wild puppy, . . . snapping at
> its own black shadow and tripping over its own clumsy feet.[2]

> Then they saw her, between chimneys, about fifty yards away.
> She lay face down on a brown blanket.[3]

This is a remarkably consistent structure, ordering both the initial encounters and their subsequent developments. In each case, it is constructed upon the basis of a *difference*: A, partaking of and integrated within one order, directs attention towards B, an element within another order, and B in turn is drawn towards C, who is either an element of the first order (as in 'One off the Short List') or of the same order ('The Sun between their Feet') or oscillating between the two, as for example in 'The Story of Two Dogs', where the third element is either the moon, equated with madness and wildness, or another dog held within the confines of social domesticity. In each case can be seen the attraction of and for the other, for the one who is different and apart.

At this point it might be useful to stress that the logic of any narrative operating within the discourse of realism (by which I mean, very loosely, any narrative which concerns itself with 're-presenting' the real) demands an oppositional structure, and uses the oppositions it creates in order to advance to its own conclusion. The two terms of an opposition might be unambiguously marked by either positive or negative value, and the narrative account be the struggle to eliminate the latter (the structure of the Western film would be a classic example here). Alternatively, the narrative may conclude without a definitive resolution in favour of one or other of the oppositional terms, in which case ambiguity enters the signifying circuit as an important factor mediating the relations of the opposition. It seems to me that the Lessing narratives partake of the latter structure – not necessarily when considering each individual story or novel, but across the *oeuvre* as a whole. The constants of the differential structure return time and again (man *v* woman, Africa *v* England, white *v* black, domestic *v* wild, dream *v* the real, self *v* the other) and yet the complex orchestration of these many elements seems either to defeat a definitive critical reading, or produces many contradictory ones, especially in relation to the notion of the self which has been variously judged to be the inner self of emotion released through breakdown, or the cool, critical intelligence which alone survives the experience. It cannot be denied there is ample evidence for both readings, and yet they cannot both be entirely accurate. To produce either interpretation demands that considerations of the narrative *context* take a second place, in the name of the search for the *truth* of Lessing's worldview. The novels and short stories are interrogated for the meanings they are deemed to contain, as if they were formal repositories for a meaningful substance to be released by critical exposition and interpretation. That this can result in such contradictory conclusions justifies, in my view, adopting a different approach, one that does not seek to liberate the 'truth' of the narrative, but, rather, seeks to elucidate the structures ordering the narrative vision and its conclusion, to examine, for example, the self of breakdown in terms of its place and function *within* the narrative; in other words, to switch the emphasis away from the narrative as embodiment of ready-constituted meaning towards the narrative as *production* of meaning, away from the identification of a product and towards the investigation of a process. It is the play of the signifying elements which constitutes a narrative, not the other way round.

In addressing myself to the question of the text as narrative order, I shall therefore be concentrating on an analysis of the language and an examination of the mechanisms constituting the actions, events and characters, in order to unravel some at least of the structures governing them. The recurring patterns and their variations are one key to reading the order in which they are inscribed, that of the logic of the narrative. This is why the function of the conclusion is crucial: summum and summation, ending and end, it inscribes the sequence of the narrative within a teleology. The coherence of its development is ordered by an oscillation between temporal and causal structures, whereby that which comes after is at the same time logically motivated by that which precedes: as the narrative now reaches the conclusion towards which it has already tended from the beginning, it irrevocably places all that has preceded it under the sign of a finality. We can therefore see that to look at any element of a narrative independently of the space and function it occupies within the narrative as a whole, is inevitably to impose a reading from elsewhere which that element is invoked to support. Isolated from the narrative structures which inform it and which it furthers, it quite literally cannot 'make' sense. Given the complexity of the process, I have restricted the most detailed analysis to just one of the stories, 'One off the Short List'.

Two major problems remain. First, the danger of reproducing once more the assumptions that the truth of the text is about to be spoken, that to concentrate upon the text somehow renders the criticism innocent of any discursive intervention. I hope that by having made the critical framework clear, it will remain apparent that this is offered as a possible reading, and a deliberately restricted one, aiming, above all, at elucidating the mechanisms by which the narrative produces itself as significant, and the elements in that process. Second, the choice of text, and the delineation of the text as unit, is far from straightforward. No analysis of one collection of short stories can claim to exhaust the narrative categories of an *oeuvre*. Moreover, as a unit it is already in some ways a factitious one, gathering together stories over several magazines, so that they become a 'text' ordered by the publishing industry, the popularity of the writer, and so on. This in turn probably explains why the 'text' should probably be seen as greater than just the sum of the individual stories, for the short introductory blurb, present in nearly all the paperback editions, not only makes these stories into a unit ordered by the one author, but also proposes which elements are to be read as significant (being in this case, woman novelist, emotions, Africa and England); the stories are already inscribed within a critical discourse – the dominant discourse on literature which privileges the author, as subjective source and site of knowledge and power over the text, and the biographical elements which will be seen to have narrative significance (even the blurb is subject to narrative finality) and which are unproblematically offered as relevant, placing the real of the text firmly outside it.

To pose these questions is hardly to solve them, merely to note the constraints and assumptions inherent in concentrating upon one set of short stories. In considering them here as a text, I am doing no more than use them as a working unit, as a convenient section ready-made within the body of work signed 'Lessing'. And there are virtues to the limitations: the very heterogeneity of the collection which predates the realignment of the stories into 'African and other' affords a fairly wide range of narrative and socio-cultural connotations. They are broadly contemporaneous. Finally, the structure of the short story is less complex than that of the novel. It is possible to define the short story as a narrative determined by the account, elucidation and resolution of one primary narrative conflict, however complex the range of oppositions, of narrative figures, of social and cultural connotations and discourses in play.

The frequency with which sight is used, on the level of both description and act, suggests that the complex structure of the observer and the observed and the multiplicity of variations which it displays, occupies a privileged position in these narratives, with many implications for the nature of the terms of the oppositions which it mediates. Seeing does not necessarily coincide with the singling out of the one observed as special, chosen or loved. It does in 'The Story of Two Dogs', where the vision of the mad puppy dancing to the moon leads the child observing the scene to conclude 'That, of course, was my puppy' (*MTW*, p. 37), but in 'One off the Short List', further developments are necessary before Graham Spence will confer his elective phrase '*Yes, that one*' upon Barbara Coles. In either case, what is privileged is *appearance*: what the appraisal of the indirect look calls into play is how the other appears, and at the moment of the initial meeting, this is what counts: that the other appear as other. The figures who embody the differential oppositions of the narrative are immediately placed within a specific relation of difference by the indirect look which both binds and separates them. There is no hint here, at the initial encounter, that appearances are deceptive – on the contrary, to appear 'other' is to *be* 'other'. Within the same structure, the first sight of Barbara Coles (see the first quotation above) suggests there is nothing to see *in* her. Even in 'Dialogue', about a meeting of two people who know each other well, appearance still exhausts being, there is just a different level of competence in play (*MTW*, p. 217):

> A single glance from a stranger (or from herself before she had
> known better) would have earned him: big, strong, healthy,
> confident man. Now, however, she knew the signs, could,
> after glancing around a room say: Yes, you and you and
> you. . . Because of the times she had been him, achieved his
> being.

The primacy of appearance and the modes of its articulation can perhaps facilitate a reading of the self and the other in Lessing's fiction. That appearance, sight, look are such important mechanisms in structuring the significant elements may also be a reason for the cultural preponderance of the visual arts in the coding of the work of many of the characters. They are designers, artists, potters, or working in television, journalism, advertising, film, sometimes famous, sometimes not. With the media and the arts predominating, they are inscribed within a cultural code which permits the preoccupation with appearance to be duplicated at other narrative levels and also to further its progress. For example, that Barbara Coles is a stage designer who wins a prize and achieves success and a certain fame is one of the ways in which she is differentiated from the Barbara Coles of the first appearance while still remaining within Spence's field of vision (*MTW*, p. 7): 'Barbara Coles was one of the "names" in the theatre, and her photograph was seen about.' Success in the arts, in design, is, through the media, a public success, and the distinction between the acclaimed artist and the brilliant but unknown one may occur as a pertinent distinction so often precisely because it is a question of being in the public eye: to appear successful is to be successful. Yet the romantic code in which the greatness of an artist is guaranteed by obscurity is completely opposed to this. Genius can only exist in so far as it is singular and different, and mass recognition (that is, both seeing and understanding) would negate it. This is no longer the only possible code of cultural practice, but the continuing dominance of the discourse on art as being a uniquely individual creation feeds it still, so it is not surprising, given the equivalence between appearance and being in this collection, that it should appear as a narrative function and counterpoint. The beginning of 'A Man and Two Women' is almost entirely devoted to placing the four characters each in their respective oppositional positions across these codes.

A similar complexity governs the figure of Graham Spence in 'One off the Short List'. Public success is essential to the choices operating in his list of 'especial women', but he himself is positioned within the code devaluing the media. His 'unique talent', and his 'struggles as a writer' have resulted, as for many others, in being dependent upon the creative work of others: 'Yet here they were, running television programmes about which they were cynical . . . or writing reviews about other people's books. Yes, that's what he had become, an impresario of other people's talent' (*MTW*, p. 9). Both his marriage and his work are inscribed within a movement from the particular to the general: in each sphere he considers his experience unique, only to discover it as part of a sameness, a multiplicity of similar experiences:

> Just as that melodramatic marriage had turned out to be like everyone else's . . . so it had turned out that his unique talent, his struggles as a writer, had led him here, to this pub and the half-dozen pubs like it, where all the men in sight had the same history (*MTW*, p. 9).

To look at them is to see himself as one of them. It is on the basis of this serial generality that the list of 'especial women' takes its place, to acknowledge his talents as he saw them, in the realm of emotion and experience: 'The formula: *Yes, that one . . .* expressed an ironical dignity, a proving to himself not only: I can be honest about myself, but also: I have earned the best in *that* field whenever I want it' (*MTW*, p. 9). The woman's function is to enable the narrator to be singled out among his peers and for himself. In one sense, the long process of watching leads to the true object of observation, himself:

> He watched the field for the women who were well-known in the arts, or in politics; looked out for photographs, listened for bits of gossip. He made a point of going to see them act, or dance, or orate. He built up a not unshrewd picture of them . . . He would be seen out with her a few times in public . . . He might have a brief affair with this woman, but more often than not it was the appearance of an affair. Not that he didn't get pleasure from other people envying him – he would make a point, for instance, of taking this woman into the pubs where his male colleagues went (*MTW*, pp. 9–10).

One of the elements creating the bitter affect of the conclusion is that Barbara Coles proves not to be a cipher for his narcissistic self-appraisal.

It has already been noted that in 'One off the Short List' the choice of the desirable object does not coincide with the moment of seeing. It is staggered across three moments of the narrative, thus proving singularly useful in elucidating the process of the articulation of desire in the text. In the visual chain of the opening paragraph quoted above, 'to see' is not synonymous with 'to notice'. Barbara Coles is only noticed because it is pointed out that she has already been noticed by Johnson; the structures of sight and choice are in fact relaying their opposite – a refusal. The notion of choice is posed as a narrative element, only to be denied at this stage to a specific narrative figure. 'Barbara Coles' is mapping out the negative space of the absence of desire, is poised on the limits between sequences of male choice: about to be eliminated from the one signed Johnson as the narrative points towards his lack of interest in her, and refused admission to the sequence of the unnamed 'he', who turns out to be Graham Spence. Spence and Johnson are aligned in implicit agreement; Barbara Coles has nothing to retain the attention. For this to change, 'Barbara Coles' has to change. In other words, the con-stituent elements constructing this figure will be modified, some added, some eliminated – though a repetition of some of the same elements is essential to maintain the fiction that this is a 'character', a person to whom the story refers or whom the story creates, offering her existence to our belief. This is one of the major narrative functions of the proper name: a name which reappears must 'be' the same figure of that name already men-tioned, even though the demands of the narrative logic have radically altered its constitution. The continuity and importance of this figure are also inscribed within temporal structures in the opening paragraph – 'when he had first seen Barbara Coles', ' "she won't last long," he remembered thinking' – and from the outset, this encounter in the past is entered into the narrative finality. It will have a sequel (that which follows it, that which it motivates). In conjunction with descriptive changes (her 'gauche' hairstyle becomes 'sophisticated'), the important differences are that her name and appearance enter the circuit of public success. This cultural cachet is accompanied by a remarkable change of positions in the observer/observed structure. Coles is now the refuser, Spence the onlooker:

> soon she went off with a group of people she was inviting to her home for a drink. She did not invite Graham. There was about her an assurance, a carelessness, that he recognized as the signature of success. It was then, watching her laugh as she

went off with her friends that he used the formula: '*Yes, that one*' (*MTW*, p. 8).

Equally importantly, this is the first time in the relating of a narrative event, that 'Graham' has been used instead of 'he'. Until this point, 'he' has read as both figure in the text and narrator – a confusion inherent in many a third-person narration. The use of the proper name separates the two levels, and places the named figure of Graham Spence on a par with the others. So the initial structure of the observer/observed is reproduced, with Spence in Coles's position (the narrator sees Graham watch Barbara Coles leave). And *this* is the moment of choice: desire is inextricably linked to a refusal, and the narrative strategy subtly negates Spence's project as subject of observation and choice.

The third moment in the sequence alters the motivation of the choice from calculation to emotional need. Once again, Coles is inscribed within another order, this time when Jack Kennaway boasts of being her lover: 'There was no doubt the two were pretty close . . . Graham Spence felt he had put his finger on the secret pulse of Barbara Coles; and it was intolerable that he must wait to meet her' (*MTW*, p. 11). 'Secret pulse' is very much a key term; the narrative circuit of otherness traced in the semantic line of pulse–throb–(heart)beat recurs time and again in Lessing. It is essential to the elaboration of the ironic 'How I Finally Lost my Heart'. Here, the secret pulse is Coles turned emotionally towards another, and the reaction is 'intolerable'. It will recur later, when Graham presumes an affair between Barbara and James, a man she works with.

This equivalence of desire and refusal, the refusal of the object of attention to return the attention, to accept the relation of dominance inherent to the structure, is equally present in 'A Woman on a Roof', and operates here at the repeated moment of sight:

> Next morning, as soon as they came up, they went to look. She was already there . . . Stanley let out a whistle. She lifted her head, startled, as if she'd been asleep, and looked straight over at them. The sun was in her eyes, she blinked and stared, then she dropped her head again. At this gesture of indifference, they all three, Stanley, Tom and old Harry, let out whistles and yells. Harry was doing it in parody of the younger men,

making fun of them, but he was also angry. They were all
angry because of her utter indifference to the three men
watching her (*MTW*, pp. 67–8).

These meetings of the observer and the observed punctuate this
story: the progression of the narrative lies in the reaction of the
observer, split across three figures. Three men are working on a
roof and see a near-naked woman sunbathing on a roof nearby. In
terms of this narrative, she is the empty space on which are
written male discourses on women. Harry, who has grown-up
children, is fatherly and protective, though not immune to the
feelings of rejection of them as men; Tom, the youngster,
nurtures erotic fantasies about the tender older woman; Stanley,
the young married man, is the most aggressive and the most
threatened:

> 'I've got a good mind to report her to the police,' said Stanley,
> and Harry said: 'What's eating you? What harm's she doing?'
> 'I tell you, if she was my wife!'
> 'But she isn't, is she?' (*MTW*, p. 69).

The two codes of woman as private possession of the man, and
woman s object of display for any man, conflict directly here, not
as contradictory discourses on women, but as contradictory
elements in male discourse: ' "Christ," said Stanley virtuously,
"if my wife lay about like that, for everyone to see, I'd soon stop
her" ' (*MTW*, p. 68). It is the refusal of the woman to participate
which allows this to be elucidated – there is no similar tension in
Stanley's flirtatious teasing with Mrs Pritchett downstairs. The
married man is inscribed within a particular discourse on women
which the woman as other specifically throws into relief. Stanley
is remarkably similar to Graham Spence:

> He went into a long, very tidy white room, that had a narrow
> bed in one corner, a table covered with drawings, sketchings,
> pencils . . . He was thinking: I wouldn't like it if my wife had a
> room like this. I wonder what Barbara's husband. . .? (*MTW*,
> p. 23).

Indifference causes each to become overtly aggressive and uncontrollable:

> 'Graham, let me go, do let me go, Graham.' She went on

saying this; he went on squeezing, grinding, kissing and licking. It might go on all night: it was a sheer contest of wills, nothing else. He thought: It's only a really masculine woman who wouldn't have given in by now out of sheer decency of the flesh! ('One off the Short List', p. 27).

Stanley whistled again. Then he began stamping with his feet, and whistled and yelled and screamed at the woman, his face getting scarlet. He seemed quite mad, as he stamped and whistled, while the woman did not move, she did not move a muscle ('A Woman on a Roof', p. 73).

However, the irremediable difference of the other is not restricted to these relations, inscribed within socio-cultural discourses of the sexes. In 'The Story of Two Dogs', set in Africa, the same narrative structure appears, articulated across the domestic/wild opposition. A similar structure is crucial to a reading of *The Grass is Singing*,[4] across which is articulated the attraction of Dick, marked by the wild, the bush, the outdoors, and Mary, marked by the order and domesticity of urban society. Once on the farm, the same opposition structures the difference between the house, the closed space indoors, and the farm, the outside. As much as anything, Mary's subsequent breakdown could be read as the breakdown of that opposition, the impossibility of maintaining that distinct order. She is irremediably marked by her removal from the order in which she was inscribed, as is apparent in her fruitless attempt to return to it in her visit to the town and her place of work. The last narrative avenue of escape and positive renewal is closed, rendering the final disintegration inevitable. 'The Story of Two Dogs' partakes of the same opposition, with its two distinct lineages, the male dogs of the wild and the female dogs of the white domestic settlements being immediately attracted to one another:

Then he lifted his head and howled, like the howl dogs give to the full moon, long, terrible, lonely. but it was morning, the sun calm and clear, and the bush without mystery. He sat and howled his heart out, his muzzle pointed away towards where his mate was chained. We could hear the faint whimperings she made, and the clink of her metal dish as she moved about (*MTW*, p. 57).

This is uncomplicated desire for the other, without any of the aggression of frustration, partly because the desire is reciprocated by the locked-up female dog, partly because in this story the aggression is located in the transgression of the spatial boundaries separating the social order from the wild as Bill the wild dog, like his father before him, and Jock, the dog partaking of both orders, harass the livestock, and at night break into the settlements to steal chickens. It is the same boundaries which impose the separation of the two orders on the dogs. But the social order is not just constituted by farming and cultivation. It is also a network of emotional and family relations spread over the male (husband and father seeing the dogs in relation to the economic unit of the farm) and the female (the mother and the obsessively emotional response to the dogs) with the children positioned in relation to these dual constraints, all of which the wild dog Bill refuses. So although the major opposition of the asocial and the social orders the attraction of the young girl for her puppy, and, coinciding with the male/female distinction, the wild dogs for the domestic dogs, the two sexes are still present as a differential structure, with echoes of the narcissistic dominance of the male:

> We set forth each morning, first, my brother, earnest with responsibility, his rifle swinging in his hand, at his heels the two dogs. Behind this time-honoured unit, myself, the girl, with no useful part to play in the serious masculine business, but necessary to provide admiration (*MTW*, p. 45).

The same structure is underlying the relations in 'Between Men', about a meeting of two women who have virtually made professional careers of being useful reflective seconds to various successful men, as one of them drunkenly asserts: 'Maureen now sat up, earnest, trying to control her tongue: "But . . . what . . . we are both *good* at, itsh, it's bolshtring up some damned genus, genius" ' (*MTW*, p. 160).

So the indirect relations of the one and the other constitute an important part of the Lessing narrative. As can be seen in the above analysis, the precise narrative positions of the various figures within this structure admit many variations, within a gamut of possibilities ranging from complete refusal to acceptance. As a structure, however, it is far from defining completely the elements constituting these figures. Across the strict spatial divisions of the African landscape the attraction of the domestic and the wild dogs is a mutual one: this interplay of the direct and the indirect is equally present in those stories where the moment of attraction is articulated across the structures of the observer and the observed. The confrontation of the two orders in the direct look constitutes a real threat to the controlling position of the observer as subject, and has important implications for the narrative construction of the emotional self.

There are many ambiguities in the structure of the indirect look. It poses the observer as subject, implicitly dominant in the relations with the observed, yet demands these relations be acknowledged and confirmed by the acquiescent look in return. When Spence's impotence provokes Coles into making him come to get the whole thing over with, it is precisely this acquiescence she refuses: 'She squatted beside him, the light from the ceiling blooming on her brown shoulders, her flat, fair hair falling over her face. But she would not look at his face' (*MTW*, p. 30). A failure on the part of the observed to comply induces aggression and anger at the implied rejection of dominance. Yet a confrontation of the two orders in the direct look is equally charged, when the observed becomes observer in turn. The other is the focus of attraction and hatred, both wanted and repulsive at the same time: it is a permanent struggle, inherent in the irreconcilable demands placed on the other, that he or she as subject enter into their given position as object. Lessing is, in this particular area at least, very close to an Existentialist analysis where the look is also used as a privileged site of interpersonal struggle. As Graham Spence pursues his physical onslaught on Barbara Coles, we read: 'And he could not stop because he could not face the horror of the moment when he set her free and she looked at him. And he hated her more, every moment' (*MTW*, p. 27). But in terms of the narrative context, it is the interplay between the direct and indirect looks which is important. 'Each Other' is an intriguing tale of incest. The opening sequence sets out the husband's hostility to the frequent visits of his wife's brother, and her ambiguous status as repulsive/desirable object of attraction for him. Initially, he surveys her indirectly through a mirror:

There's something unhealthy about her, yes . . . *Yes, dirty*, his rising aversion insisted.

> Armed by it, he was able to turn, slowly, to look at her
> direct, instead of through the cold glass . . . He now kept on
> her the pressure of a blue stare both appealing (of which he was
> not aware) and aggressive – which he meant as a warning.
> Meanwhile, he controlled a revulsion which he knew would
> vanish if she merely lifted her arms towards him (*MTW*,
> pp. 191–2).

The same interplay orders the account of the evening Spence
and Coles spend together (he has been asked to interview her for
the radio), the direct encounter which follows the sequence of his
indirect appraisal and choice of her. Coles's refusal of his dominance is not surprising – this is opened as a narrative possibility by
the extreme 'otherness' of Coles and the consequent emotional
reaction of Spence, determined to impose himself. These two
figures are opposed within the terms of all the various configur-
ations of this narrative: success (Coles is 'unique', Spence one of a
repetitive series), sex (Kennaway's boast of being her lover
induces angry jealousy, especially as Kennaway, the ultimate
media man, is opposed to Spence across the media/creation
opposition), and work (to the serial group to which Spence
belongs is opposed the theatre group, bound by a shared purpose,
to which Coles belongs and from which Spence feels excluded).
All of this means that the operation of the system of the list of
'especial women' is radically altered from the outset in this
specific instance. Usually, Spence either 'quietly pulls strings' to
meet the woman, or more often bides his time 'for there was a
gambler's pleasure in waiting.' After Kennaway's boast 'it was
intolerable that he must wait to meet her.' Usually, it was the
'appearance of an affair' with the real pleasure lying in the
'humorous complicity'. After seeing her at work and being
'shaken to his depths', he decides he has to sleep with her. 'It was a
necessity for him,' he is 'burning with this single determination'.
One might say that the primary narrative conflict is not so much
between Coles and Spence as between Coles and the list of
'especial women', pivoting around the impossible status of the
other, and it is this which will finally lead to a dislocation of the
elements constituting Spence.

The narrative resonances of the direct look are therefore
complex. From Coles, it reverses the observer/observed

positions: 'He now saw he could not possibly say this: he could imagine her cool look if he did' (*MTW*, p. 19), or 'she had been watching, since they had met yesterday, every moment of his campaign for her' (*MTW*, p. 32). Avoidance of just such a threatening confrontation dictates a turning away on Spence's part, as after a particularly crude manoeuvre at dinner when he tries to delay the order ('He looked neither at the head waiter nor at Barbara'). But avoidance of the look is also a measure of the strength of the feelings of desire or anger which a direct confrontation would reveal: 'it was only now that he imagined her as a sensual experience. Now he did, so strongly that he could only glance at her' (*MTW*, p. 18). As a mechanism, this is found again and again in this collection. Expressions such as 'with a carefully brief glance', 'with a brief reluctant glance' are frequent. The space of interpersonal conflict is primarily visual:

> Maureen said: 'Hello, Stanley, meet my father and mother.' He shook their hands and stared at her. She did not meet his eyes: rather, the surface of her blue gaze met the furious, incredulous, hurt pounce of his glares at her (*MTW*, 'Notes for a Case History', p. 241).

'One off the Short List' develops the conflicting elements involved in the choice of desirable object, that is to say the other as separate, apart, turning away elsewhere (Barbara Coles), and the other as narcissistic complement to the subject (the list of 'especial women') to such an extent that the subject Spence splits into distinct elements – the intelligent manoeuvrer shamed by his behaviour, and the aggressor, full of hate, using force to obtain the complicity he seeks: 'While with his intelligence he watched this ridiculous scene, he was determined to go on, because sooner or later her body must soften in wanting his' (*MTW*, p. 27). The conflicting emotions of hate and shame are the psychological markers of the contradictory codes towards women as desirable objects, already discussed in relation to 'A Woman on a Roof', where they are distributed across three distinct figures. Here, it is the one subject that veers from one position to the other:

> He was hurt that she still addressed the man who had ground her into sulky apathy; she was not addressing *him* at all (*MTW*, p. 28).

> He was stung back into being the boor because she had not the
> intelligence to see that the boor no longer existed; because she
> could not see that this was a man who wanted her in a way
> which she must respond to (*MTW*, p. 28).

Appearance is all. To be someone who behaves differently he has
to be seen as such. The response he needs is unrealisable by the
very constitution of the narrative – Coles as other, as refuser, is
not only essential to that figure, but equally essential to the fact of
her being chosen by Spence. Spence's hope of a possible unity is
there only to be closed by the logic dictating its impossibility. It
would be a unity that would reconcile, not only the self and the
other but also, in Spence, the elements of desire and complicity:

> Seeing the small damp flesh of her face, he felt kinship,
> intimacy with her, he felt intimacy of the flesh, the affection
> and good humour of sensuality. He felt she was flesh of his
> flesh, his sister in the flesh (*MTW*, p. 28).

But the two elements are mutually exclusive – the attempt to
unite them only serves to eliminate Spence as sexual figure:

> As he did so, knowing he was putting himself in the position of
> raping a woman who was making it elaborately clear he bored
> her, his flesh subsided completely, sad, and full of reproach
> because a few moments ago it was reaching out for his sister
> whom he could have made happy (*MTW*, p. 29).

After the fiasco of the night, the narrative merely chronicles his
further humiliations. In spite of his insistence on accompanying
her back to the threatre, to be seen with her (to have at least the
'appearance of an affair'), he is once more eliminated, this time as
subject of the observer/observed structure. It is Coles who offers
him to the gaze of others with *her* insistent reminders of his visit
there the previous evening; apart from that he is virtually
invisible, hardly seen, not recognised. The stage hands no more
remember him than did Barbara at their second meeting. The last
sentence of the story confirms his return to the seriality of the
media group ('this evening he had to interview a young man (for
television) about his new novel', *MTW*, p. 33). The impossibility
of accommodating Barbara Coles within the structures of the list
of 'especial women' has effectively negated its entire function.

'Each Other' is an interesting variation on the elements of 'One off the Short List'. The relations of the sister and her husband are those of indirect contemplation, direct aggression and desire. The self and the other are irremediably separate. But the relations between the brother and sister realise what was for Spence an impossible unity, for the duality of the self and the other is also the reflective duality of the self to itself here:

> She now stood, frowning, in front of the long glass in the new wardrobe: a very tall girl, stooped by her height, all elbows and knees . . . She brushed her short, gleaming black hair, stared at length into the deep anxious eyes, and got back into bed (*MTW*, p. 193).

> in came a very tall, lank, dark young man. He sat on the bed beside his sister, took her thin hand in his thin hand (*MTW*, p. 193).

> Again the two pairs of eyes stared into each other at an inch or so's distance . . . he kissed the perfected copies of his own ugly eyes (*MTW*, p. 194).

Aggression still governs the relations of the direct encounter, but it is a mutual aggression – 'In a moment they were pulling each other's hair, biting, sinking fingers between thin bones' (*MTW*, p. 195) – and in this reciprocity where each is subject and object, the divisions of the self and the other are annulled:

> They had become one person, abandoned against and in each other, silent and gone (*MTW*, p. 195).

> Slowly they quieted, in love and in pity, in the same way that they quieted in their long silences when the hungers of the flesh were held by love on the edge of fruition so long that they burned out and up and away into a flame of identity (*MTW*, p. 199).

The nature of the sexual activity is also subordinated to the differing sets of relations. The brother and sister refuse orgasm. With their respective partners, the men make the women come (which is exactly what Coles does to Spence) and the women scream. The dominance inherent in the structure culminates in the figures of aggressor and victim, which is opposed to the reciprocity of the incestuous relation, yet, as in all oppositions, both terms are necessary: 'Perhaps if you and I didn't have Charlie and Alice for coming, we wouldn't be able to do it our way, have you thought of that?' (*MTW*, p. 198). The different distribution of the various elements has not changed the structure: the one (brother and sister) and the other (Charlie and Alice) are still necessarily bound together by their very division.

The observer observed: structures of the self

> Meanwhile he sat looking at her, seeing himself look at her, *a man gazing in calm appreciation at a woman*: waiting for her to feel it and respond (*MTW*, 'One off the Short List', p. 15).

Throughout 'One off the Short List', Graham Spence never loses sight of himself. To watch his companion is simultaneously to watch himself. He is as he appears to Barbara. The sight of other marriages, other media employees in the pub, allows him to see the nature of his own marriage, his own career. To be able to see what he considers his unique flair for emotional experience, he needs his list of 'especial women'. In this narrative, the self is both subject and object, observer and observed, self and other for itself. But this structure is often temporarily overridden by a sudden, immediate emotion, by jealousy or anger or something which drastically alters his vision of himself. In short, Graham Spence is constantly *surprised*, surprise is the mark of the moment of rupture in the continuous process of self-appraisal. He lived through his marriage with 'such surprise of the mind and the senses', he is 'surprised by his jealousy over James'. For a moment, observer and observed collapse together in a flux of emotions, which in this narrative is a measure of the unsuitability, to say the least, of Barbara Coles as choice. It is not usually Spence who is the victim of such confusion in his series of affairs: 'his real pleasure came when he saw her surprise at how well she was understood by him' (*MTW*, p. 10).

It is clear that the duality constructing the relations of the self and the other, articulated through the narratives across the interplay of the direct and the indirect look, finds its counterpart in the structures of the self, experienced both directly and indirectly, either at the moment of direct, immediate experience, or at the term of a mediation. It is something of a truism of Lessing criticism, to state that the self is fragmented in her work, yet it seems to me that the nature of that fragmentation, and the manner of its production in the narratives which articulate it, could bear further examination, for, in terms of fictional structure, it would be difficult to say that one was any more true or real than the other: the position and function of immediate experience only makes sense in relation to the mediated self. Like the elements constructing the divisions between the self and the other, they are bound by their oppositional structure, their co-presence is mutually determinant. Together, they form a consistent vision which founds the self as irremediably conscious of itself, and yet to which all possible discourses of self-expression are inadequate. Mediated across the terms of a difference which articulates its relation to the other, and hence to itself, self-consciousness is its hallmark. The term is taken from a passage in *Going Home* which elucidates the mechanism particularly clearly:

> One of the reasons why I wanted to return was because so many people had asked me how it was I had been brought up in a colour-bar country and yet had no feeling about colour. I had decided that a lucky series of psychological chances must have made me immune. But it was surely impossible that I should be entirely unlike other people brought up in the same way? Therefore *I was watching my every attitude and response* all the time I was in Africa. For a time, the unconsciousness of a person's colour one has in England persisted. Then the miserable business began again. Shaking hands becomes an issue. The natural ebb and flow of feeling between two people is checked because what they do is not the expression of whether they like each other or not, but deliberately and consciously considered to express: 'We are people on different sides of the colour barrier who choose to defy this society.' And, of course, this will go on until the day comes when self-consciousness can wither away naturally. In the meantime, the eyes of people of a different colour can meet over those formal collective hands, in a sort of sardonic appreciation of the comedies of the situation (emphasis added).[5]

The self is traversed by the social, moral and personal codes which construct it, and which it displays to itself for its own sardonic, or bitter, or calculating appreciation, yet still they do not exhaust it. In many of the narratives there is something else, either unspoken or unspeakable, often silenced by the inherent contradictions in the codes in play. For the self also speaks with many voices: it listens as much as it watches, which brings the question of language, the very stuff of narrative, resolutely to the fore.

In 'England versus England', the divisions of the central figure, Charlie, are mediated through a multiplicity of voices and languages. Charlie, a final year student at Oxford, makes one of his brief visits to his home in a northern mining village. The story chronicles what Charlie calls a 'clash of cultures': the pressure on the young man, for whom all the family is making sacrifices, to succeed, and the discrepancy in values and attitudes between the upper class and the working class. Each has its own language to which Charlie conforms:

> The third man, adding his tribute to this, the most brilliant son of the village, said: 'You'll be coming back to a right Christmas with us, then, or will you be frolicking with t'lords and t'earls you're the equal of now?' . . .
>
> 'For a day or so, any road,' said Charlie . . . 'That's time enough to spend with t'hewers of wood and t'drawers of water.' The third man nodded, as if to say: That's right! and put back his head to let out a relieved bellow (*MTW*, pp. 113–14).

It is a division which constructs Charlie as irremediably and always other to himself, and is displayed in the voices which are always speaking for him: the inner voice, 'nagging', 'painful', 'didactic', 'rational'; the voice of critical judgment, analysing the contradictions of the difference from within a political, class-conscious discourse; and the voice outside, the jeering voice of derision, mocking the discourse itself, turning judgment into cliché:

> Charlie said: 'It's not as bad as that, I'll pass.' The inner enemy remarked softly: 'I'll pass, and I'll get a nice pansy job in a publisher's office with the other wet-nosed little boys, or I'll be a sort of clerk. Or I'll be a teacher – I've no talent for teaching,

but what's that matter?' . . . The enemy behind his right
shoulder began sartirically tolling a bell and intoned: 'Charlie
Thornton, in his third year at Oxford, was found dead in a
gas-filled bed-sitting-room this morning. He had been
overworking. Death from natural causes.' The enemy added a
loud rude raspberry and fell silent (*MTW*, p. 117).

The relations of the self, conscious of the difference in which, at
every level, it is displayed to itself as other, also govern the
relations to its surroundings. The hostility of the direct look is
often traced in the connotations of reflection as well as in an
aggressive stare or glare. Moreover, the same semantic line also
traces the hostility of the inanimate which pervades this story:

The pub had been panelled in dark wood. It was ugly and
comforting. Now it had half a dozen bright wall-papers and
areas of shining paint, and Charlie's stomach moved again,
light filled his eyes (*MTW*, p. 121).

The shine on the leather confused Charlie's eyes; he glanced
over at the magazine, but its glitter, too, seemed to invade his
pupils (*MTW*, p. 130).

The girl now sat, . . . staring him out. Her blue eyes glinted
into his, and he looked quickly away (*MTW*, p. 131).

In the train on which he leaves, the beginning of his crisis is
sited in the sudden immediacy of the moment of rupture, as he
watches the elderly woman opposite him:

For some reason, the sight of her clean pinkish scalp shining
through the grey wisps made Charlie wild with anger. He was
taken by surprise, and again summoned himself to himself,
making the didactic voice lecture (*MTW*, p. 129).

But the didactic voice is overlaid with the jeering voice and the
'fusion of the two' terrifies him, especially when it takes over
completely and silences 'Charlie'. The final breakdown is the
breakdown of language: 'His eyes were shut, his tears running.
Words, no longer articulate, muttered and jumbled somewhere
inside him, a stream of frightened protesting phrases' (*MTW*,
p. 132).

The narrative tensions of the gap between the mediate and the immediate are clearly illustrated in 'The Sun between their Feet'. Two dung–beetles roll a ball of dung up a small slope watched by the narrator. This simple narrative event is the basis of a series of actions, where the sun and the rain are as much active figures as the beetles and the narrator. Set in Africa, both the beetles and the landscape are the site of paradoxical discourses of nature and culture and the oppositions between them. With the road to the mission as a sort of boundary, the rough land behind, where the beetles are seen, is opposed to the cultivated land in front. The former is unpeopled, the latter 'thick with white farmers'. But once across the divide, the wilderness itself is shown to be a cultural space, filled with the signs of past occupation, such as defensive earthworks and Bushmen paintings. The opposition between nature and culture is historically bounded – the wilderness is only such in terms of white culture now. The action of the beetles is similar inscribed within the structure of two discourses, science and culture, with a book quoted to explain the process, which again the observation of nature contradicts: 'Sacred beetles, these, the sacred beetles of the Egyptians, holding the symbol of the sun between their busy stupid feet' (*MTW*, p. 63). Busy stupid feet, because the beetles do not conform to the action prescribed them: ' "The slope is chosen," says the book, "by a beautiful instinct, so that the ball of dung comes to rest in a spot suitable for the hatching of the new generation of sacred insect" ' (*MTW*, p. 64), whereas these two beetles resolutely attempt to roll the ball up a surface too steep and too rough, and fail completely after a whole day's effort. The interplay between the discourses which mediate the action of the beetles inscribes it within an order which the behaviour of these particular beetles, or the discourse of nature, directly refutes, and the paradox governing the contradiction is such that neither can be said to be correct or incorrect.

It seems to me that this irreducible difference between the established discourse, the mediating process of the book, and the immediate experience which both should and cannot be accommodated within it, is one of the constants structuring the self in these narratives. In 'To Room Nineteen', the account of a marriage and the gradual breakdown of the woman, Susan Rawling, leading to her suicide, the code in which a marriage is founded upon intelligent relations between reasonable people could be said to constitute the 'book' which cannot explain Susan's disintegration except in terms of irrationality and madness. In 'How I Finally Lost my Heart', the language of romance is the discourse which both speaks the self and yet is also to be read and observed as appropriate or not:

> I was in that state of mind (in which we all so often are) of thinking: He might turn out to be the one. (I use a woman's magazine phrase deliberately here, instead of saying, as I might: *Perhaps it will be serious*) (*MTW*, p. 78).

This is an amusing, fantastic tale, where the exaggerations of romantic pronouncements are given literal force. The narrator's heart leaves her body, gets stuck to her fingers until she manages to give it to a woman on the tube. The demarcation lines between mediacy and immediacy, presence and absence of self-consciousness, are completely blurred. The contrast between the two women is clear: the narrator whose concentration on her own feelings, whose self-observation, has brought her to this state, and the other, quite 'unconscious' of herself and of her surroundings, the focus of attention for all around in the tube while she sees only the absent person she is talking to, who coincides perfectly with what one might call the 'already written':

> A passionless passion – we were seeing unhappiness embodied, we were looking at the essence of some private tragedy – rather, Tragedy. There was no emotion in it. She was like an actress doing Accusation, or Betrayed Love, or Infidelity, when she has only just learned her lines and is not bothering to do more than get them right (*MTW*, p. 86).

The emotional self is no less constructed than the rational self. Here, it is lived within the terms of the 'book' of romantic discourse. The paradoxical contradiction written into 'The Sun between their Feet' is here governing the relations of the self; the book is not extraneous to the self, as the very existence of the occasional passionate affair for the central figure has already taken its place in the code. Yet the interplay between the heart as clichéd site of the emotions and the externalisation of the biological heart, 'a large red pulsing bleeding repulsive object, stuck to my fingers' (*MTW*, p. 80), enables the code to be seen as strange, made unreal by the very literalness of the mechanism. And the heart, having materialised as a real object within the narrative by a linguistic conjuring trick, is immediately reinvested within the romantic, with a certain ironic inappropriateness, by being covered with the tinfoil, for both practical (indexing the reality of the heart) and emotional (shame reintroducing the signifying circuit of the self as other to itself) reasons:

> The tinfoil was effective, and indeed rather striking. It is quite pliable and now it seemed as if there were a stylized heart balanced on my palm, like a globe, in glittering, silvery substance. I almost felt I needed a sceptre in the other hand to balance it (*MTW*, p. 81).

This is considered in such 'bad taste' it has to be covered further. It is finally got rid of by the sight of the woman in the train, as the externalisation of the code in another narrative figure allows the heart to be transferred from one to the other. This is the moment of rupture already announced when the narrator becomes so absorbed in a scene in the street that the heart loosens:

> I understood that sitting and analysing each movement or pulse or beat of my heart through forty years was a mistake . . . What I must do is to take myself by surprise, as it were, the way I was taken by surprise over the woman and the pigeons and the sharp sounds of heels and silk wings (*MTW*, p. 83).

The first-person 'I', both figure in the text and overall narrator, is the basis on which the several narrative voices speaking the text position the very process of narration within the same structure, either in a gesture to the code, 'At this moment, dear reader, I was forced simply to put down the telephone with an apology' (*MTW*, p. 80), or reflectively, 'I simply cannot go heart-beat by heart-beat through my memories. A pity, since I suppose this is what this story is about' (*MTW*, p. 81). The text self-consciously writes itself into the code it displays, or holds itself up to its own contemplation as narration.

A similar fluctuation between the text and its narration occurs in 'Notes for a Case History', where the account of the formation and development of Maureen Watson is, by virtue of its very title, also inscribed within a social and psychological discourse of behaviour. Maureen's life is both story and history, that is to say, the resolution of the narrative cannot be final but points towards a future which, by its very ambiguity, retrospectively orders the reading of the narrative. The import of the story of Maureen's childhood, her determination to use her attractiveness and her intelligence to get the best she can, which in practical terms means to make the best possible marriage, culminating in her engagement to a young architect, cannot be fixed, for the discourse informing the title cannot be fixed. It could be that of narration – in which case the short story looks forward to a greater fictional project; or social history or psychology – where the unique narrative becomes an exemplar of a pattern of behaviour; or the discourse of medicine, psychiatry or social work – where the narrative unfurls itself as a ready-constituted past governed by the future conflicts towards which it tends and retrospectively explains. On the level of the narrative as process, 'Maureen' is the site of intersection of the multiple readings which variously display her as behavioural object. As narrative figure, 'Maureen' is the self on display for the other, and hence visible to itself as other: her prettiness is her capital, her assets which her intelligence will use to the greatest advantage. The question of the constitution of the self is the essential one here, through the various elements which mediate it. The description of Maureen's childhood experience of the war is immediately followed by a 'social reviewer's' description. The ambiguities of personal experience and the parental discourse which speaks that experience are highlighted: 'Maureen and Shirley remembered (or had they been told?) that once Nelson's Way was a curved terrace of houses' (*MTW*, p. 227); or again: 'The sigh annoyed Maureen, because it contradicted the absolute certainty she felt (it had been bred into her) about her future' (*MTW*, p. 228). Her knowledge of herself as different is the basis of her self-consciousness – like so many other key figures, she exists in relation to the other:

Shirley had put in six months of beehive hair, pouting scarlet lips, and an air of sullen disdain; but Maureen's sense of herself was much finer. She modelled herself on filmstars, but with an understanding of how far she could go – of what was allowable to Maureen. So the experience of being Bardot, Monroe, or whoever it was, refined her: she took from it an essence, which was learning to be a vehicle for other people's fantasies. So while Shirley had been a dozen stars, but really *been* them, in

violent temporary transmogrifications, from which she
emerged (often enough with a laugh) Shirley – plump, good-
natured, and herself; Maureen remained herself through every
rôle, but creating her appearance, like an *alter ego*, to meet the
expression in people's eyes (*MTW*, pp. 229–30).

Yet the calculating appraisal of herself for the other, the deliberate
utilisation of the discourses of class, culture and 'romance' finally
fail, because the other in this story is split into two figures, Tony
Head and Stanley Hunt. Tony watches and understands her
careful plans, but remains outside them. Stanley watches and
understands them because he is doing exactly the same for
himself, and so is similarly caught within them. This duality of
the other logically has its effect on the level of Maureen's identity:

> It now seemed to her that for the last week she had simply not
> been Maureen; she had been someone else. What had she done
> it for? Why? Then she knew it was for Tony: during all that
> ridiculous scene at the tea-table, she had imagined Tony
> looking on, grinning, but understanding her (*MTW*, p. 242).

Stanley returns a mirror-image, but Tony, who, it is suggested,
sees her as she is, not as she sees herself through the eyes of others,
returns no image at all. To see herself in his eyes, she acts out
under Stanley's gaze the negative image of what she is for Stanley.
The immediate self has no means of realising itself in time, only in
the disruptive moment, which here is carried by the frequent
breakdown of tears. Even then, the dual responses are at times
ironic imitations of each other:

> But did that mean Tony thought *she* was nice? Unlike Stanley?
> She did not think she was, she was moved to tears (concealed)
> that he did (*MTW*, p. 239).

> 'Stanley, it was only a joke, you aren't really angry, are you,
> Stanley?' The tears sounded in her voice now, and she judged it
> better that they should (*MTW*, p. 243).

Just as the movement of her tears smears her make-up, the
demarcation lines of emotion and calculation are hopelessly
blurred, because of the impossible demands of the double figure
of the other. The confusion inherent in 'Tony' is that of the
immediate, inexpressible, non-reflective self which can never be

realised (significantly, when she finally turns to him, he is not there to hear her), though her attempt to do so means she loses with 'Stanley', too, for in the battle for supremacy between the self and the other, he wins: 'she was in Stanley's power now: there was no balance between them, the advantage was all his' (*MTW*, p. 243).

So the self-reflective self, founded in the never-ending oscillation between appearance and being, is also caught within an inescapable contradiction: the various discourses constituting the 'book' are both essential, for it is through them that the self materialises as both substance and process for its own observation, and inadequate, for they cannot account for, and therefore will be constantly disrupted by, the direct immediacy of either experience or emotion. They are two incompatible orders. The discursive structures are articulated through a process of mediation which has no purchase on the immediate – it can neither prepare, nor rehearse, nor even expect a moment which by its very nature falls outside its terms of reference, and yet which might always disrupt it. But it is this incompatibility which guarantees their co-presence: neither can be integrated into the other. On the level of Lessing's vision of society, one could perhaps argue that it is the very suddenness of the holocaust which makes it inevitable, as no social structure could possibly render it unavoidable. On the level of the self, the reflective process is the basis of its own disruption, for the privileged site of the Lessing narrative is precisely its inadequacy.

This externalisation of the mechanisms by which the self is constructed, this self-consciousness, the necessary corollary of the duality at the heart of being, is the reason why, in my opinion, a reading based upon the dichotomy of reason and emotion, or the rational and the irrational, is inadequate to an understanding of these narrative structures. Informed by assumptions which oppose the linear control of rational thought to the private domain of emotion which is properly unthinkable, it is essentially a romantic reading. In many of these narratives, the processes of the emotions or dreams are not at all 'unthinkable', and admit no clear demarcation lines between reason and unreason. In 'How I Finally Lost my Heart' or 'Two Potters', the division between dreams and reality, or the emotional and analytical modes, is eroded in favour of an examination of the various levels of literalness of the real – language and representation. The complexity of the narration which is also implicated in the same process tends to be lost if the critical method relies on the model of an individual's thoughts and feelings. The reading remains trapped on the surface of the narrative, characters are accepted as such, at face value, and unproblematically equated with distinct individuals, whereas separate 'characters' may in fact be the several vehicles for one narrative element, as in the observer/ observed structure in 'A Woman on a Roof'. This valorisation of the individual as an independent agent, site and source of consciousness set down in its social habitat, has meant that too often Lessing's fiction has been read in terms of a behavioural sociology, or a psychology, and the radical quality of her writings on the self as construct ignored.

Lessing's impact on her women readers is far from surprising. The didactic implications of an ironic mode of writing in which the mechanisms of both personal and interpersonal relationships are not taken for granted, but are on display, holding the 'characters', and indeed the narration, too, at a critical distance, place the reader in a position of insight and knowledge into processes which elsewhere were discursively structured as pre-given reality. The romantic discourse of love and marriage is a case in point here. Her fiction also easily enters the feminist analysis which refuses the various discourses on the nature of women in the name of an elucidation of the mechanisms by which they construct 'woman' as 'natural'. Nor is it surprising that her fiction concentrates so often on the figure of the woman, for the social discourse of the woman as other, as object of visual display, coincides perfectly with the narrative vision of the differential otherness of the self to the other and itself. But perhaps there is a fundamental ambiguity here; many of the female figures are 'givens', as is the social typology of the male and female. One has only to think of the woman lying on the roof, and the parents in 'A Story of Two Dogs', or 'Notes for a Case History', to realise the contrast with Maureen Watson or Susan Rawlings. But it is an ambiguity inherent in the structures of the self and the other, and of the self: this is what governs the positions of the various figures, that they bear the significance of the other or of the divided, self-reflective self. If to appear other is to be other, then there is no space in this immediate duality for the mediating factors – social, political or personal – to be displayed. Only if the self can appear to itself can the complex variety of the discursive structures orchestrating it become visible.

Notes

1 *A Man and Two Women*, MacGibbon & Kee, 1963. Edition used here: Panther, 1965. All the short stories quoted are from this collection, which is referred to as *MTW*.
2 'A Story of Two Dogs', *MTW*, p. 37.
3 'A Woman on a Roof', *MTW*, p. 66.
4 *The Grass is Singing*, Michael Joseph, 1950.
5 *Going Home*, Michael Joseph, 1957, p. 17.

6   The more recent writings: sufism, mysticism and politics*

Ann Scott

In an often quoted introduction to a recent North American edition of Olive Schreiner's *The Story of an African Farm*, Doris Lessing describes having read Schreiner's novel at the age of fourteen, 'understanding very well the isolation described in it; responding to [Schreiner's] sense of Africa the magnificent – mine, and everyone's who knows Africa. . . I had only to hear the title, or "Olive Schreiner", and my deepest self was touched.' As she says, it was the first 'real' book she had read which had Africa as a setting. But, as she acknowledges herself, she is also making a larger claim for the book: she is suggesting the existence of a perennial and universal stream of human creativity, which she feels the imagery and part of the story of *African Farm* belong to and typify. She illustrates this point by drawing a likeness between Schreiner's allegory 'The Hunter' and a fourteenth-century Sufi parable. What she says is that 'a version, or germ, of this tale appears in Attar's *Parliament of the Birds*'. The Schreiner allegory depicts a man who goes in search of a famous Bird of Truth, his journey involving social ostracism, physical danger, and sensual temptations, and the Bird attained only at the point of his death. Lessing describes one of the manifestations of the Simurgh, the great bird in Attar's story – which she calls 'God or what you will' – as taking place in somewhat similar circumstances to scenes in Schreiner's allegory.[1]

I'm not concerned here to reproduce the subject-matter either of 'The Hunter' or of 'Parliament of the Birds', but to point to the fact of the comparison and to one aspect of the way Lessing makes

* I am grateful to Tim Bond and Jenny Taylor for discussing the first draft of this chapter with me.

use of religious language. She is using the term 'God' in a very liberal way; in a sense she is weakening or even disavowing the word's usual affiliation with the religious as denoting either a personal deity, or a way of talking about the supramundane, or the ground of all creation. Further, she sets the stage for her own way of using religious language when she concludes: 'What Olive makes of this tale is both all her own, and from that region of the human mind called Anon.' What are we to make of this notion of a 'version' or 'germ', of Sufism as the cultural antecedent of the novelist's imagination?

In this chapter I am looking at some of the many meanings encoded in the notion of a 'turn to mysticism' in Doris Lessing's more recent fiction. In that Lessing's interest in Sufism is well known, and that Sufi teaching stories and fables make an appearance in *The Four-Gated City* and *Briefing for a Descent into Hell* as well as the commentary on *African Farm* that I've just referred to, we might take it that talk of her fiction as being mystical signifies only a comment on her overt or didactic use of a particular religious tradition and its symbols. That is, one would be positing some overall telos in her writing in the light of which one might want to reinterpret the earlier work. My own contention, rather, is that the explicit concern with Sufism can be read as constituting a meta-language, a pointer to issues about 'visibility' and resolution within a narrative in a more general way; but that a formalist reading of this kind, which by definition secularises 'mysticism' in putting it to work as one of the materials of a text, cannot dispense with the possibility that Sufism, along with other religious narratives and symbols that Lessing refers to, does also represent itself and the ultimate unexplainability of things to which Lessing considers we all must yield.[2] These are separate, though related, issues, and are perhaps combined in the notion of the *Bildungsroman* by which Lessing has identified the *Children of Violence* series: that is, here we would be seeing the power of the Sufi legacy of belief to sum up, even to subsume within itself, a striving for knowledge.

I illustrate these ideas with reference to a cluster of Lessing's writings from the late 1960s and early 1970s: her novels *The Four-Gated City* and *The Memoirs of a Survivor*; the preface to the 1971 edition of *The Golden Notebook*; and two essays on Sufism, 'An Ancient Way to New Freedom' and 'In the World, Not Of

It'. In doing this I concentrate on three main areas which are raised by her use of religious, and, most frequently, Sufi imagery: first, the question of anti-psychiatry, 'Eastern thought' and our own cultural history; second, the tension to be discerned between the role and meaning of Sufi and Christian imagery in her writing; and, third, some issues in the philosophy of mysticism which I want to refract through her own non-fiction writing on the subject.

At the outset, however, one has to ask the question: whose Sufism, which Sufism? To call Lessing's unwillingness to define Sufism idiosyncratic, by contrasting it with the work of Western academics in the field,[3] would be to miss the point that Lessing, avowedly following Idries Shah, is trying to make. For, whereas someone like A. J. Arberry, a twentieth-century translator of Attar, wrote unambiguously that Sufism was 'the name given to the mystical movement within Islam; a Sufi is a Muslim who dedicates himself to the quest after mystical union (or, better said, reunion) with his Creator,'[4] Shah, one of the most widely read popularisers of Sufism in the West, considers that such particularity of vision destroys the meaning of Sufism, which by definition cannot be put into words, and bears witness only to 'the unproductive struggle of scholastics'.[5] Further, Shah rejects the idea that the study of Sufism can be approached 'from the single standpoint that it is a mystical system designed to produce ecstasy and based on theological concepts.'[6] What, then, is Shah's Sufism? According to *The Way of the Sufi*, it is 'the transcending of ordinary limitations':

> The Sufis claim that a certain kind of mental and other activity
> can produce, under special conditions and with particular
> efforts, what is termed a higher working of the mind, leading
> to special perceptions whose apparatus is latent in the ordinary
> man.[7]

Shah does not specify these perceptions; nor, usually, does Lessing. The most Shah will say is that Sufis do not stick to any one convention.

> Some quite happily use a religious format, others romantic
> poetry, some deal in jokes, tales and legends, yet others rely
> on art-forms and the products of artisanship. Now, a Sufi can

tell from his experience that all these presentations are legitimate.[8]

Shah, therefore, holds that Sufi currents are to be found in all kinds of literatures which do not on the face of it have to do either with religion or with the doctrines of Sufism itself. His *The Way of the Sufi*, wherein he quotes from or refers to a diversity of poets, psychotherapists, scientists and historians, all of whom he sees as embodying some kind of unconscious Sufi influence, shows this very strongly. Correspondingly, if we talk about mysticism in Lessing's fiction we're not necessarily talking about the literal advocacy of a particular set of beliefs about the nature of reality, space–time categories, transcendence, and so on; but about defamiliarisation, a writer's attempt to make use of a form of language, a way of looking at narrative, or an interpretative framework as a whole which the Sufi tradition seems to have provided.

There is a fairly classic ambiguity here. By excluding almost nothing from his temporal and intellectual reference – indeed, by combining authorial intention, unconscious influence, and cultural parallel so freely – Shah leaves Sufism virtually undefined and certainly unlimited. But in his own defence would he not say that this is precisely the approach of the authentic Sufi? Or, by extension, that of the true mystic, who falls silent in the face of systematisation?[9] For here even the concepts of God or Allah or mysticism become limiting. Lessing has made the analogous point, in a discussion about the limitations of language, that the writer is always prey to mistaken attributions of intent. In a recent television interview she spoke scornfully about the different labels which had been attributed to her at different times: 'And then I was *mysticism*, in quotes'. She said she wanted to emphasise something about the way that in our culture we used words like spirit, soul, or collective unconscious: 'You could use a word like collective unconscious and people would think "Jungian", and you might not have or want that association.' She had begun to use metaphor, therefore, because so many words had become inadequate for what she wanted to express.[10]

In 'An Ancient Way to New Freedom', similarly, Lessing does not identify Sufism as a form of mysticism, but speaks of Western attitudes *to* mysticism. She talks initially about information and its communication, but in a very unspecific way, and the conceptual vagueness that lies at the heart of this essay sets in:

> Recently, a feeling that the kind of education most of us get is not giving us information we ought to have has led to curiosity about Eastern cults, Buddhism, gurus of various sorts, or the dozen or so Yogas.[11]

Her Sufism, described in the roundabout way of someone who rejects categorisation, especially the categorisation of mysticism as an occasion for eccentricity, sensationalism, and so on, emerges as a peculiarly indistinct force:

> A Sufi would say that people living in a society where Sufism has been openly at work, and respected for what it offers, must regard all these attitudes towards mysticism I have described as ill informed, to say the least. 'You will have to learn through that most banal of all things,' says the Sufi to the would-be student. 'You must learn through ordinary life'. He is likely to have nothing to say to people looking for excitements and sensational experiences.[12]

Like Shah, Lessing says that Sufism works through jokes, lectures, and books; a Sufi can be a scientist, politician, poet, housewife, usherette in the cinema, Sufism may have nothing to do with outward appearance and behaviour. People offer it, or they may teach it secretly. Sufism can't be defined in a dictionary sense; all that can be acknowledged is the difficulty of defining something that has to be experienced.

As in the introduction to *African Farm* Lessing reiterates the principle of a timeless and uniform symbolising capacity, the claim that all knowledge is fed from the same stream. Given Sufism as the core of Islam, she says, and Islamic civilisations lying at the cradle of history, a 'river of knowledge' has run since Adam through the Prophets, through Jesus and Mohammed, these men being different aspects of the same 'Truth' or 'Way', Jesus and Mohammed both starting world religions and both feeding an 'inner heart' of religion. Thus Sufism can be hostile to no true religion since all religions are the outer faces of (the same) inner truth. But in early Christianity, the argument continues, this inner knowledge was available but then went underground or was lost. Our creativity is still potentially available to us, but can only be developed with the aid of a guide. Sufis say that man has the possibility of conscious development, but the education system twists and distorts and confines individual talents; flashes, intuitions, hunches, and intimations of dreams – when they stem from a process of intense concentration – represent the first stirrings of an evolving part of humanity which could be called a 'Sufi current'.

Lessing is extremely flexible about what would constitute manifestations of this Sufi current – a person, a book, a 'sharply angled statement' at a conference, a new trend in fashion, a poem, a play, a garden planted and tended in a certain way. Even more liberally – and speaking of a basically secular context – she closes on this note:

> Sometimes, when we look back on our lives, we may think: 'I have learned more through that experience than in all the rest of my life put together.' The experience may have been a tough job of work, a phase of marriage, a serious love, an illness, a nervous breakdown. This way of learning, a time of crammed, thoughtful living, is perhaps nearer to the learning of the Sufi Way than any other.[13]

It's clear that when one proceeds from Lessing's 'direct' exposition of Sufism in this essay to the role of Sufi narrative forms in her fiction, different rules of reading are involved. Now, for instance, would the principle of a 'time of crammed, thoughtful living' be enacted in a novel like *The Four-Gated City*? In the essay she is attempting an account of what Sufism 'is' in the everyday world; in the novels the 'use' of Sufism is, presumably intentionally, considerably more oblique. Again, Lessing follows Shah in his definition of a teaching story:

> Teaching–stories are told in public and form a part of the outer activity of dervishes. They are intended to lay a basis of knowledge about Sufism and its characteristic methods of thought. They are seldom employed for didactic purposes.
>
> The 'inner dimensions' of teaching–stories, however, are held to make them capable of revealing, according to the stage of development of the student, more and more planes of significance.

It is this theory that 'one may work on different layers of the same material' which is unfamiliar to many people, who tend to prefer being told that a story has one message or one use only.[14]

The Sufi voice in *The Four-Gated City*, therefore, works both overtly and, if it's meaningful to speak in this way, since Lessing herself is so attentive to the relation between spoken and unspoken, as the 'unconscious' of the text. The body of the novel calls on a range of different vocabularies: those of psychotheraphy (ideas of 'containing', and 'working through'), telecommunications (radio sets, and being 'plugged in'), and of religion (Christian images of the Stations of the Cross, Martha's experience of the devil). As a whole it exists on the interface between psychiatry and politics, its 'real' setting depicting a group of people who have experience of both; whatever mysticism the novel embraces (and some have seen it represented by the post-holocaust landscape of the appendix) exists as part of a triangle, its other two points being supplied by the two terms just mentioned: specifically, their failure to 'explain' or 'resolve' human suffering. Significantly, however, Sufi sources as such virtually appear only on the 'edges' of the novel – in the dedication, and then in the transition between parts three and four of the book.

The dedication consists of a dervish teaching story (about a fool who was sent to buy flour and salt and contrives to empty his dish of both), and the opening of part four is preceded by an extract from Idries Shah's *The Sufis* about man's evolution to a 'certain destiny' which will necessitate the emergence of new organs of the body, and a fable on parallel lines by the thirteenth–century Sufi poet Rumi. These are set against lines from a (Western) schools broadcast about zoology which touch on the encoding of information in the cells of a toad. What are they doing here? They raise the question of information and its transmission, less directly than in 'An Ancient Way', by making a demand on the reader to allow the text to exist in her/his mind at many levels. In Lessing's 1971 preface to *The Golden Notebook* the same theme emerges, when she depicts a continuity of repression linking the child in junior school and her own experience as a published writer receiving requests for 'information' about the critical reception of her own works.[15] She is asking us to rethink our definition of the transaction called 'education', to reformulate the proper relationship of teacher and student, and to experiment with ways of reading which could not only illuminate issues which the conventional forces of socialisation hold down, but allow new ways of being or thinking to be 'born' (as in Shah's determined though elliptical reference to the Sufi belief that there exists 'a form of mentation more valuable than mechanical thought').[16]

Dedication
Once upon a time there was a fool who was sent to buy flour and salt. He took a dish to carry his purchases.
'Make sure,' said the man who sent him, 'not to mix the two things – I want them separate.'
When the shopkeeper had filled the dish with flour and was measuring out the salt, the fool said: 'Do not mix it with the flour; here, I will show you where to put it.'
And he inverted the dish, to provide, from its upturned bottom, a surface upon which the salt could be laid.
The flour, of course, fell to the floor.
But the salt was safe.
When the fool got back to the man who had sent him, he said: 'Here is the salt.'
'Very well,' said the other man, 'but where is the flour?'
'It should be here,' said the fool, turning the dish over.
As soon as he did that, the salt fell to the ground, and the flour, of course, was seen to be gone.[17]

If we underline certain phrases in the dervish story – 'fell to the floor', 'fell to the ground', 'the flour, of course, was seen to be gone' – what we seem to be talking about is failure, emptiness and disintegration. But perhaps there are different levels of order that would mirror the different levels of meaning referred to by Shah in his definition of a teaching story? Perhaps the disorder on the surface alerts us to an 'interior' layer of meaning or plane of significance that leads us to ask (though not necessarily to provide answers to) questions like why the man failed to see what was there to be seen, or why he had thought that one dish could contain both flour and salt and keep them separate. On the face of it, such questions are banal, but they help one to see through the man's (one's own?) confusion and lack of clarity; thus, they hint at possible rebirth and regeneration within or alongside the account of dissipation and loss. I think these questions are always involved in reading *The Four-Gated City*, because at a first or 'conscious' reading it seems so forcibly to be a depiction of failures: of relationships between individuals and within a group; a failure to achieve certain kinds of ideals; but, most explicitly, a failure to understand and identify 'what is going on' in society and the mind. Lessing is suggesting that the language of the parable can serve as an appropriate meta-language with which to grasp the 'heart' of what is happening in time and space.

Indeed, if one follows through the idea that she is trying to invoke in the reader a new and original attitude of mind to the activity of reading by drawing on Sufi writings, then something different is seen to be at work from the notion, sometimes put forward, that mysticism – or the transcendence of space–time categories – is the advocacy of an *escape* from reality. Lessing is not, apparently, trying to describe or advocate such a thing: what she wants the reader to see is precisely the reality of the world ('reality' and 'world' here in their common-sense usage). She is not saying that reality is spiritual, or that all is one, but that the 'truth' of a situation is obscured by a false, because limited, perception of it. It remains an open question, of course, whether our ordinary experience of the world does indeed have to be transcended on the basis of a belief in the primacy of the 'spiritual'; this ambiguity in interpreation stems from the lack of a clear status for the term 'mystical' in the writings of both herself and Shah. In terms of the Sufi 'boundaries' to *The Four-Gated City* all we can go on is the fact of their placing in the novel and their overt concern with multiplicities of meaning and of evolution.

As to the body of the novel itself, it's also possible to speak of Sufi ideas, forms, practices, or 'theory' (if we can borrow the term for a moment to denote this conviction that ordinary perception is mystified) as a thread informing certain kinds of actions, motives, and responses, whether those of the author or of the characters. Almost without exception, though, they are introduced casually; only towards the end of Martha's breakdown, when she confronts the 'sacred books of the world' directly, can we be assured that it is religious language which is under scrutiny; for the rest, ideas which seem 'Sufi' could equally well be part of a wide-ranging social psychology. About a third of the way through the book, for instance, during the period when Lynda's breakdown engages the time and energy of the people in the household more and more, and where Martha begins to feel that she herself needs psychiatric attention, we hear that Martha is attempting to resurrect her lost past.

> Every day more of it was slipping away. Sometimes she felt like a person who wakes up in a strange city, not knowing who he, she, is. There she sat, herself. Her name was Martha – a convenient *label* to attach to her sense of herself (my italics).[18]

A couple of pages later we find that, from her vantage-point of mental breakdown, 'she felt as if she had been blind' before: 'For suddenly far from mental illness (as distinct from neurosis) being something that happened somewhere else, it was all around her; and, which was odder, *had been all around her for a long time*' (my italics).[19] Somewhat further on in the book we find the comment, in Martha's voice, that the key fact about 'this great machinery of psychiatrists, psychoanalysts, psychologists, social workers, clinics, mental hospitals' is usually ignored: 'In any situation, anywhere, there is always a key fact, *the essence*. But it is usually every other fact, thousands of facts, that are seen, discussed, dealt with. The central fact is usually ignored, *or not seen*' (my italics).[20]

Very shortly after this, a period of fantastic dreaming begins for Martha in which she feels 'something' needs to be expressed, and although she's not sure what it is she begins to pick up on ideas or emotions belonging to others in the house; one wonders whose emotions they were, whom they belonged to – she's simply 'tuned into' them. Martha remembers the paradox that 'one could never be told what one did not already know, though of course the "knowledge" might be hidden from oneself.' I think this links up with the first point that I made, where I described the way in which Lessing situates Schreiner's allegory 'The Hunter' in the context of an ongoing though unconscious 'stream' of human creativity. For although 'human creativity' isn't just a synonym for interpersonal communication of the kind Martha is engaged in, it's quite possible that what Lessing is talking about, or positing, in the novel is a similar state of affairs where there exists a pool of knowledge, feeling, sentiment, and perception, to which people may or may not be able to tune in, and which is logically prior to the individual. If this is the case, then the model of the 'true' and 'false' self could represent a Sufi voice in the text, bearing in mind Sufism's teaching that the notion of self-centred selfhood is illusory,[21] and that, paradoxically, only when she/he has seen through the illusion can an 'authentic' selfhood – in which all sense of a separate individuality is lost – be attained. To that extent, Lessing is asking the question: is what we attribute to individuals such as Martha – personality, life-history, etc. – not a distortion? Is there not some kind of universal reality – not necessarily going under the name of God, Allah, or Atman – of which we, like her, are all an aspect?

It's significant that in the passage to part four of the novel we find the Rumi fable about evolution, forgetting, ignorance and sleep; and, near the beginning of this section, the idea that society is characterised by an inability to diagnose its own condition.

> From realm to realm man went, reaching his present
> reasoning, knowledgeable, robust state forgetting earlier
> forms of intelligence. So, too, shall he pass beyond the current
> forms of perception. . . There are a thousand other forms of
> Mind. . .
>
> But he has fallen asleep. He will say 'I had forgotten my
> fulfilment, ignorant that sleep and fancy were the cause of my
> sufferings.'
>
> He says 'My sleeping experiences do not matter.'
> Come, leave such asses to their meadow.
> Because of a necessity, man acquires organs. So, necessitous
> one, increase your need.[22]

There is an implied critique, in Lessing's own voice, of the possibility of the self-understanding of society, and the comment that Martha's next step is 'under her nose' but she can't see it: from that we pass to the protracted experience of breakdown within the basement of the house.

The symbol around which this experience is organised is the symbol of the wall, and the experience introduced within reference to two meanings of the word: an account of Lynda's thudding against the wall of her room, and the account of Mark, who covers his wall with facts about mental hospitals and the state of mental patients around the world. The wall contains Martha and Lynda. But the wall is also the medium through which they must pass: they have symbolically to understand that the wall both contains or protects them, and that it requires them to transcend its boundaries in order to feel, free of its constraints. In this sense the wall stands for the self, which both defines and confines the person. Not that the women are positioned in the experience in the same way: there comes a point where Martha knows that her experience has *ended*, and that 'her mind was her own again'; this is the transition back to 'ordinary' reality, whereas Lynda's mind is never her own. We're told that Lynda didn't eat or drink, she continued for two days to thud around the wall; and this process develops – Martha begins to find a 'potential explosion of energy' in herself and begins to move and exercise and behave as Lynda has done. Lynda's obscenities in the bath take on a 'rapid, repetitive, almost ritual sound' (one of the first hints of the 'religious' ideas which are to come), her mind is alert and clear, as though 'seeing' or recognising the alarm and concern that people feel for her for the first time. As for Martha's mind, it becomes a texture through which other textures can pass: she begins to remember her childhood experiences, to understand that the walls of the room stand for the walls of Lynda's mind; she feels 'plugged in' to an impersonal current linking herself, Mark and Lynda; she shakes, and lets the energy accumulate; her head is clear and receptive; she hears what is in Lynda's head and it strikes her as being the contents of the 'human' mind.

An authorial voice intervenes to ask a direct question which, I think, contains the unspoken referent 'religion': Is this process, this questioning that Martha is engaged in about communication, necessity, sound, dreams – is this madness, an even keel, is it just a 'way of thinking'?[23] From then on, the discussion does take, to a certain extent, an implicitly Sufi direction in terms of propositions about reality: the notion of humanity being defectively evolved, for instance, or a sermon on the deflection of energy and true or authentic perception into mundane concern and illusion; and taking the form of a critique of contemporary society rather than a call to piety or withdrawal from the world.

Soon, however, we find the introduction of an overt religious language, where Martha becomes absorbed in the religious books of the world; she feels that from St John of the Cross to the Upanishads all faiths and sets of ideas describe the same thing, but that the ideas embodied in them usually struck people as insane. The sound-ocean that she begins to explore, experience and initially name as hysteria gradually takes shape as a madness that she can define more neutrally, *pace* Rumi, as the possession of certain faculties in embryo. But when we come to the passage where the Stations of the Cross are referred to as a metaphor for the experience that Martha is undergoing, we're dealing with the Passion story of Christianity and the Christian model of a voyage, not with Sufism alone. We have notions of devil, God, 'retreat'. All these terms delineate a new field of concern in the novel: that of the applicability, or extension, of religious symbols – especially from celebrated religious narratives which function here as a tale within a tale – to the attempt to make sense of or heal the continuities and dysjunctions of subjective experience. These tensions between Christianity and Sufism come up again in *The Memoirs of a Survivor*, but for now Sufism speaks 'louder': an authorial voice lays down the fantasy of a future where those individuals with the capacities which Martha is beginning to discover would be considered to be in the main line of evolution.

Martha's experience of catharsis, self-isolation, and purging comes fairly near the end of the 'realist' narrative of the text, and very shortly before the point where Martha's career in the novel is summed up. Martha is now presented as having arrived in London over fifteen years previously without any idea of what she was going to do, and being in a similar situation once again. Does this mean we are at the end of a teaching story? 'No longer was the house her responsibility; she contributed nothing, held nothing together: the holding operation was long over,'[24] which recalls the parable of the flour and salt that fall to the floor that starts the book. And it is at this point that the appendix, which ends the novel on a deconstruction of continuous narrative, takes over.

The Four-Gated City, as I've said, exists on the interface between psychiatry and politics, and in the appendix some of these issues are refracted through the breakdown of the group who have known each other in Radlett Street for so long and have been dispersed in the 'Accident'. Interestingly, however, it is only in the appendix that words like 'mystical' or 'esoteric' are used overtly for the first time.[25] Lessing herself said, in the television interview that I've already quoted, that the word 'dream' quite deliberately didn't appear in *The Memoirs of a Survivor*, even though it could at one level be interpreted as a book in which dreams are central; almost the same could be said about the appendix to *The Four-Gated City*: it's only here that Lessing gives a name to what she has been referring to, in a sense, throughout the body of the text – but it has always been only one of the levels of language to be found in the novel. So we have the notion that individuals who have developed the extraordinary faculties first hinted at within the 'ordinary' narrative are known to exist: a rumour developed that 'in such and such a house lived people who could hear what others thought, could see through walls, "knew" when lies were told.' Like the words 'mystical' and 'esoteric', the word 'occult' figures in quotation marks, all this indicating the ambivalence that the terms hold as definitional categories.

Lessing's work is always open to a variety of readings. So far I have been looking at *The Four-Gated City* and 'An Ancient Way' as texts which, in different ways, raise the relatively 'perennial' issue of religion: on the one hand, its definition, on the other, its possible meaning in a work of fiction. Now I want to turn to the specifics of culture and time. I've tried to show how problematic the term 'mystical' becomes when it's applied to the account of breakdown, psychological development and closure in *The Four-Gated City*, and I want to go on to look at what the word might mean in the context of the cultural space that Lessing occupies or is depicting. We are used to thinking of *The Golden Notebook*, especially within women's liberation, as a key text for our self-understanding as post-war people and our sense of a historical dimension to feminism; *The Four-Gated City* published at the end as opposed to the beginning of the 1960s sums up a rather different history and perspective – one originating with the publication, in 1960, of R. D. Laing's *The Divided Self*. Thus I take it as no accident that some of the main themes pursued in *The Four-Gated City* – those of the split self; of the individual as being made up of 'different' selves, part authentic, part not; of 'perception' as a problematic category at the most general level – have all the resonance of anti-psychiatry. This is not to say that Lessing is 'Laingian', but, rather, that her work belongs within a group of roughly contemporaneous writings – polemical, fictional, etc. – that concentrate and theorise a similar range of concerns.[26] What unites the statements of Laing and Lessing at this particular point in time is that both are addressing questions which they see

Marxism and psychoanalysis as having inadequately resolved: specifically, the intelligibility of individual and social events.[27] Further, the matrix for the development of these ideas within the novel lies explicitly in the practice of psychiatry, and there are a number of striking parallels between the development of Lessing's ideas about social madness in *The Four-Gated City* and of R. D. Laing's ideas in a paper entitled 'The Obvious', given to the Dialectics of Liberation conference at the Roundhouse, London, in 1967.

Laing opens in this way:

> I want to draw attention to a few of those features of North
> American and European society that seem to be most
> dangerous, because they seem to help, or perhaps even to be
> necessary, to maintain and to perpetuate our component of a
> social world system that as a whole presents more and more the
> appearance of *total irrationality* (my italics).[28]

It's an interesting paper, drawing briefly but succinctly on a diversity of sources: work on contemporary China, the American experience of Vietnam, the mirror stage of development seen through the psychoanalytic perspective of Donald Winnicott, and some experimental psychological work on authoritarian conditioning done in a North American university. Laing's basic point is about the invisibility of social events, as is that of one of the authorial voices in *The Four-Gated City*. The notion that society has lost its capacity to diagnose its own condition is echoed in Laing's work: 'This talk is also an attempt to exhibit for your inspection some facets of my present effort to diagnose, to see *into and through* social reality' (my italics). Laing considers that the system generates both ignorance of itself and ignorance of this ignorance, a point reiterated throughout the essay. Lessing assumes a similar cultural competence in the reader, but she goes one step further – she wants to expand the interpretative framework of that reader; in this sense, 'using Sufism' or her 'mysticism' can be understood in terms of 'needs' or lacunae within our own cultural conceptual apparatus. She is taking up a point about man's cognitive capacity being 'underused' (as in the words of Laing – things are there to be seen, but we're not seeing them) as a key to understanding our social malaise and hence to acting on it.

What does all this amount to, and why does it get labelled

'mystical'? Both Lessing and Laing have made their interest in meditation and Eastern styles of thought known, Lessing in book reviews and Laing in a series of interviews.[29] Because of this enthusiasm and because Lessing concedes or believes that certain things, by definition, cannot be verbalised;[30] because she would seem to regard political radicalism as one stream of activity among many, and the generation and sustaining of an even psychological and physical *energy*[31] for one's work or projects as a problem of equal magnitude – so her refusal to arrange forms of language in a hierarchy has made her, in my opinion legitimately, something of an intellectual relativist. Up to a point, then, I can agree with her and Shah when they deride the 'common-sense' Western notions about mysticism for depriving the word of all substantive meaning. Even if one were to assess the 'role' of Sufism in her writing on the basis of orthodox Western academic discussion about mysticism, her reluctance to write about God or Allah – or to indicate whether her concern with Sufism in the novels represents something other or more than a narrative strategy, a way of posing questions – should alert us to the difficulty in coming to conclusions about the relationship between the 'political' and the 'religious' in her texts.

Here, I am primarily concerned with one aspect of the conventional classification of Lessing's work. In this context we can take the word 'mystical' as a term of attribution, rather than one that Lessing has claimed for herself; put another way, as a signifier whose signified is response-to-text. 'Mystical' is thus encoded as meaning 'non-political' – a personal endorsement, on Lessing's part, of some brand of idealism – as when a positive concern with religious language is juxtaposed against the apparent failure of a political movement. The social background to such a move would be the proliferation of spiritual disciplines, books, centres, retreats, and ashrams in the West[32] inspired by different Eastern religions in the last fifteen years or so – and, further, of the innumerable mutual language-blocks felt by 'politicos' and 'mystics'.[33] That having been said, one has to concede that an interest in a religious tradition, a 'borrowing' of its concepts and their representation in a novel, suggests something about what the writer takes to be 'true' about reality. Again, I can only point to ambiguity in the status of Lessing's concern with a tradition in Islam which Western academics call mystical and which she and

Shah, as I've said, will only loosely call 'a form of mentation more valuable than ordinary thought'.

Yet even if we were to accept that mysticism is largely a 'code' or descriptive word about or *for* the writings rather than intrinsic *to* them, we should not overlook the fact that another, equally important religious tradition is represented in Lessing's writing of this period: that of Christianity. In 'An Ancient Way to New Freedom' Lessing reveals her ambivalence about Christianity when she says:

> In the West we all live beside one version or another of
> Christianity, and believe, or half believe, or have to put up
> with, some pretty bizarre ideas. Perhaps the most useful thing I
> personally have been invited to do in my approach to Sufi
> study is to find out why I believe the things I do believe, to
> examine the bases of my ideas.[34]

This would seem to suggest an articulate distance from the traditions and cultural legacy of Christianity, but that is not the case when one consults the fiction itself. At this point it seems that the fiction corroborates the non-fiction statement that she makes in 'An Ancient Way': 'Individually each one of us may or may not be Christian, but like it or not we are steeped in Christian history.' There are indeed formal parallels between the Gospel stories and some of the naming and structure within both *The Four-Gated City* and *The Memoirs of a Survivor*.[35] Martha Quest's surname, for instance, has often been commented on as symbolic of the voyage which the five novels of the sequence depict, but her first name has been rather overlooked. Martha is a Biblical name, the Aramaic 'mistress', or mistress of the household,[36] and her situation is recounted in the Gospels of both John and Luke. Now, Carol P. Christ, in *Diving Deep and Surfacing: Women Writers on Spiritual Quest*, makes quite a play of the way in which Martha gradually jettisons the role of caretaker and mother,[37] and discovers her own 'self'; Christ's is essentially an account of a 'gathering together' of a coherent or unified personality. What seems equally relevant to an understanding of *The Four-Gated City* is that Martha's situation is actually a triangular one involving Lynda and Mark, just as the Biblical Martha existed in a triangle involving Jesus and her sister Mary: in an important sense, her 'self' *cannot* be her own.

In the Luke version,[38] Jesus comes to a village where Martha receives him; Mary sits at Jesus' feet. Martha is said to be 'cumbered about much serving', paralleling the Martha/caretaker in *The Four-Gated City*, and says to Jesus: 'Dost thou not care that my sister hath left me to serve alone. Bid her therefore that she help me.' Jesus responds: 'Martha, Martha, thou art careful and troubled about many things, but one thing is needful, and Mary hath chosen that good part that shall not be taken away from her.' Roughly translated: Martha, heavily involved with preparations for a meal for Jesus, complains to Jesus that Mary is too preoccupied with her spiritual needs. Jesus tells her that Mary's devotion is of a high order and that Martha must not dissuade her from it. In short, Mary exemplifies a path that Martha must struggle to understand. Similarly in *The Four-Gated City*. where Lynda is in a position to be Martha's guide: she has given up the 'active's' work of a daily routine and has surrendered to the demands of her mental life. It is open to Martha Quest to follow her. Further, in John's account of the raising of Lazarus it's made explicit that Martha's faith enables 'the man' to work miracles – in the case of the Gospel story, Jesus to heal the dead;[39] in the case of the Martha Quest story, Mark Coldridge to prophesy in *A City in the Desert*. But it is her constancy which is pivotal for all of them, and in that sense the Biblical Martha is not 'separate' from her sister or Jesus, just as Martha Quest's autonomy is attained only when she opens herself to Lynda.

An analogous point is made in one commentary on the Martha/Mary story in particular, – *The Cloud of Unknowing*, written by an anonymous medieval Christian mystic. Whereas many interpreters distinguish Martha and Mary sharply from one another, with Mary strongly esteemed for serving Jesus as a contemplative and the active Martha chided for undue attention to domestic concerns,[40] *The Cloud of Unknowing* links the two women in a relation of overlapping dependence, such that their two lives combine to express what the author calls the 'second part' of the two types of life, active and contemplative.

> Though there are only two lives, these two lives have between them three parts, each one better than the other . . . the first part consists of the good and honest physical works of mercy and charity (as performed by Martha, for instance). This is the

first stage of the active life, as we have already said. The second part of these two lives consists of good spiritual meditations on our own wretchedness, on the sufferings of Christ, and on the joy of heaven. The first part is good: the second is better, for it is the second stage of the active life and the first of the contemplative. In this part the contemplative and active lives are knit together in a spiritual relationship, and made sisters like Martha and Mary.[41]

That is, Martha and Mary can meet and can share the same experience: to that extent they lose their individuality as persons. But this second stage is defined as much in relation to what comes beyond it – 'the third part of these two lives is caught up in this dark cloud of unknowing', which is 'between' the individual and God and about which absolutely nothing can be said.[42] To that extent, too, Martha and Mary are equals in this (worldly) life, even though Mary has also chosen to go beyond it.

The fact that the situation continues to be triangular, that the appendix is recounted not by Martha but by Francis Coldridge, one of the second generation, that Martha's death is introduced in such a low-key way – she is simply reported presumed dead just before the appendix ends – this underlines the unconventionality in the novels placing of its 'central' protagonist, Martha, the identity of whose 'self' is so much in question. Further, she and Lynda reappear in *Canopus in Argos*, in a very different setting, this time as a dyad – a structure which could equally well support a Sufi/mystical notion of a 'universal' or non-personal reality in which individuality is a subordinate or inauthentic factor.

These two religious traditions, then – Sufi and Christian – make a variety of claims on the text. That they embody different 'senses of an ending', to paraphrase Frank Kermode, is clear from the resolution of *Memoirs*. Here, the Christian–redemptive notion of death and disciple-hood is brought to the foreground.

> There followed a small shower of stones: from the windows above us catapults were being trained on him, perhaps worse than catapults. A stone hit [Gerald's] shoulder: it might have hit his face, or even an eye. Now he deliberately turned and faced the building, and we saw he was presenting himself as a target.[43]

Very shortly after this, the narrator begins to see what she thinks is the hidden pattern behind the wall. 'My feeling that this was what we had been waiting for was so strong that I called to the others, who were still asleep.' When the group do, in fact, 'walk through the forest', we have a sense of completion and salvation quite unlike the loss of narrative boundary and definition in the ending of *The Four-Gated City*. Emily is 'transmuted' and in 'another key'; the yellow beast Hugo 'fitted her new self' and had become handsome, splendid. Then, at the very last moment, Gerald's children 'came running, clinging to his hands and his clothes, and they all followed quickly on after the others, as the last walls dissolved.' It is a notion of dissolution that invokes the concern with eschatology and Revelation intrinsic to Christian metaphor.

Even so, there is within the ending of *Memoirs* one of the rare points in Lessing's writing of this period when the 'classic' language of mysticism seems to be enacted. The narrator arrives at an 'inability to speak':

> The one person I had been looking for all this time was there. There she was. No, I am not able to say clearly what she was like. She turned her face just once to me, and all I can say is . . . nothing at all.[44]

Could we then say that we deal with three religious traditions: Sufi narrative and imagery, Christian narrative and imagery, and what could be called an agnostic or non-theistic mysticism?

It is not as if Lessing leaves us without any clues as to her general assumptions about language and what it can organise. Two-thirds of the way through *Memoirs*, for instance, the narrator asks the reader to think about 'it' – the 'thing' or external 'event' or 'atmosphere' or 'change' which the narrator and Emily and the inhabitants of the city witness and share. What could 'it' be?

> – the ground-swell of events, experience
> – something visible in times of crisis
> – a force, a power, earthquake, a comet
> – pestilence, war, tyranny, climate, savagery or religion
> – the word for helpless ignorance, or helpless awareness;
>   perhaps a word for man's inadequacy?
> – above all a consciousness of something ending.[45]

But she will not allow such 'positive' definition, and in the process explicitly recalls the medieval mysticism I quoted above when she ends this section by saying:

> Perhaps, after all, one has to end by characterizing 'it' as a sort of cloud or emanation, but invisible . . . 'It' was everywhere, in everything, moved in our blood, our minds, 'It' was nothing that could be described once and for all, or pinned down, or kept stationary; . . . 'It' was, finally, what you experienced . . . and was in the space behind the wall, moved the players behind the wall, just as much there as in our ordinary world where one hour followed another and life obeyed the unities, like a certain kind of play.[46]

Although Lessing has not set out to give an account of the relation between an individual and her/his God – and thus can allow herself to locate 'it' in the relatively mundane realms of 'what you experienced' – she follows *The Cloud of Unknowing* in affirming the intrinsic unknowability of things, the final unimportance or inapplicability of definitions. If the concept of a cloud has any empirical referent here it is a spatial one, just as it has in *The Cloud of Unknowing*, albeit as metaphor: in *The Cloud* the sinner dares to '*press into* that cloud of unknowing between him and God', or Mary's urgent love '*reaches out* into it' (my italics);[47] in *Memoirs* the cloud is 'in the space behind the wall'.

We can see *The Golden Notebook* as being concerned with the depiction and analysis through various devices of conscious and unconscious process: the technique of (Jungian) psychoanalysis, the exploration of memory, the attempt to represent experience with immediacy in the dairy. I am saying that in the later fiction another device is used – the Sufi teaching story – but invoked to address questions that, as I've argued, Lessing considers to remain unanswered by the language and explanatory systems offered by Marxism and psychoanalysis. If the notion of conscious development is central to Sufism, then it can be seen as central to the development of the narrative of *The Four-Gated City*. But Sufism also stands for a return from exile, because it represents both the dependency on a providing culture and because it is *not* about personal withdrawal from society. It is about being *inside* society, but seeing the significance of the 'total situation' therein ('Be in the world, not of it,' in Lessing's words). It then becomes possible to see 'Sufism', within the dynamic of Lessing's writings, as an attempt to negotiate the early split in her fiction between, on the one hand, the historical and, on the other, the mythic. Thus, we have the notion that Sufism is always 'present', but manifesting itself in different ways at different times. Or the wall in *Memoirs*, which is always there, potentially available to the narrator, *inside* the block in which she lives. The wall doesn't involve a voyage *or* a dream, and on the latter point Lessing has been explicit, as I've said.

Finally, in Lessing's various aesthetic statements, 'realism' is a special form of knowledge, and I would say that 'mysticism', too, stands for another pole, or form of knowledge: as a strategy employed to complexify narrative, or to complete it; to describe relations between persons, but not necessarily, in a classical mystical sense, to describe relations between persons and God. It is to do with being at the heart or kernel of 'reality', and thus having a unique vantage-point on it – but always the earthly world, or so it seems. Even if one were to follow A. J. Ayer in his discussion of mysticism, in *The Central Questions of Philosophy*,[48] and concede that mysticism does not have to include talk about God – that is, the fact that Lessing doesn't talk about God would not rule out the possibility that her insights could be termed 'mystical' – one can see that Lessing's way of depicting the post-holocaust landscape in *The Four-Gated City* really doesn't fulfil the criteria that Ayer sets out. In his discussion of mystical experience there is no mention of God, but there is certainly the stress that, for the mystic, reality is spiritual, time and space are not ultimately real, and that everything is one. But this is not the position that Lessing is taking. Here I can return to the most casual statement Lessing makes in 'An Ancient Way': 'Perhaps the most useful thing I personally have been encouraged to do in my Sufi study is to examine why I believe what I believe.' This is essentially an ethical question. Ironically, almost the same point was made by the philosopher John Wisdom in relation to psycho-analysis,[49] which he also saw as a form of official practice, or as a discourse on discourse, a means of examining why one thinks what one thinks. For Doris Lessing at no point asserts that through her study of Sufism she has abandoned concepts or beliefs which inform her earlier fiction.

If we turn now to questions about the nature and assessment of mystical experience as a whole, then some other problems present themselves in relation to Lessing's use of Sufi imagery. I've said that she ends on a distinctly secular note in 'An Ancient Way to New Freedom'. To her, a Sufi current is one which opens the individual to a new way of looking at things, which she uses, I think, in a deliberately open-ended sense. Ronald Hepburn, in his discussion of the nature of mysticism, calls mystical experience 'religious experience' in a 'broad but meaningful' sense of the word,[50] and I think it's a possibility that Lessing's advocacy of 'a new way of looking at things' could be seen as embodying what many would call a religious sentiment or feeling about the world. But problems about the nature of mysticism also lie in the area of what object of knowledge mystical language is assumed to be referring to.[51] Hepburn remarks that mystical experience, in the first place, is a vision of the world that is free to a very unusual extent from the interposition of concepts; he continues:

> When concepts are withdrawn and fundamental distinctions obliterated, it is understandable that our ordinary sense of the limits and boundaries between thing and thing, person and person, should also temporarily disappear. In this we may have an important clue to the mystic's claims about the overcoming of finite individuality, and mergings and meltings into the infinite.[52]

At one level, how strongly Lessing departs from any notion of this kind. The mysticism that she is talking about in the writings of the late 1960s and early 1970s is something of a mysticism 'in quotation marks': in *The Four-Gated City*, the other two points of the triangle are supplied, as I've suggested, by psychiatry and politics – they exist, interdependently, as three ways of looking at the world, with 'mysticism' standing as a 'general' model for the human being's potential. Lessing's mysticism is not, on the face of it, linked with any sense of a unitive state, of a merging into the Absolute or the Infinite, or even with any special experience of bliss. In this novel, at least, she is talking in a time-specific sense about what goes on in a given society at a given period; she dates the reality after the holocaust (we're in 1997); she's talking about countries which can be named, although their geographical identity may be obscure; she is not simply constructing a vision-ary landscape. And even though the breakdowns and mergings that take place between Martha and Lynda do seem to mirror certain technical aspects of the Sufi path, they do not orient themselves to an identification with an Infinite reality; they are essentially about living 'in the world', in the context of a group of discourses about madness and individuality, and are always rooted in the relationship between the individual and the social formation.

I have tried to show how Lessing's use of religious symbolism constitutes an attempt at transcending ordinary limitations in language by drawing on a variety of conceptual and written traditions and integrating facets of them in her fiction. That is, she is trying literally to resolve the problem of generating new types of narrative, metaphor and story. If she turns to religion, of course, she will discover that language is usually deemed inadequate to the task of representing 'ultimate' (or God's) reality; hence the deliberate insubstantiality of 'it', the cloud, in *Memoirs* – the recourse to a notion of the structuring absence. This aspect of things, perhaps peculiar to the religious sphere, underlines the difficulty one faces in combining 'religious' and 'fictional' discourses: there is no straightforward correlation between the objects of discussion, representation, or experience. Religions and their truth-claims are, *par excellence*, the field for debate as to whether one is talking about a subjective or private truth only, or an objective existence of a deity or spirits of some kind. Any attempt to negotiate that issue while remaining alert to the rather different 'truth-claims' or demands of a literary text is bound to be flawed, if only because the categories of analysis will not always be convergent. The 'truth of a doctrine' might be a valid notion, for instance, the 'truth of a text' a mystification. Whatever comes to be felt, in general, about the place of mysticism in Lessing's more recent fiction, the word and its meanings are certainly over-determined now: resonant with all the associations of cultural and religious life, on the one hand, and Lessing's practice as a novelist, on the other. Our first step can probably only be to disentangle some of them – to paraphrase Laing, 'to see into and through' them.

Notes

1 See Doris Lessing's introduction to Olive Schreiner, *The Story of an*

African Farm, New York, Schocken Books, 1976, pp. 2, 7. In fact the glossary to C. S. Nott's 1954 translation of Farid ud-Din Attar, *The Conference of the Birds* (London, Routledge & Kegan Paul, 1978, p. 146), indicates clearly that the great bird is to be taken as a symbol of God.

2 See Florence Howe, 'A Conversation with Doris Lessing (1966)', in A. Pratt and L. S. Dembo (eds), *Doris Lessing. Critical Studies*, University of Wisconsin Press, 1974, pp. 2–3.

3 See, for instance, Ninian Smart, 'History of Mysticism', in P. Edwards (ed.), *The Encyclopaedia of Philosophy*, New York, Macmillan and The Free Press, 1972, vol. 5, pp. 419–29; W. Gerber, 'Sufi Philosophy', in Edwards, op. cit., vols 7 and 8, pp. 40–3; R. C. Zaehner, *Mysticism Sacred and Profane*, Oxford University Press, 1978, pp. 156–66; H. A. R. Gibb, 'Sufism', in R. C. Zaelmer (ed.), *The Concise History of Living Faiths*, London, Hutchinson, 1977, pp. 189–95.

4 Farid al-Din Attar, *Muslim Saints and Mystics*, trans. A. J. Arberry, London, Routledge & Kegan Paul, 1979, p. 1.

5 Idries Shah, *The Way of the Sufi*, Harmondsworth, Penguin, 1979, p. 15.

6 Ibid., p. 36.

7 Ibid., pp. 14–15.

8 Ibid., p. 30.

9 Ibid., p. 31.

10 Interviewed by Malcolm Dean, BBC Television, 7 May 1980.

11 Doris Lessing, 'An Ancient Way to New Freedom', in Leonard Lewin (ed.), *The Elephant in the Dark and Other Writings on the Diffusion of Sufi Ideas in the West by Idries Shah and Others*, New York, Dutton, 1976, pp. 73–4.

12 Ibid., p. 74.

13 Ibid., p. 81.

14 Shah, op. cit., p. 215.

15 Doris Lessing, *The Golden Notebook*, St Albans, Herts, Panther, 1973, pp. 17–18.

16 Shah, op. cit., p. 34.

17 Quoted in 'Do More then Laugh at Fools', in ibid., pp. 232–3. The story ends as follows: 'You have laughed at the joke of the fool. Now, will you do more, and think about your own thoughts as if they were the salt and the flour?'

18 Doris Lessing, *The Four-Gated City*, London, Panther, 1979, p. 236.

19 Ibid., pp. 237–8.

20 Ibid., p. 333.

21 See the particularly clear exposition of 'Sufism and Selfhood' in Kenneth Cragg, *Islam and the Muslim*, 'Man's Religious Quest', The Open University, Units 20–1, 1978, pp. 71–7.

22 *The Four-Gated City*, p. 461.

23 Ibid., p. 517.

24 Ibid., p. 603.

25 Ibid., p. 635.

26 The bibliographies on 'One-Dimensional Society' and
    'Underground' in T. Pateman (ed.), *Counter Course, A Handbook for
    Course Criticism*, Harmondsworth, Penguin, 1972, provide a
    representative sampling of this literature.

27 See R. D. Laing, 'The Obvious', in D. Cooper (ed.), *The Dialectics of
    Liberation*, Harmondsworth, Penguin, 1971, pp. 13–33. Sheila
    Rowbotham describes the Dialectics of Liberation conference and its
    impact on her in *Woman's Consciousness, Man's World*,
    Harmondsworth, Penguin, 1974, pp. 22–3.

28 Laing, op. cit., p. 13. The fact that Laing later dissociated himself
    from his paper doesn't negate its historical importance.

29 For Lessing, see her comments on the dust jacket of C. Naranjo and
    R. E. Ornstein, *On the Psychology of Meditation*, London, Allen &
    Unwin, 1972. For Laing, see the interviews with him in R. I. Evans
    (ed.), *R. D. Laing, The Man and His Ideas*, New York, Dutton, 1976,
    pp. lviii–lxiii, and 'The World Opens Up in Different Ways', pp.
    71–81; and the interview with him by Peter Mezan, *Esquire*, January
    1972.

30 See 'In the World, Not of It', in Doris Lessing, *A Small Personal Voice*,
    ed. Paul Schlueter, New York, Vintage Books, 1975, p. 134.

31 Jonah Raskin, 'Doris Lessing at Stony Brook: An Interview', *New
    American Review*, 8 (1970), pp. 166–79.

32 See, for instance, good journalistic accounts like S. Annet (ed.), *The
    Many Ways of Being, A Guide to Spiritual Groups and Growth Centres in
    Britain*, London, Sphere, 1976, which lists forty-eight such groups,
    not including the 'human development groups', many of which use
    (or used, if now defunct) Eastern techniques as one type of therapeutic
    resource. Anne Bancroft's *Twentieth Century Mystics and Sages*
    (London, Heineman, 1976) gives potted biographies of about twenty
    men and women, from Gurdjieff to Krishnamurti, whose ideas have
    been influential in the West.

33 A typical example of this is Peter Sedgwick's discussion of Laing's
    later work, 'R. D. Laing: Self, Sympton and Society', in R. Boyers
    and R. Orrill (eds), *Laing and Anti-Psychiatry*, Harmondsworth,
    Penguin, 1975, pp. 11–47, especially 'Postscript, April 1975', pp.
    45–7. See also Alison Fell and Michele Roberts, 'All a Girl Needs is a
    Guru', *Spare Rib*, 59, June 1977, for some stereotypical feminist
    objections to Bhagwan Shree Rajneesh, and the correspondence on
    the article, *Spare Rib*, 61, August 1977. A more optimistic account of
    the possibility of integrating such 'mystical' (in this case, Buddhist)
    ideas into the work of mental health professionals is provided in Gay
    Gaer Luce, 'Western Psychology Meets Tibetan Buddhism', in
    Tarthang Tulku (ed.), *Reflections of Mind*, California, Dharma
    Publishing, 1975.

34 'An Ancient Way', p. 76.

35 My thoughts on this were influenced by Simon During, 'The
    Structure of Messianic Narrative: Daniel Deronda and The Gospel

of St. Mark', unpublished paper given at King's College, London, 1980.

36 I. H. Marshall, *The Gospel of St. Luke. A Commentary on the Greek Texts*, Exeter, Paternoster Press, 1978, p. 451.

37 Carol P. Christ, *Diving Deep and Surfacing: Women Writers on Spiritual Quest*, Boston, Beacon Books, 1980.

38 Luke 10: 38–42.

39 John 11: 20–7, 40.

40 See, for instance, accounts ranging from F. C. Cook (ed.), *The Holy Bible With Commentary By Bishops and Other Clergy of the Anglican Church: New Testament*, vol. 1, London, John Murray, 1878 and M. G. Easton, *Baker's Illustrated Bible Dictionary* (Grand Rapids, Michigan, Baker Book House, 1978; first published 1903), to *The Interpreter's Bible, Vol. 8, Luke; John* (Tennessee, Abingdon Press, 1952, pp. 197–9) and *The Interpreter's Dictionary of the Bible* (Tennessee, Abingdon Press, 1962, vol. 3, p. 287) and Marshall, op. cit., pp. 450–4.

41 Clifton Wolters (trans.), *The Cloud of Unknowing and Other Works*, Harmondsworth, Penguin Books, 1980, p. 88.

42 Ibid., pp. 89, 79.

43 Doris Lessing, *The Memoirs of a Survivor*, London, Pan Books, 1980, p. 186.

44 Ibid., p. 190.

45 Ibid., p. 136.

46 Ibid., p. 139.

47 Wolters, op. cit., pp. 81, 83.

48 A. J. Ayer, 'Evaluation of Mystical Experience', in *The Central Questions of Philosophy*, Harmondsworth, Penguin, 1978, pp. 4–7. R. C. Zaehner, 'Mysticism without Love', in *The City Within the Heart* (London, Unwin, 1980, p. 17) makes a similar point about talk of God.

49 J. A. Wisdom, 'Critical Notice of C. H. Waddington and Others, *Science and Ethics* (1943)', reprinted in his *Philosophy and Psychoanalysis*, Oxford, Blackwell, 1969, p. 107.

50 R. W. Hepburn, 'Nature and Assessment of Mysticism', in P. Edwards (ed.), *The Encyclopaedia of Philosophy*, New York, Macmillan and The Free Press, 1972, vol. 5, pp. 429–34.

51 Cf. C. A. Keller, 'Mystical Literature', in S. Katz (ed.), *Mysticism and Philosophical Analysis*, London, Sheldon Press, 1978, pp. 75–100.

52 Hepburn, op. cit., p. 433.

7 'If you mate a swan and a gander, who will ride?'*

Marsha Rowe

The Marriages Between Zones Three, Four, and Five is the second book in the series Canopus in Argos: Archives which Doris Lessing is writing, having turned to the genre of science fiction. Why had she taken this course, I'd found myself wondering, had she travelled beyond me? Also, despite Ursula Le Guin and a novel by Naomi Mitchison – the handful of science fiction I've read – I remained bemused by the cold modernity, the metallic ring of the description itself. Science fiction – almost like a contradiction in terms – as if there could be some alchemical metamorphosis which would produce a story out of the spanner, the laser, the atom. Doris Lessing gives her reasons for adopting science fiction in her preface to Shikasta, which is the first of this series. Science fiction – or, nowadays, space fiction – is impressively, concurrently relevent – morally, politically, aesthetically. It 'maps' our world for us. It projects us into the future to reveal and examine the logical, perhaps disastrous, consequences of present policies, of 'scientific and social possibilities'. It presents new and inspiring ways to broach conjecture about our world, to question, to probe, to fantasise. This demanding genre has also stretched and fractured the 'realistic' form of the novel and, by its very popularity and its manifold proliferation, is unquestionably affecting and influencing it, while itself representing a definite break with realism. Despite this, Doris Lessing says, academia persists in turning up its nose and ignoring the genre, and she emphasises that these writers are 'dazzlers', telling 'truths the respectable siblings do not dare'.[1]

* I would like to thank Jenny Taylor for her sisterly insistence that I think my ideas through.

There is none of that manipulation of technology which confirms the supremacy of the human species over the planet and the future in her series (in the first two, that is, which have been published so far – which means that this is an arbitrary cut-off point and the view will change when the series is completed). *Shikasta* fictionalises a galactic history and an epochal overview of Earth's history. It is not about the 'real world', since it constructs a cosmology, yet the planet Shikasta is also recognisably Earth. That is, its characters appear human (there are no insectoid people for instance), although their dimensions of size, age and significance are elasticised beyond the commonplace – and the sources from which Doris Lessing has drawn to create the 'history' of the planet after often recognisable, though far-ranging: from archaeological supposition to religious history, or the sacred texts of the world to which she refers in her *Shikasta* preface when she makes the comment:

> The sacred literatures of all races and nations have many things in common. Almost as if they can be regarded as the products of a single mind. It is possible we make a mistake when we dismiss them as quaint fossils from a dead past.[2]

In an introduction written some time ago, Doris Lessing placed the novel in a sort of middle ground where Culture, 'the high arts', meets culture, meaning a way of living: 'the novel being that hybrid, the mixture of journalism and the *Zeitgeist* and autobiography that comes out of a part of the human consciousness which is always trying to understand itself, to come into the light.'[3] She is careful not to reduce her novelistic intentions to any singular aim or cause. Of course, when we read her 'It is possible that . . .' we do proceed to wonder whether or not 'the sacred literatures' have a common origin and whether or not we think it is a question we want to ponder. This idea of truth being buried in the past, like some illuminating treasure which will only be disclosed when it can be 'seen' – as and when it fits the shape of the times – is one she explores in *The Marriages Between Zones Three, Four, and Five* at many different levels of meaning, including that of image-making or story telling itself.

Shikasta blows through and unclutters your perspective. Through it, Doris Lessing questions any residual clinging to the belief that we have attained the pinnacle of progress. One way of reading it is that she has turned to Hindu ideas about reincarnation and kharma, 'For the Hindu . . . rebirth . . . is a prosaic and routine occurrence, as common as birth and death. Each birth is a re-birth, in fact, the literal re-embodiment of a self sundered from its most recent body in its latest death.'[4] She uses this in a loose way to create characters who, we gather, have more than one chance at life – we are shown them in a shadowy nimbus between lives, before rebirth on Shikasta. The actual life-cycles on Shikasta are presented as challenges for spiritual transformation which will release the characters from the cycle of rebirths, and also, eventually, from some sort of spiritual bondage. (Since none of this is explicit – it appears by way of the characters' 'experiences' in the novel – perhaps a more prosaic use of rebirth will occur in the later books. It is not clear whether all the characters in *Shikasta* have such a choice or whether it is only a method used by the governing galaxies.) She applies the Christian concepts of conscience and duty, not as an externalised set of rules, like a moral mechanism, nor to earn kharmic benefits, but in the sense of intention and motive being naked and exposed to judgment. So the novel appears to be dealing with ethics, and with essentialist states, those we associate with terms like 'soul' or 'spirit'. Yet Doris Lessing appears to stress engagement with the world as the choice which must be made – one of the women characters is portrayed as losing a chance to transcend her individual soul to some sort of post-spirit state because she makes escapist decisions in her 'human' life on Shikasta. There is a delicate balancing of social responsibility and self-interest. Doris Lessing is exploring an idea of an overall pattern being possible to life – the characters are shown to have a destiny but not a fate – they are free to choose to listen to and to fulfil an inner purpose which will serve society, or to fail. Therefore, whom they meet, where they are reborn . . . such incidents are not accidental, but opportunities. From a ghostly dimension may come nudges to encourage a character along the way intended by the outer-galactic purpose, and such nudges will be perceived as dreams, persistent doubts, phantoms in a corner. Ideas about technology are not ignored, but taken back into the mythic past – there, geometric shapes characterise various localities and the people who live within them. They have a harmonic, symbolic place in the psyche of the people in that area and they service as a galactic energy link.

The vast carpet sweeping over history and legend, collecting up and using notions such as that of human mortality only coming at a time of the 'Flood' which appears in *Shikasta*, is quite compressed in *The Marriages Between Zones Three, Four, and Five*. At its simplest, the plot is Woman, AI.Ith of Zone Three, marries Man, Ben Ata of Zone Four. Are these archetypes or stereotypes? It's romantic fiction put through a space transformer. The images flicker . . . a majestic Cleopatra and Antony . . . Where did Ben Hur come in? Perhaps he is the Marlboro man – that distant sun–smoke gaze . . . No, it is the Sheik, and AI.Ith in floating veils is about to be carried off – she's a cool one, bare-back riding, what nerve, a reassuring feminine lilt to her name.

You can't help feeling like the three monkeys as you read *The Marriages*. You watch yourself spellbound, knowing that if you took away one pair of hands you'd hear your own laughter, or again and there would be a chorus chant, or again and you'd see the manipulator of shadow puppets. The part of you which recognises that all this is going on is addressed by the 'chronicler' in the novel, a voice which Doris Lessing uses to extemporise on story telling, listening and imagination. She wrote in the *Shikasta* preface that *The Marriages* 'turned out to be a fable, or myth. Also, oddly enough, to be more realistic.'[5] Darko Suvin noted that the difference between science fiction and myth was mainly that, while both were opposed to 'naturalism or empiricism', 'SF sees the norms of any age, including emphatically its own, as unique, changeable, and therefore subject to a *cognitive* view,' whereas, 'The myth absolutizes and even personifies apparently constant motifs . . . claims to explain the eternal essence of phenomena.'[6] *The Marriages* departs from certain particulars of the science fiction *novum* set up in *Shikasta* – it does not have the galactic empires of Canopus, Sirius, and the evil Pruttoria. It does not roam over possible time. It is closer to myth in the way it postulates a world above time, in components of its plot and in its gender archetypes. On the one hand, the gender archetypes are embracing and inescapable in this novel, and, on the other hand, change is presented as the nucleus of things: no 'realism' appears constant. It is illustrated as a time–and–again dialectical continuity of process, and, in the self, as a movement of desire reaching resolution only to have to begin again at a new level.

The dreamy contours of the landscapes in *The Marriages*, and the formalised, ballad cadence in the narration evoke the uncertainties and anticipations of the fairy-tale. The different zones are plausible as regions – a mountainous area, one of watery plains, one of hills and desert – but they are conveyed by metaphor rather than naturalistic detail. Colours, shapes and atmosphere are accumulated as backdrops against which the characters are delineated by contrast. This deliberate distancing intensifies an epic effect in their presentation. The narrator's role is similar, as if setting up a chorus to stage the characters as representative figures, since he is one of the historians, or 'chroniclers, poets, songmakers and the Memories' of Zone Three. The method could also be compared to that analysed by the Russian Formalists – characters in fables are *actants*, created and made by the function and roles they play in the story. On one level, however, Al.Ith and Ben Ata function as real people. We follow their relationship, their journeying into each other's depths, related in an intimate, personal way. At another, they emerge from this as larger-than-life figures, gesturing towards their zone chorus. There is, too, the constant play between archetypes and stereotypes of gender. Feminist criticism of stereotyped representations of women is based on the way stereotypes fix things into patterns of monotonous, predictable regularity. Stereotypes are moulds. Stereotypes reduce. Archetypes are not rigid. Archetypes produce. They are prototypes from which we can pull a multiplicity of meanings. Both are suggested, and to disentangle them, the characters have to be related to their zones, since it is through the symbolism of their zones that the characters attract their meanings – like magnets.

Here again, complexity meets us. The zones are ambiguous. The accounts of each zone appear as a pentimento of allegories, and the relationship between them shifts according to the different placements of interpretation. The underplaying theme through it all, like fish swimming in and out of the reeds, is the setting up of oppositions. Like fish or soap, these are never still, and your reading will see what mine doesn't. The zones are substantiated by such eclectic reference to categories of the self, and genres are so shuffled – romantic fiction, fable, space fiction – that the use of conventions both reinforces and undercuts their expectations.

At the end of the novel, Al.Ith is leaving both her own Zone

Three and Zone Four (which she experienced by marriage), for the transports of a nebulous region, Zone Two. She is trying to formulate, or to remember, a song which will relate to this. She finally overhears it sung by someone else (the significance of the chance event). She discovers it has come from the zone most distant from the one she is trying to enter. It has come from Zone Five. But Zone Five is sensuous, earthy, a primitive, matriarchal past. She is going into the future. She is ascending – Zone Two is literally and figuratively higher, the sky, the spiritual; or descending – it is numerically lower, it is an emblem of a nether-region; she is leaving the life she has known, 'I shall ride my heart thundering across the plains. Out distance you all and leave my self behind.'[7] The expression of what she seeks comes from the past. (She searches for the right *rhyme and meaning* throughout the novel.) The song's composition supposes a synthesis between the zones at the extreme points of difference, just as the uniting forces – brought about by the marriage – between Zones Three and Four have already begun to transform each zone into its opposite. In the final pages of the novel, Al.Ith tries to clarify this to her sister, Murti., her 'other self', who replaces her as ruler of Zone Three, 'And now, instead of lethargy, and listlessness, and sorrow, instead of a falling birth rate and animals who will not mate, we have the opposite. The opposite, Murti.!'[8] In Zone Four, a general complains about the same thing, 'But suddenly, from one day to the next, everything is its own opposite, black is white.'[9]

At first, the idea of oppositional energy and tension is presented as irritating, difficult, even unnecessary: 'The nature of Zone Four – it was conflict and battle and warring. In everything. A tension and a fighting in its very substance: so that every feeling, every thought held in its own opposite.'[10] Undoubtedly, we are shown, this is a problematic state of things. Zone Four has analogies to our world, aspects exaggerated into bold relief. The masculine sex is dominant. The values esteemed are linked to warfare, brutality, hierarchical social stratification and organisation, enforced obedience. Women's subjugation is deep and bitter. The sexes, living largely separate lives, fear each other. Boy children go to military camp at age seven. Women's strength is locked into survival. There is an underground movement of women. The women practise secret rites where they turn the tables on men, and where they stare up at Zone Three (Al.Ith's zone). This is forbidden – a fact which signifies all sorts of self-delusion, repression, ideological blind-folding, national chauvinism. The agriculture and the capacities of the zone are poorly and unevenly realised, its potential barely tapped, so it is not only poverty-stricken, but ugly – both appearance and economy reflect the distortions of a stark sexual division of labour. However, depending on which other frontier or zone we turn to compare or relate to Zone Four, we will choose a different label for its, and the other zones', naming.

If we relate Zone Four to Zone Three, which is AI.Ith's zone, and the zone of the 'chronicler' of the novel, the one which takes up equal space in the novel to Zone Four, then Zone Three is a dream of the future compared to Zone Four taken at face value. Zone Three is a pastoral Utopia. It represents what Zone Four might become, if the creativity lodged in human labour were to be released by a transformation of the relations of production and reproduction, if 'feminine' values like responsiveness and nurturing were released through the entire social texture. Zone Three has no exploitation or oppression, no hierarchy based on force, privilege or possession. Childcare is shared between the sexes and between biological parents and others. There is no sexual ownership – sexual monogamy is only ever temporary, and, while a special value is attributed to nurturing the soul from the moment of conception onwards (in this idealised world no abortions are needed since conception only ever occurs by choice), a woman will conjoin with other men during pregnancy, men whose vibrations she feels are right for her and the child-to-be. Sex itself is not lustful, eroticism contains no threat. Individuals have only to be patient to understand each other, since all have heightened intuition and feeling sensitivity. Words are often unnecessary and they communicate with animals. Young girl children who show an aptitude for organising will participate in adult council meetings. The fact that there is no polarisation between existence and essence shows itself in the results of all this unalienated activity – the buildings have an indescribable beauty, harmony is everywhere apparent.

It is definitely a 'feminist' Utopia, in the sense of being a feminised world, one in which women are independent and men do women's work. As a feminist I observe, too, that its imaginative breadth is circumscribed by some of today's gender patterns

– it is unhesitatingly heterosexual, so that biological sexual difference still holds as a directing force in some personality traits and preferences. For instance, women exclude men from childbirth, and when women relax together, as do AI.Ith and Murti. as co–rulers of the realm, they don't chat about anything too abstract, but about dress and manners. Are these my quibbles or are they clues? We move here to Doris Lessing's play on archetypes, I think, because this apparently Utopian zone also has its problems, which necessitate the marriage between it and Zone Four, the exchange of energies transmuted through AI.Ith and Ben Ata.

Throughout the Utopia, as the novel begins, stasis is setting in. By the end of the novel, the immobilisation is ended, transformed. To put it baldly, Zone Three has been fertilised, energised, by Zone Four – as AI.Ith reminded Murti. in the conversation quoted, 'instead of a falling birth rate . . . we have the opposite. The opposite, Murti.!' So, at one level, these two zones represent 'femininity' and 'masculinity' as archetypal, primal forces, the yin and the yang of t'ai chi. Yin is 'feminine', receptivity, form, matrix – Zone Three; yang is 'masculine', creativity, energy, dynamism – Zone Four. In his introduction to *The Book of Changes*, Richard Wilhelm explains that both yin and yang and their gender ascriptions of femininity and masculinity are historically later additions to the original concepts,

> In its primary meaning yin is 'the cloudy', 'the overcast', and yang means actually 'banners waving in the sun', that is, something 'shone upon', or bright. By transference the two concepts were applied to the light and dark sides of a mountain or of a river.[11]

Originally, 'The terms used for the opposites are "the firm" and "the yielding", not yang and yin.'[12] The idea that the change and interplay of these two forces produce the 'world of being' is one that Doris Lessing would appear to be using. It is applied to both zones, the 'masculine' as well as to the 'feminine', since Zone Four is similarly slowing to a halt and needs energising by its opposite.

There's quite a long ride from the archetypal symbols of t'ai chi to a personalised, even fetishistic stereotype of a man or a woman. In *The Marriages* this is achieved by the juggling of images, the to and fro of movement between describing AI.Ith and Ben Ata as characters, and describing the qualities of their respective zones. Both AI.Ith and Ben Ata are represented through more concrete and precise detail. They are the only two characters created in the round. The others are more cardboard since they give outline to the zones as backdrops. We are told what AI.Ith and Ben Ata look like. AI.Ith has long, dark hair. Ben Ata is sunburned. There are limits here, too. Do they have moles? Big or small feet? We are only given so much detail as will give them each body, so as to provide the minimum texture for us to understand their relationship and their changes. Through their appearance we see the habits of their respective zones. AI.Ith has light and grace, and eats fruits and nuts. Ben Ata is more gross, relies on animal protein. Some of the stereotypes which comes to mind are, therefore, obviously for him, macho, 'into steak', rough, and, for her, gentleness, sexual, delicate. As we are told of their experience of self-realisation and self-transformation through the marriage, these characteristics change. Their faculties of perception appear vulnerable, are shattered by experiencing opposite values. They are only identity tags. Are they false? Are they necessary? Are their identities, at a deep level, also only habits?

So far, it would appear Doris Lessing was asking whether each sex needs to find the energy of opposites within, that she was criticising asymmetrical power relations between the sexes, also intimating that idealistic, futurist fantasies can be one dimensional, that emotional separatism closes in on itself and is self-defeating. She is making a play on representations and examining the role of image and symbol in identity. Since the character predicates by which AI.Ith and Ben Ata define themselves differ according to their two zones, she is also breaking the false solidity between the self and the social. She is questioning whether the sense of the self as unique is illusory. The permutations and allusions in the novel don't stop there. They branch off in other directions – temporally and spatially through the other zones, and inwards, so that, at another level, the sum of the zones represents the self. I imagine it was some fun and games conceiving these textual complexities.

If we turn our heads and relate Zone Four, not to Zone Three, but to another zone altogether, to Zone Five, we find the archetypes have done a double de-clutch. New stereotypes zip across our windscreen, reflections of the past existing in the present zoom from behind.

Sometime after AI.Ith has a child with Ben Ata, they both receive 'Orders' to separate from the mysterious, extra-zone 'Providers'. These orders are described as an 'inner listening to the Law'.[13] They are an invisible, unconscious sense of direction and acceptance which needs to be brought to the surface to be understood, to be enacted. Are they understandings from Doris Lessing's 'over-mind'? Ben Ata recognises he should seek out the queen of Zone Five and marry her. To his surprise she finds him first, albeit in a rather odd fashion, since his soldiers dump her, a bound and struggling captive, at his feet. Whereas before Zone Three was refined and Zone Four, Ben Ata, was barbaric, now it is Ben Ata who appears civilised and Vahshi, Zone Five, primitive. Whereas, within his zone, Ben Ata had sought refuge from women in a dark-womb-comfort and had not recognised them as persons in their own right, now that he is a changed man (because of the influence of AI.Ith) the child–parent relation is turned about and it is he who is the parent, he who becomes the father–teacher to the child, to Vahshi, Zone Five. This does not occur only sequentially in the novel, since the meetings between Zone Four and Zone Five begin earlier and dot the fabric throughout. Hence, the archetypes represented by their relations are summoned as part of the whole. At one level these archetypes are those of dualistic gender –worldly comments about the qualities projected by both sexes onto the other, the animus and the anima. Zone Four, Ben Ata, is the animus – the qualities listed by Jung as 'obstinate, harping on principles, laying down the law, dogmatic, world-reforming, theoretic, word-mongering, argumentative, domineering'.[14] For example, he bores Vahshi silly with his drawn-out account of his victory in a race and he verges on well-meaning pomposity when he talks of guiding her primitive zone towards 'ordered anarchy'. Zone Five, Vahshi, has the qualities of the anima – 'sometimes fickle, capricious, moody, uncontrolled and emotional, sometimes gifted with daemonic intuitions, ruthless, malicious, untruthful, bitchy, double-faced and mystical'.[15] Her tribe lives by plunder and banditry, and play exuberant, exhilarating games to test daring and physical prowess. Through her relationship with Ben Ata, Vahshi learns to think, to consider and to reason. At first she thinks it too slow a process to bother with.

Just as Zone Three was a Utopia in the sense described by William Morris, as 'a steady expression of the longing for a society of equality of conditions',[16] so here I am reminded of him, 'Morris thought it was a very good thing for Europe that the corruption and evil and *organization* of the Roman Empire had been destroyed by German barbarians "fresh from their tribal communism".'[17] The zones and archetypes are drawing in historical shadows and valuations: Zone Five, for example, for all its barbarism, displays a cunning, quick wit, its hill tribes have always been one step ahead of Zone Four, whose armies they have watched march and manoeuvre in militaristic formation with great amusement. And Ben Ata partly envies the way they carry their dried meat around in handy pouches – no need for soup kitchens, tents and queues. Thus, the archetypes represented by Zones Four and Five move towards concepts related to social organisation and connected psychic structures, from the animus and anima to patriarchy and matriarchy. The relativity of things slows you down. Each zone is a stage in both senses – an enactment and a plane of development. Zone Four, the 'patriarchy', has advantages – for example, of sharing, against robbery – over the 'matriarchy'. But the matriarchy, Zone Five, has vitality and flexibility.

Zone Five is a matriarchy in a number of ways. It is *naturally* ruled by women: when Vahshi becomes pregnant with Ben Ata, 'They have no doubt at all it would be a girl: she because the strength of her wild femaleness could only give birth to itself.'[18] And it is matriarchal in the psychoanalytic sense, as a metaphor for consciousness at the pre-Oedipal stage (the Minoan-Mycenaean civilisation of Freud's reference).[19] Ben Ata describes Vahshi as having 'no self-consciousness at all'. Earlier, there is a sort of *double-entendre* on Vahshi's 'unselfconscious sensuality', meaning both the missing functions of thought and feeling, concealing a deep insecurity, as well as a positive freedom from inhibition. Zone Four is patriarchy in parallel – there the psyche develops through a version of the Oedipus complex (by which the rule of the father becomes rooted in the unconscious and hence in the structure of the sexed personality). After Al.Ith has had her child in Zone Four, she is astonished by a dream in which she initiates him sexually. This turns out to be common to all Zone Four mothers who interpret it as the time for weaning. Where does the dream cóme from, they ask significantly. As in the other references employed by Doris Lessing, there is no exact replication of theory, since the juxtapositions of meaning work by free association.

So there are by now three sets of archetypes in duplex – a real Wimbledon of matches – there is yin and yang, and anima and the animus, and matriarchy and patriarchy. We find stereotypes in replay. Nor is the ball all in that court.

When Al.Ith enters Zone Four to 'marry' Ben Ata, she arrives at a pavilion which he has built according to the 'Orders' – in other words, to cosmic specifications. The pavilion is mundane, the place where they live together; it is official, the social sign of their marriage; it is the ziggurat, the antechamber and the birth place, where a drum beats to symbolise the mystical significance of their sexual union, the cultural effects sent like sound-waves through the zones – the movement of the oppositions. These interpretations are not conjured out of thin air, but from the architectural composition given by Doris Lessing – the vaulting roofs, the sides open to the sky and to gardens, the fountains in special numerical arrangements. Thus, it becomes a mandala. Not only the place for the regeneration of Al.Ith and Ben Ata, but the centre, the focus of the *self*, where the zones cross. The splash and reflection of meanings play like the fountains.

Each zone represents one of the four, traditional psychic qualities. Zone Five is sensation, Zone Four is thinking, Zone Three is feeling and Zone Two is intuition. Zone Two is the realm where Al.Ith goes when she and Ben Ata separate. It is here we may open our eyes again after spinning round for a new relationship between the zones, because if we begin with Zone Two from the point of view of astrological symbolism, the qualities don't match up. For example, in astrology, the symbol for thought (Zone Four) is air (Zone Two), or the symbol for feeling (Zone Three) is water (Zone Four). So Doris Lessing deals another set of cards: Zone Two represents air, all flickering blueness; Zone Three represents fire, movement and contrast; Zone Four represents water, the plains criss-crossed by rivers; Zone Five represents earth, hills and desert.[20] Each zone is lopsided on its own: the 'thinking' of Zone Four is obessional, lacking moral

self-consciousness, hell-bent on activity – in other words, externalised. Similarly, the 'feeling' of Zone Three is externalised;
'feelings', explains AI.Ith, 'are meant always to be directed out-
wards and used to strengthen a general conception of ourselves
and our realm.'[21] Eventually, we are shown, such feeling leads to
superficiality, to lethargy. Each zone needs the energy of its
shadow side. With these four sides reflecting different oppositions
according to perspective, the experience of individuation represented by the zones becomes a holistic one, like the astrology
chart: the horizon of the conscious and the unconscious is pierced
by the axis from mid-heaven to nadir, the apex being the self-in-
the-world, above the self-for-itself, sweeping the horizon again
from the point of I-consciousness to the point of relationship-
consciousness, and so on. The lines and arcs of the birth chart are
to be pulled out metaphorically, as if they were a Xmas decora-
tion, making a three-dimensional symbol – an orb – for the self.[22]

Representing the zones as planes of being by this method
enables Doris Lessing deliberately to draw the reader inwards.
For example, she doesn't write merely that Zone Three moun-
tains had such and such a shape. Instead, she includes the sense of
being there, the atmosphere, as integral to the outward appearance of things,

> with us the eye is enticed into continual movement and then is
> drawn back always to the great snowy peaks that are shaped by
> the winds and the colours of our skies. And the air tingles in the
> blood, cold and sharp.[23]

This is heightened with Zone Two, the least realistic of the zones
in the ordinary sense, its allusions being more immediately culled
by adjectival reference. It is blue. As mentioned before, blue is
sky, representing also the colour of illusion, and blue is traditionally the colour of the spiritual – but, in case we might miss
anything, Doris Lessing makes a point of blue being the colour of
mourning in Zone Three, so its links with death – the idea of Zone
Two as a hiatus, an ethereal, meditative, other realm – are all
drawn in. Its 'flames' are inspiration. Again, when AI.Ith has
spent more time there, she begins to look emaciated, to be leaving
her physical body, and such associations with the unconscious
(oceanic blue) are emphasised again by the time-warps in Zone
Two and its uncertainty of dimensions – its elf-like existences, the

fairy-tale manifestations, personifications of the 'forces of nature'.

Phew, it must be time for some tea. I'll just mention the parable – AI.Ith, for example, experiences deep guilt concomitant with love in Zone Four – the zone which shocks her out of apathy. Her experience of descent into Zone Four is also an act of redemption.

The 'chronicler' is the most distinct voice of the chorus. He has told us all along how key events are shown by the picture-makers of the various zones, how they are fixed for a moment in an ideological version and then reconceived, repainted, as the social reality of the zone changes. Is he asserting the materiality of language or an idealist imagination mocking any reality other than itself, when he says,

> I also share in AI.Ith's condition of being ruler insofar as I can write of her, describe her. I am woman with her (though I am man) as I write of femaleness – and Dabeeb's. I am Ben Ata when I summon him into my mind and try to make him real. I am . . . what I am at the moment I am that.[24]

He warns of the power of the image, 'The most innocent of poets can write of ugliness and forces he has done no more than speculate about – and bring them into his life,'[25] while giving us, in the style of myths, the 'essence of phenomena': 'Without this sting of otherness, of even – the vicious, without the terrible energies of the underside of health, sanity, sense, then nothing works or *can* work.'[26]

Notes

1 Doris Lessing, 'Some Remarks', *Shikasta*, London, Jonathan Cape, 1979, p. x.
2 Ibid.
3 Doris Lessing, introduction to Olive Schreiner, *The Story of an African Farm*, New York, Schocken Books, 1976, pp. 2–3.
4 Arthur C. Danto, *Mysticism and Morality*, London, Pelican Books, 1976, p. 36.
5 Lessing, 'Some Remarks', p. ix.
6 Darko Suvin, *Metamorphoses of Science Fiction*, New Haven and London, Yale University Press, 1979, p. 7.
7 Doris Lessing, *The Marriages Between Zones Three, Four and Five*, London, Jonathan Cape, 1980, p. 227.

8 Ibid., p. 241.
9 Ibid., p. 235.
10 Ibid., p. 114.
11 Richard Wilhelm, Introduction to *The I Ching or Book of Changes*, London, Routledge & Kegan Paul, 1971, p. lvi.
12 Ibid., p. lvi.
13 Lessing, *The Marriages Between Zones Three, Four and Five*, p. 56.
14 C. G. Jung, 'The Psychology of Rebirth', in *The Archetypes and the Collective Unconscious*, Collected Works of C. G. Jung, vol. 9, part I, London, Routledge & Kegan Paul, 1971.
15 Ibid.
16 James Redmond, introduction to William Morris, *News from Nowhere*, London, Routledge & Kegan Paul, 1974, p. xxviii.
17 Ibid., p.xxii.
18 Lessing, *The Marriages Between Zones Three, Four and Five*, p. 216.
19 See Juliet Mitchell, *Psychoanalysis and Feminism*, London, Allen Lane, 1974, pp. 109–12.
20 See Stephen Arroyo, *Astrology, Psychology and the Four Elements*, Vancouver, CRCS Publications, 1975, pp. 18–19, 95–9.
21 Lessing, *The Marriages Between Zones Three, Four and Five*, p. 5.
22 See Dane Rudhyar, *The Astrological Houses*, New York, Doubleday, 1972, pp. 1–28.
23 Lessing *The Marriages Between Zones Three, Four and Five*, p. 23.
24 Ibid., p. 198.
25 Ibid.
26 Ibid.

8 Doris Lessing: exile and exception*

Rebecca O'Rourke

Introduction

This essay explores the phenomenon of Doris Lessing as woman writer. However, to make sense of her as a woman writer, it is necessary to start from her relation as a writer to British literary culture more generally. Two elements come into play: first, the nature of exile and its significance for Lessing as a writer; and, second, general issues in thinking about women's writing. My starting-point is that exile – as woman, communist, white Rhodesian living in England – is the means to explain Lessing's achievement as a woman writer within British literary culture. Exile is central to Lessing's writing, mainly as a precondition for the forms of its reception, but also to its actual production. It is possible to be very clever with words and extrapolate from the historical account of exile a suggestion that the fundamental condition of exile exemplified and lived out by Doris Lessing is a woman's exile from womanhood. To see the acceptance of her as an 'author only' by the British literary establishment as evidencing her alienation from women. It could be taken as an index of her desire not to be thought a woman writer based on awareness of the limitations that would entail. There is some mileage in this argument, but at the end of the day it is a mean, ungracious argument that denies the writing she has produced.

* I would like to thank Jenny Taylor, Toby, Janet Batsleer, Michael Green, Esther Frankish and Jane Reast for their help.

Women, criticism, writing

Recent debates within feminism over issues of cultural production and consumption have problematised the concept of
women's writing. There is no simple means of defining women's
writing apart from men's writing, or from writing in general.
There are no easy justifications for doing so. In the last analysis
the concerns of feminist criticism must be with gender, as division and difference. The representation of this in fiction must be
organised around sexuality, not one sex – woman; but I find it
necessary to begin from and come back to women's writing. This
necessity is a political imperative.

The modern Women's Movement, unlike previous feminist
struggles, organised around a primary assertion that all women
have more in common with each other than they do with men.
Movements prior to the 1970s asserted the rights of women
against the wrongs done to them. They were, in a sense, structured around a negative pole; whereas sisterhood and the appeal
to the strengths of and pleasures in women as women, stresses
something positive. It would be naive to insist upon that unity as
unproblematic. Obviously, there are tensions and divisions
between women – over particular issues or originating in class or
race – and these can generate a situation where the issues that
divide us can seem greater and to have more political urgency
than those which unite us. But, taking that all into account, it is
impossible to accept as feminist a position which denies common
experience to women – differently determined though it may be
and, importantly, is. Moreover, stressing a commonality
between women need not imply that women are necessarily or
inevitably revolutionary in political terms. Nor that all women
consciously identify and act upon their common interests.
Indeed, estrangement from and lack of identification with other
women is one of the most recurrent elements of that common
experience.

Bringing these general points down into focus on the area of
literary production, they can be taken to imply the necessity of
considering women's writing as *women's* writing, while at the
same time analysing and calling into question the very category.
But doing this argues against the idea generated through a substantial body of feminist criticism; that womanhood guarantees

or predicts a certain form of content. There is no female essence of style, subject-matter or imagination. That is, biology does not produce culture: gender acts upon and determines cultural production in complex, non-reductive ways. The key factors are social: the meaning and consequence of a situation defined biologically – sex – are realised in social terms – gender. For women, who are socially constructed as being within the natural or the biological, the push is always towards the body, towards biology. Whether writing from within subordination or against it, these elements of a social division, seemingly ratified by nature, are always in play for women: 'Men may congratulate themselves upon the productivity of their own mental wombs, but they are displeased to come upon women with mental penises.'[1]

Gender determination is not restricted to the writing of women. Men, too, write as gendered subjects from within patriarchal relations. Analyses which focus on gender determination within women's writing predominate because it is women who, historically and materially, experience subordination and have formed the focal point of a politics of liberation. The reading, rereading and reinterpreting of fictional writing and, increasingly, the production of new kinds of writing, has played a significant part in the development of a new consciousness of womanhood and femininity for contemporary women.

Women who write and publish do so as women. Woman writer – a woman who writes. Women's writer – a women who writes and is assumed only to be read by women. Feminist writer – a woman who is a feminist and a writer. Women's writing – that which all these women produce. These categories need to be explored and active within feminist critical practice because their currency within our culture testifies to the dominance they have exerted and continue to exert within it.

The descriptive term 'women's' carries with it a negative implication. It connotes the less than whole, the less valuable, the trivial. Writing, unlike other creative or professional pursuits, is one area in which women have claimed a public voice. This claim has not been without struggle. Charlotte Brontë's 'vague impression that authoresses are liable to be looked on with prejudice', came at a time when it could be pronounced with certainty that:

There certainly have been cases of women possessed of the properly masculine power of writing books, but these cases are all so obviously exceptional, and must and ought always to remain so, that we may overlook them without the least prejudice to the soundness of our doctrine.[2]

It was, if anything, a trifle naive. These exceptional women, 'possessed', as if by devils, were Jane Austen, Fanny Burney, Maria Edgeworth, Charlotte, Anne and Emily Brontë, Elizabeth Gaskell and scores of by now lesser-known eighteenth- and nineteenth-century women writers who dominated, in productivity and sales at least, the literary markets of their times. It points to a paradox current even to the present day. Women write and publish in larger numbers than men, they use public libraries more frequently, buy more books than men and outnumber them as students of literature. Yet in no sense can it be claimed that within the field of writing or within literary culture generally women exert a power of definition or control consonant with this apparent bias in their favour.

In the light of this, Doris Lessing's ambivalence towards other women writers and, as the parodies within *The Golden Notebook* suggest, the idea of writing as a woman, indicates a consciousness of the possibly undesirable consequences of such an identification. Whenever Lessing has addressed this area, either implicitly or explicitly, it has been in such a way that the claims of art and being an artist take precedence. Art, in some sense, is understood to be beyond the humdrum claims of gender, class or race. One is, or should aspire to be, an Artist creating Art. The shrill trumpet of explicit political claims rules out both the possibility of the small personal voice being heard and the play of *Canopus in Argos: Archives* being precisely, at one level, *play*.

Debates about the propriety, ability or otherwise of women writing have been resolved – no one today would suggest that women cannot or should not write. But questions about the nature of what women write continue. If we consider defining characteristics of women's writing at the most general level we can detect an interesting process at work. There is a common sense about women's writing which remains largely unchanged from generation to generation. At the same time, though, there is a historically specific and changing definition of what constitutes

women's writing. The play between these two means of definition organises the field of women's writing internally, as the
relation between certain female authors and their books, and
externally, as the relation between women's writing and writing.
Real writing: men's writing.

The relatively constant characterisation of women's writing
begins from the commonest assumption that women's writing
and the women who write it constitute a unified, undifferentiated
whole. The pejorative ends to which this definition has been put
account for two impulses within feminist criticism which seem at
first to have little in common. The impulse towards laudatory
gender criticism, which reaches its apotheosis in the work of
Patricia Meyer Spacks,[3] is best understood as a reaction against
the lumping together and denigrating of women writers. The
female imagination, which is the key concept to her thinking,
becomes an immanent force, mysterious and mystical, binding all
women writers together, irrespective of their own time or place
in history, at a deep level of identity. The purpose of feminist
criticism then becomes rescue, rehabilitation and celebration:
activities important as preconditions for a developed critical
practice, but not in themselves enough. The limitations of
laudatory feminist criticism rest in its misrecognition of the
political challenge that is constitutive of feminist criticism. It is as
if Simone de Beauvoir's comment that women writers have had
to expend so much energy negatively in order to free themselves
from outward restraints that they arrive somewhat out of breath
at the stage from which masculine writers of great scope take their
departure,[4] has been taken as license simply to sit back and delight
in the fact that any woman ever put pen to paper or signature to
publisher's contract. Feminist criticism, like the feminism which
has produced it, is not 'about women' in any straightforwardly
empirical way. It is rather about oppression and subordination:
experientially, it concerns being oppressed, but it is also centrally
concerned with that which structures and determines oppression.
The second impulse within feminist criticism which can, in part,
be understood as developing out of the characterisation of
women's writing as a unitary body of texts is that associated with
structuralist and later discourse theorisations of literary texts and
literary production.[5] Briefly, the impulse here is to break up, to

deconstruct, both the text's internal relations and the preconceptions the reader brings to it.

However, this relatively constant characterisation of women's writing as a unified whole also involves certain dominant assumptions being made about the nature of that writing. It is assumed to deal with the same plots, subjects and themes in the same ways. Its characterisations are predictable. Its male characters never 'fully realised'. Women's writing is understood to be obsessively concerned with questions of personal relationships and the emotional–sexual sphere. It is as if within the dazzling and inventive range of fictional writing there is an ungainly, dowdy body of texts labelled 'women's writing' which, unclaimed, is at best consigned to the margins and footnotes of literary history. One initial reason for retaining the category of 'women's writing' is that, behind these stereotypes, we can find a diversity of writing too summarily dismissed as merely the writing of women. The project, though, must not remain at the level of simple rescue. Rescue in itself is problematic in the literary sphere because of the degree to which women writers and women's writing have visibility. Women have had their contribution to the development of literary forms recognised – albeit in highly ambiguous ways – and even discussions of feminist criticism in radical contexts can flounder on a very genuine puzzlement in men about the nature of the problem. A useful means of clarifying the form of appearance of the problem can be found in the theory of muting developed in anthropological work.

> The theory of mutedness, therefore, does not require that the muted be actually *silent*. They may speak a great deal. The important issue is whether they are able to say all that they wish to say, where and when they wish to say it. Must they, for instance, re-encode their thoughts to make them understood in the public domain? Are they able to think in ways which they would have thought had they been responsible for generating the linguistic tools with which to shape their thoughts? If they devise their own code will they be understood?[6]

To recognise difference is not the same as to insist upon or endorse it. Indeed, given the extent to which gender difference is naturalised and masked by a series of conventions and customs which represent relations of dominance and subordination as matters of preference or aptitude, an insistence upon difference which also combines a privileging of 'women' can be a way into beginning to break with and transform those power relations.

Knowledge of women's writing, gained formally through research and study, or informally, shows how ill founded is the assumption that women's writing is all alike: narrowly and obsessively concerned with personal relationships, moralistic, lacking in humour, self-indulgent and of interest only to women. We can see how women writers go beyond the boundaries set by their supposed narrow concerns. More importantly, though, we see how denigrating the writing for what is defined as narrowness implies an evaluation which is transformed if we take our perspective from women's experience and consider the writing as part of a process of negotiation and exploration within women's consciousness and everyday life.

The fields of women's writing (post-war)

There are a number of problems involved in dealing with recent and contemporary fiction. Our reference-points in thinking the field are not generally derived from the institutionalisation within educational practice that is inescapable when thinking about writing prior to 1945. This is because in Britain, though not in the United States, all debates over what is and isn't Literature, capital L, keep one thing constant: literature exists in the past. Reference-points can, however, be derived from the literary establishment: reputations are made, competitions and prizes won, the media increasingly intervene and construct literary 'stars' for us. A sense of current writing – the issues, the names, the favourites – is easily enough obtained. For my generation it is the decades just out of living memory that cause problems: the 1940s, 1950s and the 1960s. They have yet to be caught and categorised by history or literary history, and knowledge of them is a confused, imaginistic jumble of remembered public events and atmospheres which are all shot through by intensely important private events. We can think about the 1840s, the 1920s, with a certain degree of detachment, but coming close up to the 1950s or 1960s, the history and our analysis of it has to struggle to take account of private and public events mixed in our own lived experience.

Literary history, at the institutional level, constructs a series of periodisations within its chronology of literary texts. The Romantics, the Victorians, the 1930s – generally non-materialist in conception. History, when it enters into the account at all, does so as the spirit of the age or as a rather nebulous context. The focus is clearly on the text, as an object detached from the social relations of its production and consumption. The advent of a socialist, specifically Marxist, criticism reinstates history as an important category. The materialist conception of writing, in its relation to other social processes and ideas, and the making of literatures and Literature initially served only to reproduce within itself the absence of women and gender concerns. History and culture aren't male, but they often appear to be so. In developing a materialist periodisation of women's writing we need to be very clear about whether we are fitting women into an account structured in patriarchal ways or whether we have located the internal dynamics of women's changing relation to form and content in their writing.

Women's writing can be seen as an internally structured field of relations between writing, publishing, reviewing and reading. This for the moment suspends its relation to dominant literary values and practices, though it is important to note that this implicitly subordinates 'women's writing' to writing. This is materially the case. Writers, of whom Lessing is a key example, who transcend the limits of women's writing, become above their sex: honorary men.

What different kinds of women's writing are possible within a periodisation? Following the success of Elaine Showalter's *A Literature of Their Own*, an assumption has been generated within feminist criticism that women writers consciously position themselves in a unitary tradition of writing. Showalter's dependence on a sub-cultural model of women's writing occludes the relations of resistance, subordination and interdependence which structure the field of writing and the relation of women within and to it. The assertion that all women's writing follows a staged progressive movement from the feminine to the feminist to the female is not, for me, sufficiently complex to account for women's writing.[7] Against Showalter's model, I would argue that the field of women's writing, at any given moment, is composed of different modes of writing. Genre writing – romance, science and detective fiction – has to be thought of as a mode in order that we may see discontinuities and continuities between it and other modes of writing which women inhabit, rather than reproduce the value-laden divisions between popular fiction, the novel and literature. Categories which have been used to subordinate women's writing are recuperable in only limited ways in the formation of new forms and relations of writing. These modes of women's writing are not static and changes within them are differently paced. Thus, for example, we would need to take a longer perspective on the romance mode than we do for the modernist. In order to periodise women's writing we can't approach the dynamic of the field through an account of its internal relation as, at one level, Showalter does. Nor can we do it by a dependence on the isolated figures so beloved of the literary tradition. Autonomous literary individuals do not shift the boundaries of a nation's writing profile. It is possible to see that within the range of modes available to women writers one dominates. Reviewers, publishers, and, to some extent, the authors themselves, consent to a definition of women's writing against which all other women's writing is tested and valued. The nature of the dominant mode's dominance lies in the capacity to define appropriate women's writing. These defining dominant modes of women's writing do change across time and are articulated with a common sense about women's writing that inflects and emphasises, but never questions, aspects of the identification of women's writing with the personal. Finally, as a kind of overarching means to understand the various modes' interrelations, we can map them in relation to romance and realism, taking these as the central generative matrices of women's writing.

To summarise: the field of women's writing has three characteristics. First, all writing stands in relation to romance and/or realism. Second, there is a dominant mode of women's writing which acts as a definer in relation to other women's writing. Third, there is a range of modes operating which stand in an internal relation to each other, over and above the relation given by the dominant mode. The modes of women's writing are defined primarily through the public discourse about them. This discourse includes considerable areas of silence: much women's writing is never publicly spoken about. It provides feminist criticism with a starting-point: the current version of women's relation to literary production as endorsed by the establishment.

We take this starting-point not necessarily to assent to the version of importance and significance it implies – although a social history of reading and readers cannot ignore this public moment – but to use them as a means of appropriating the excluded women's writing of the time. They provide a material route into the processes whereby women's writing is marginalised, validated and valued. A dominant mode of women's writing is defined, usually, through one exponent and involves such matters as the appropriate subject-matter, the method of characterisation, the style and form. For the immediate post-war period, that is roughly 1945–59, we could, from contemporary sources, ascertain that the dominant mode of women's writing was that of sensitivity increasingly superseded by a moral realism: the mode of sensibility. Writers involved in these modes include Rosamund Lehemann (*The Ballad and the Source*), Elizabeth Bowen (*The Death of the Heart*), Rose Macaulay (*This World My Wilderness*), and Elizabeth Taylor (*A View from the Harbour*). Throughout this period, as throughout the twentieth century, there is a bedrock of archetypal women's writing, generally within the romance mode but quite other than mass formulaic romance writing. These novels tend to be long, and the authors prolific. As a mode of writing, it changes on a much longer time-scale than other modes. Pre- and post-war differences do exist, but those between the 1950s, 1960s and the 1970s are slight. These writers and the writing are positioned within a tradition going back to – but much transformed in the twentieth century – the popular novelistic traditions of the nineteenth century. If we consider the relation of this mode of writing to the romance mode we can begin to see a number of differences. One concerns the material level of production: the romance mode exists within an extensive and diversified production and distribution process: paperback and hardback novels, magazine short stories and novellas; in terms of consumption, actual buying and library borrowing are about equal. The archetypal fiction is, on the other hand, mainly published in hardback and distributed and consumed via library borrowing. The major narrative difference is that this mode of writing starts from within marriage, rather than ending with it as the romance mode does. Ordinary situations are preferred to the aristocratic, and the tendency is towards the generation and the family, rather than the couple.

The romance and archetypal modes of women's writing stand, in the 1950s, in direct relation to a third. It is linked to both by the importance it gives to the smooth progression of the narrative and the singling out of a heroine. Where it differs is that its site of action is neither the family nor the couple but the world of paid work outside the home. The romance interest, when it is present at all, is very definitely subordinate. Throughout the 1940s and 1950s, this is the fictional site for a discussion of the impact of the Second World War, a theme absent from most women's writing at this time. Writers who can be considered part of this mode include Honor Tracy, Jane Duncan, Monica Dickens.

The defining mode in the late 1940s and early 1950s within women's writing is the mode of sensitivity. A major defining characteristic of this mode was a 'fine' use of language: the endorsement of a literary language. This contrasts directly with the social realism of pre-war writing where, in writers such as Winifred Holtby, Phyliss Bentley and Stella Benson, women struggled with and towards a language for and of everyday life and experience. A second defining characteristic was the exploration of personal relationships in terms of moral questions. Its writers demonstrated a sensitivity towards and perception about human emotion in the context of personal relationships. The distinctive treatment of personal relationships – which singles it out from the general identification of women's writing with the personal – is that, rather than explore the romance, romantic or passionate dimension of those relationships, these novelists are concerned with questions of morality. Choices and preferences in personal relationships, understood as familial and to involve friendship as well as sex, are cast in moral terms as actions having effects beyond the individual's conscious or unconscious desires. A helpful way of differentiating women's writing is to trace out the continuities between twentieth-century women's writing and that of the nineteenth century. Within this, reference back to George Eliot and the Brontës forms the commonest strand and this mode stands out for its formal connection to the writing of Jane Austen. Its range, in both subject-matter and characterisation, was narrow and, on the whole, it refused the experimental modernist techniques developed in the early twentieth century. This narrowness was seen by some contemporary critics as a limitation, a judgment which had its effects. For example, many of these works are no longer in print, they do not figure very much in general discussions of the novel or post-war fiction, and they are little known to generations of readers who grew up in the 1960s and 1970s. The most typical of these writers is Elizabeth Taylor, but the grouping also includes Isobel English, Elizabeth Jane Howard, Rachel Trickett, Monica Stirling and Barbara Pym.

From the mid–1950s onwards, the dominance of this mode is contested and eventually superseded by the novel of sensibility, which, in its turn, enables the assertion of a moral realism which continues throughout the 1960s. In the same way that romance, common–sense and archetypal modes are differently articulated towards romance (understood as story, happy ending, magical resolution and mystery) so we can see these modes: sensitivity, sensibility and moral realism articulated in relation to realism. The actual writers involved are Elizabeth Bowen, Rose Macaulay, A. L. Barker, Ivy Compton-Burnett, in the mode of sensibility; Pamela Hansford Johnson, Nina Bawden, Olivia Manning, Kay Dick, Gillian Freeman, Penelope Mortimer and, with considerable ambiguity, Doris Lessing in the mode of moral realism.

I want to conclude this discussion on the field of women's writing by briefly indicating the areas upon which we have no purchase through this method of analysis. It doesn't, for example, tell us very much about the genre type popular fiction (excepting romance) which women were writing and publishing at the time: detective, thrillers and science fiction. Another consideration is that in taking the mode to define the period, we find that authors, unfortunately, do not live, write, publish and die in order. Certainly, most periods do give us a strong grouping of writers whom it is useful to discuss as a whole, but this shouldn't lead us to ignore other generational groupings or other ways of differentiating the field. In terms of generational groupings, for example, we have the existence of writers who had published and made their reputations some years before, yet who continue to write and publish during the years where we have drawn our lines: writers publishing at the beginning of the twentieth century, such as Lettice Cooper, Storm Jameson, Anna Kavan, Naomi Mitchison, Ethel Mannin, and Rebecca West; writers who made their reputations and consolidated their writing careers in the periods immediately preceding, such as Daphne Du Maurier, Stella Gibbons, Rumer Godden, Pamela Hansford Johnson, Mary Renault and Margery Sharp. At the other extreme of generational difference we have to take note of writers who publish maybe one or two works in this period, but whose reputations and modes of writing are consolidated later, often forming the generational core of a later mode. In this instance, writers such as Brigid Brophy, Iris Murdoch and Muriel Spark.

The case of Doris Lessing

How does this very schematic account of the organisation of the field of women's writing in post-war England help us to understand the particular place that Doris Lessing had within it? To what extent does it explain her distanced and distancing position *vis-à-vis* women writers?

The main benefit is to emphasise ambiguity, tangential relations to traditions, the native culture and available forms of writing. The ambiguity which marks Doris Lessing's relation to moral realism as a mode of writing is the starting-point. This ambiguity signals areas of difference between herself and other contemporary British women writers.

Her writing career has throughout been marked by a struggle with and over form. *The Golden Notebook* most clearly illustrates the degree to which problems of representation constitute the actual creative impulse for Lessing. But other texts signal, in somewhat more muted ways, the skirmishes with form. Lessing's ability to range easily between forms marks her out in comparison with other contemporary writers whose writing careers consist of settling into and refining one of the formal options open to them. As a general proposition this suggests a comfortable, unproblematic relationship between British women writers and their writing, which is more or less the case.[8] What is more distinctive about Lessing though, is that she continues to *write through* and *write out* her problematisation of form. Other women writers who consciously experience a crisis over representation have, by and large, ceased to write. Tillie Olsen, in her book *Silences*, is eloquent upon this point, a clear example of which can be found in Zoe Fairbairn's account of her relation to writing prior to joining a feminist writers' group and publishing

Benefits.[9] Finally, Lessing has warranted serious critical attention which is in itself and in its nature qualitatively different from the critical response to most other women writers. The nature of Lessing's achievement here and its reception is determined by her entry into the British literary formation.

This began long before she arrived in England and found it full of 'quiet, mad maniacs – behind closed doors'. England came to her, defining her in a colonial relation to the land she lived in. Literary culture came in the form of books from England, reading them an activity to 'counter balance' life in Rhodesia: 'All white-African literature is the literature of exile: not from Europe, but from Africa.'[10] Lessing's arrival in England and subsequent development as a writer is determined by the social consequences of a biography which defined her as a white Southern Rhodesian female communist. There's a problem in that description: where to assign the greater weight? I wanted to put 'woman' first, but couldn't then sustain gender as the primary determinant on her life and writing. Gender determines whether or not you want it to, but there is still a difference between being consciously or unconsciously defined as a woman that affects actions and their explanations. Lessing, a writer and a woman who took very conscious choices about her life, questions any easy identification of herself or her writing with contemporary feminism. I feel, therefore, that I cannot impose that definition on her. During the 1950s it was race: exile from Rhodesia which determined, or at least, which she acknowledged as a primary determinant. Had Lessing continued to live in Rhodesia it is possible that, assuming her relation to feminism continued broadly as it did in England, her communism would have been the key factor organising her relation to ideas and writing. Communism because it was the form most easily available to, the only stance from which to, oppose racism and colonialism. In England, the situation in which racism was appearing was different: an anti-colonial position did not necessarily need to be allied to communism: Lessing's early reputation in England was as a writer concerned with race and the colour bar. Based on the outstanding success of *The Grass is Singing* it was, unusually, consolidated through realist short stories later published in collection form as *The Sun Between Their Feet* and *This Was The Old Chief's Country*, and through documentary writing.

There is something odd in the acceptability of white writers voicing – and being fêted for doing so – an anti-colonial position: a voice denied, even today, to the black. A problem of which Lessing herself is conscious. Perhaps here, unstated though it remains, we can see gender determination at work transforming the political impetus behind the writing about colonialism into a feminine impulse of concern about suffering.

Gender, however, also operates in Lessing's favour. She encountered the literary establishment as a woman but also as a 'foreigner'. The signalling of difference and the consequent code of appropriate behaviour to her *as woman*, was inflected in a way it never can be for women of the native literary culture. Not only are women writers situated and perceived in subordinate relations by the dominant literary establishment, they also situate themselves within it: it's a two-way, collusive process. Lessing cuts across this in much the same way that Sylvia Plath did. Arguably, it is no accident that the only two women Britain contemporarily acknowledges as artists of classic stature – producers of Literature, capital L – both experience(d) exile from their countries of origin and birth. They enter into a critical relation with the dominant culture that later valorises them.[11]

Published women writers, until very recently, came predominantly from the professional and upper middle class. To that extent, they share obvious interests with the literary establishment. However, as women, there is an equally obvious dysjunction: a perception of distance between themselves and the dominant culture: culture which is normatively, though not essentially, male. Until, as is beginning to happen, women as writers, and in society generally, assert their collective interests against this status quo, it remained impossible for individual women to articulate a generalising voice of opposition. There are two reasons for this. First, for women, to be socialised into patriarchy is to be socialised into complicity with a system of power, control and definition. Second, the nature of the perceived difference historically involved division into the public and the private as spheres of influence and location. Women, even in speaking of the public, do so from the private – that small personal voice which is defined as other than a serious critique. Because of the subordinate position they occupy within culture, women generally have not assumed positions of confrontation.

Lessing, because she came to British literary culture via an extreme encounter with it: that of the colonial experience, is sufficiently knowledgeable of, and sufficiently distant from, it to be able to comment – as was outlined. The particular social facts of her biography ensure that she will. Perceived by the literary establishment as woman, but not, perhaps, as a 'real' woman, the codes of chivalry or patronising belittlement of women's literary production become inappropriate, given the absence of a culturally recognisable femininity.

One of the conditions of exile for Lessing as a writer was a self-consciousness about form and a sense of strangeness in the content of her writing, both of which derive from her peculiar mix of knowledge and unease about British literary culture. That this is their great achievement is not in question. What I question about the constructed figure of Doris Lessing is the comparison drawn between her and other women writers. She is, in a very insidious way, a token woman for the literary establishment, used to police its standards and mask their conditions of existence. I am not elaborating exile as a key to this process, as psychological atmosphere, translating it into fictional terms as a source of artistic inspiration. Her African writing's relation to British culture operates both within a 'Novels of Empire' tradition and as a critique of it. Lessing, particularly at the height of her acclaim as an African writer, showed herself to be very conscious of the place of white African writing in the British literary institutions. Africa was a starting-point in her writing, but one that could not continue. In later writings, its importance becomes problematic and it constitutes a shifting focus. But the irony of her condition of exile is sustained.

The African short stories, particularly in her later prefaces, evidence an obvious link between Africa and her writing. But they are not the only point of engagement: the documentary accounts *In Pursuit of the English* and *Going Home* are one form it takes; the *Children of Violence* series and the black notebook in *The Golden Notebook*, another. Finally, in *Canopus in Argos: Archives*, colonisation is a subject write large – the African experience becomes a mirror for the universe:

> an exile ever afterwards from an inexplicable majestic silence
> lying just over the border of memory or of thought. Africa

gives you the knowledge that man is a small creature, amongst other creatures, in a large landscape. [12]

But Africa was, for Lessing, also the source of a quite different knowledge: a knowledge of politics that contributes to the tension in her writing between the urge to describe and to delineate, the political faith in social realism, and the urge to question this faith, the speculative stance that finds its formal outlet in the Utopian and dystopian modes. And that constant feature of Lessing's narratives: the split, unstable, unreliable narrative voice. Only in the African stories is the narrative persona fully consonant with the authorial and unobtrusively present: reporting, describing and commenting. Even when, as in 'The Old Chief Mshlanga', there is a play with the narrative as it shifts from 'she' to 'I' this only confirms the realism of the story, securing, rather than disturbing it. Further, here the processes of recognition and identification between the author and the authored appear powerful:

> This child could not see a mbaba tree, or the thorn, for what they were. Her books held tales of alien fauna, her rivers ran slow and peaceful, and she knew the shape of the leaves of an ash or an oak, the name of the little creatures that lived in English streams . . . for many years, it was the veld that seemed unreal. The sun was a foreign sun and the wind spoke a strange language. [13]

Conclusion

Lessing's writing career was forged through Africa. Not only in terms of a professional reputation which enabled her to make a living as a writer, but in the very act of writing itself. The problems of what to represent and how, which increasingly come to dominate Lessing's fictions, are arguably grounded in the problem of how, as a white settler, to represent the relation of oppression: the internal and external dimensions of her situation as exile, both within and when distant from 'her' country.

The unreliability of the narrator, a symptom of unease about the process of writing itself, reaches its final stages in the *Canopus in Argos* series. [14] It would be too easy to see the series as a logical, progressive stage in Lessing's development. It does, after all, rehearse the dominant concerns of her fictional writing: how societies operate efficiently and inefficiently; whether they have an internalised destructive cycle; how sexual and emotional relationships are to be worked at and through – what they mean; how an individual identity is forged through social interaction, yet retains an inner, separate core; the degree to which writing – as a made thing – re-presents, interprets and selects reality; the concern with cross-cultural experience. Furthermore, it presents a panoramic, totalising scene. It is, as *Children of Violence* before it, very largely conceived, totally inclusive. Lessing is loath to leave things out. But, if we avoid the teleological trap, how do we begin to account for this series, situate it in relation to her other work, her place within literary culture? Lessing takes up the Utopian or science fiction mode as a means to establish a critical relation to, and thus be in part a solution to the problem of, the realist novel. To this extent it is part of a general re-evaluating of that mode by women writers, especially those with some explicit commitment to feminist politics. Lessing shares a common project with writers such as Marge Piercy, Monique Wittig, Zoe Fairbairns, Joanna Russ and Ursula Le Guin. It is a project succinctly outlined by Joanna Russ who, in an essay entitled 'What Can A Heroine Do – Or Why Women Can't Write',[15] pinpoints the problem for women writers as that of their inability to create characters and fictional situations which break with

> innumerable variants on FALLING IN LOVE, on courtship, on marriage, on the failure of courtship and marriage. HOW SHE GOT MARRIED. HOW SHE DID NOT GET MARRIED (always tragic) HOW SHE FELL IN LOVE AND COMMITTED ADULTERY. HOW SHE SAVED HER MARRIAGE BUT JUST BARELY. HOW SHE LOVED A VILE SEDUCER AND ELOPED. HOW SHE LOVED A VILE SEDUCER ELOPED AND DIED IN CHILDBIRTH.

With the exception of three types of writing – detective, science fiction and Gothic – women can only break with the above by writing 'How she went crazy'. More recently, we might add 'How she became a feminist' as an alternative to death in childbirth.

But, just as Lessing's entry into British literary culture and the whole history of her relation to the realist novel is slightly skewed, so, too, is her relation to this cultural conjunction around women's writing and Utopian modes. Joanna Russ provides a starting-point for rethinking whole areas of women's writing – detective fiction in the 1920s and 1930s, science fiction from the mid-1970s onwards. It becomes possible to see how the form, superficially rule-bound and closed, enables degrees of freedom with regard to content which are not available to women within the mainstream modes. Raymond Williams, in his essay 'Utopia and Science Fiction', situates the Utopian mode within a political culture generally, and, although he doesn't recognise them as such or address himself to the area, puts on the agenda a set of questions and observations that link the development of a feminist culture, contemporary women's writing and the politics of cultural practice. He makes an important distinction between heuristic and systematic modes. The former: 'offers a strength of vision against the prevailing grain; the systematic utopia a strength of conviction that the world really can be different.'[16]

He understands the crucial contemporary question as concerning the impulse towards dystopias in Utopian writing. The absence of dystopic impulses within women's Utopian writing suggests something of the relative health of socialist and feminist culture. All of which is very useful when thinking about Marge Piercy or Zoe Fairbairns, but when we bring Doris Lessing's Utopia into line with these critical observations we find her way of inhabiting the mode is singular. Her concerns are with the sacred, the all-embracing, fundamental conditions of humanity. At one level, she does totalise a set of relations around colonialism, race, class oppression, familial patterns – but she almost wilfully refuses to take responsibility for that.

> If I have created a cosmology, then it is only for literary purposes! Once upon a time when I was young, I believed things easily, both religious and political; now I believe less and less but I wonder about more . . .
>
> Why is it that writers who by definition operate by the use of their imaginations, are given so little credit for it? We 'make things up'! This is our trade.[17]

This refusal of meaning or significance to fiction sits strangely with the constant repetition in *Canopus in Argos* of the importance of story and song as a means of knowledge and instruction.

Three years earlier, in a preface to *Shikasta*, the first in the *Canopus in Argos* series, Lessing had described her latest work as sociological space fiction. She had also then been prepared to acknowledge such writing as commentary on life:

> These dazzlers have mapped our world, or worlds, for us, have told us what is going on and in ways no one else has done . . . played the indispensable and (at least at the start) thankless role of the despised illegitimate son who can afford to tell truths the respectable siblings either do not dare or, more likely, do not notice because of their respectability.[18]

Here the distance from the received and taken for granted is marked and echoes back along her writing career. Lessing has always noticed and, in her way, told truths silenced in the legitimate daughters of the British literary tradition.

Notes

1 Mary Ellmann, *Thinking about Women*, Harcourt Brace, New York, 1968, p. 13.
2 Coventry Patmore, 'The Social Position of Women', *North British Review*, 1850. Quoted in Elaine Showalter, *A Literature of their Own*, Virago, London, 1978.
3 Patricia Meyer Spacks, *The Female Imagination*, Allen & Unwin, London, 1976.
4 Simone de Beauvoir, *The Second Sex*, Penguin, London, 1972, p. 718.
5 See, for example, Mayor Jacobus (ed.), *Women Writing and Writing about Women*, Croom Helm, London, 1978.
6 Shirley Ardener, 'The Nature of Women in Soceity', in *Defining Females*, Croom Helm, London, 1978.
7 My treatment of Elaine Showalter's work here is very brief, which may appear as dismissive. Although I do have major disagreements with her work, I also recognise and appreciate the major contribution to feminist criticism which it represents.
8 Experimentation with and across forms has become a feature of women's writing in the 1970s. Arguably, this is under the impact of feminism.
9 Zoe Fairbairn, 'Playing with Words', *Spare Rib*, 97, August 1980, pp. 24–6.
10 Doris Lessing, 'The Lost World of the Kalahari', *New Statesman*, vol. 56, no. 1444, 15 November 1958, p. 700.
11 Terry Eagleton, *Exiles and Emigres* (Chatto & Windus, London, 1974, p. 18) contains a more detailed analysis of this process.
12 Doris Lessing, *African Stories*, Michael Joseph, London, 1973, p. 8.

13 Doris Lessing, *This Was the Old Chief's Country*, Michael Joseph, London, 1973, p. 11.
14 Doris Lessing, *Re-Colonised Planet 5: Shikasta*, Michael Joseph, London, 1979, *The Marriages Between Zones Three, Four and Five*, Michael Joseph, London, 1980, *The Sirian Experiments*, Michael Joseph, London, 1981.
15 Joanna Russ, 'What Can a Heroine Do – Or Why Women Can't Write', in Suan Cornillon Koppleman (ed.), *Images of Women in Fiction*, Bowling Green Press, Ohio, 1972.
16 Raymond Williams, *Problems in Materialism and Culture*, New Left Books, London, 1980, p. 203.
17 Doris Lessing, *The Sirian Experiments*, preface.
18 Doris Lessing, *Shikasta*, preface.

9 *Memoirs* was made of this:

an interview with David Gladwell, director of *Memoirs of a Survivor*

Jenny Taylor

Doris Lessing's fantasy, *The Memoirs of a Survivor*, has recently been made into a film, directed by David Gladwell and partly sponsored by the National Film Finance Corporation. Described by Doris Lessing as 'an attempt at an autobiography', the novel combines different forms of fantasy or fabulation. Most clearly it is a dystopia – a piece of future fiction which presents a recognisable though transformed world, a world in a state of cultural and social decline following an unexplained catastrophe. The central figure, the unnamed narrator, acts as a link with the reader, describing the attempts of the young gang leader, Gerald, and Emily, the abandoned child consigned to her care, to rebuild functioning social relationships in the face of the collapse of social rules, communication systems and, eventually, the breakdown of language. The narrative opens with a meditation on the workings of the memoir itself: 'we – everyone – will look back over a period in life, over a sequence of events, and find much more than they did at the time. . . At any rate, the past, looked back on in this frame of mind, seems steeped in a substance that was foreign to it, was extraneous to the making of it,' and this self-consciousness about the status of language and narration persists through the novel. The narrator constructs alternative visionary worlds – both mythic and individual – in exploring scenes of Emily's infancy, which open up behind the wall of her flat, and into which the real world finally dissolves through both a willed and a magical transformation.

This shifting between different forms of fantasy is crucial to the way that *The Memoirs of a Survivor* works as a literary text. How might these different processes translate into the visual language of film? What material possibilities and constraints are involved? This interview concentrates not only on the texts themselves, and questions of the relationship between verbal and visual language, but also the broader cultural and economic factors that helped to shape this film: the language, narrative and cultural position of the novel itself; the different power structures in the British and American film industries; the detailed practical problems of production; the difficulties of developing more experimental editing techniques within the parameters of contemporary British and American cinema.

JT   What first gave you the idea to make a film of *The Memoirs of a Survivor*?

DG   Actually I was working on something of my own. When I start thinking about a film, I think about it primarily in visual terms, what I think would look good on the screen. I'm an editor, so I am constantly receiving a wealth of different material from all sorts of different people's films. This can't help but give one all sorts of ideas, because you're always having to stop frames and run backwards and forwards and fast and slow. You become very aware of the possibilities of different sorts of images used in different sorts of ways. So ideas for films for me don't come as stories usually, but as visions, as chunks of action that I would like as an editor to be presented with. So that's how it starts. I was writing fragments of ideas for a film. In fact what I was working on included something of a crib from another book, Henri Babousse's *Hell*. That's a story of a man who looks through the hole in the wall and sees the whole gamut of human life in the room beyond, and becomes obsessed with it. I was using this as a starting-point for developing a similar idea through film. Anyway, I was writing all these ideas down and my wife happened to see them. She had just read *Memoirs* and she said I ought to read that, which I did. Although there wasn't much similarity in the narratives, apart from the motif of the wall, I was really drawn into the book and thought here was something which would make a very interesting film. It wasn't just the explicit fantasy element that interested me, but the whole diversity of images which I thought could be juxtaposed through montage in a surrealist way. And also its kaleidoscopic range, the way it combines personal and political history.

JT What was the next stage in getting the script written, organising funding, and so on?

DG I've never written a script for a large film before, only documentaries or semi-documentaries, so I thought I'd try and find out for myself how it could be made into a film, whether it could, what sort of shape it would take just at the beginning. So I went through the book and wrote the script, a script straight from the book which was the first version, the only dialogue here was dialogue taken directly from the book. There's a lot of dialogue in the book, and this translates into dramatic dialogue very well.

JT How did you deal with the persona of the narrator there, did you have a voice-over effect?

DG Yes. I had a voice-over narrator, but that's been an area of contention. One of the sponsors of the film is the National Film Finance Corporation which has a very lively and involved chairperson, who is a film-maker. He was very strongly against the voice-over technique and he holds the view that direct narration is not suitable for film, that it's using a different sort of language that is not suitable for film language. That is a view that I don't share. I can think of lots of good films that aren't 'literary' in the bad sense that use direct narration, it can be essential. One of my favourite films is *Hiroshima Mon Amour*, which is based on direct narration. But he won in the end. In fact, the script which finally emerged actually did not need narration though this did not become clear beyond doubt until the film was almost complete. The NFFC had committed themselves to half the budget or rather half the budget of which they said the film must not exceed. That is, they would say if the film cost more than this, it is no longer a valid proposition for us to invest in. So there was a top figure above which we were not able to go.

JT What sort of film did they envisage it being, what would

it compare with in terms of funding and publicity? Would it be a major feature film?

DG Yes. They saw it as a relatively large-scale, but fairly small-budget feature film. The previous film they'd sponsored was *Babylon* which had a smaller budget, but which was completely different in style and far less complex. Anyway, we had half the money and then sources were sought all over the place for the rest of the money, largely in America. It was thought that it would probably be from some private funding in America, neither the producer nor the NFFC thought that it would be funded by one of the major American distributors. In fact, it's not the sort of thing they'd go for and we were turned down by lots of them, even by EMI – in fact twice by EMI at an early stage.

JT That quite surprises me because one of the problems I find with *The Memoirs of a Survivor* is that it can easily be read as a book that sensationalises violence, shows a society that has fallen into a state of degeneration and decay in an almost social Darwinian way, particularly as in the scenes of the children from the underground. That's one of the ways that perhaps it could be seen in terms of translation into a film. Those are my political reservations about it as a book, in any case, that it could be compared with *The Lord of the Flies*, a story about a society's inevitable relapse into barbarism. Obviously, that's a simplification, but on one reading it can be seen to do that. Do you know what I mean?

DG Yes. That would be the appeal for some people, I suppose. And if it had been presented like that, it would, as you say, have got support from some big American companies. But when you go to these big American companies, you don't go and say, 'Look, here's the book that we want to make a film of, go and read it,' because they don't read books. You just have a very brief outline, a suggestion for the shape of the film. And it is the way that that is written which shows the sort of film it is intended to be. There wasn't a strong emphasis on that 'degeneration' aspect of it in the outline, and in fact as the film's turned out, I think there is too little of the portrayal

of the outside world, of how it works, or of how it
doesn't work. It's very much just a background that's
hinted at.

JT But it's very central in the book, isn't it? And that's why I
think the narrator is so important, to act as a link between
what's going on outside and the reader, as well as giving
some sense of the different codes by which people live
their lives: what people regard as 'normal' and what isn't.
That has to be done very carefully, I think, for it not to be
seen just as some old lady looking out of the window at
everything disintegrating around her. But to return to
the problems of production, how did the script
eventually go through and how did you choose the set,
and so on?

DG One of the first things was to decide on somebody to play
the narrator, D, as we called her. It became clear very
early on it would have to be some sort of a star because
people in film finance business had never heard of Doris
Lessing and certainly hadn't heard of me. There was the
slight help of having Michael Medwin as the producer
and Memorial Films as the production company because
they have quite a good track record. They had produced
Lindsay Anderson's films, *If* and *Oh Lucky Man* and
Gumshoe and *Charlie Bubbles* – the best British films over
the past ten years, or so. But that wasn't a great asset, it
was just a small asset. So it was obvious that a star would
be the asset. I had seen the narrator definitely as an older
woman, middle fifties really, the first person that came to
mind as a possibility, who I thought would be valuable in
all respects was Ingrid Bergman, and I talked to her about
it. That must be three years ago now. She had just said
categorically that she wasn't going to do any more films,
she had just done a film – Ingmar Bergman's film *Autumn
Sonata* and that was going to be the climax of her career,
because there weren't any reasonable parts for women –
for older women that is – apart from somebody's mother
or somebody's grandmother. Anyway, I persuaded her
that she might be interested in it, and it was left that I
would let her have a script as soon as there was one and
that she would seriously consider it. But then things

were held up, and there wasn't a script for several months after that, and, by the time there was one, I was told that Ingrid Bergman was very ill and wasn't going to be taking on any more film parts. And then I thought of Jeanne Moreau. I couldn't think of a British actress who would be seen as attracting the kind of box office success in America, which is what the American backers ask for financing films, and American finance is all there is around, really, at the moment. I went to see Jeanne Moreau and she was very interested, very keen, she turned out to be a Doris Lessing fan; but then I discovered that we couldn't raise money on Jeanne Moreau because they weren't interested in Jeanne Moreau in America. Then Mamoon Hassan of the NFFC, which by then was fully supporting the project, had heard that Julie Christie was interested in doing something, preferably British, preferably not a blockbuster, but something that she considered was worth while. But she wouldn't consider a film of any new director without knowing his work or seeing his work. So I showed her a film of mine called *Requiem for a Village*, which is a semi-documentary and had been sponsored by a grant from the British Film Institute. Luckily, Julie liked it and agreed to read the script of *Memoirs*, and agreed to do it. And it was with her that we renewed our efforts for sponsorship in America from various sources and in Scandinavia and France as well. But things just fell through financially for various reasons. We didn't try Germany, perhaps we should have done. I know that Germany was investing in the *Grass is Singing* at the time, but that was something to do with an African interest.

Incidentally I should say that it was on the strength of Doris Lessing liking *Requiem for a Village* so much that I got a free hand and a free option on *The Memoirs of a Survivor*. She's been very supportive all along, but she specifically didn't want to be involved herself in the screenplay. Having decided that I was to do it, she wanted me to do it completely without her. She's been very interested in the film's progress and came to some of the shooting. She hasn't seen the results yet, and I'm very apprehensive about showing her. She was quite right about not getting involved, of course – it couldn't have worked without her having to throw up everything and getting involved in what writing for film really meant, and at this time she was deeply immersed in the *Canopus in Argos* series.

JT   So to return to the funding and setting up *Memoirs*, what role did Julie Christie need to play in getting promotion and backing?

DG   Well there was more interest in the project from potential financers with her involved, but it still didn't come to anything for ages. We had contacts in California and the West Coast and all over, trying to raise finance from various sources, and it was getting late in the summer and I knew that it had to happen then, because I didn't want us to have to start shooting in the winter. Filming is a very seasonal thing. One is at the mercy of the weather. It is in fact easier to fake the winter in the summer than the summer in the winter. And then there is the problem of the short daylight hours and the cold, and so on. It was really getting late. I was about to go back to editing, thinking it would have to be next year now, but then the NFFC said they couldn't guarantee financing it the next year. Costs were likely to go up, the budget would have to be raised. That meant everything that had seemed to be settled was thrown into the melting-pot again. Then suddenly EMI agreed to support it, but by now we couldn't possibly shoot until the middle of October. That was almost the worst possible time and we had absolute minimum time for preparation because you can't really start to prepare a film until it's absolutely got the go-ahead. Until *all* the money is made available, none of the money is made available. We couldn't even get the art director involved, or get down to casting until we knew that we had got the go-ahead from EMI because nobody was willing, or in a position, to put speculative money into it. So, because it was so late, everything had to be done so quickly and we decided that the maximum preparation time had to be six weeks, but that turned out to be terribly inadequate. Nearly all of the six weeks was taken up for me with casting for Emily, while there were so many other things I should have been doing.

JT   Why did it take so long?

DG   Well, we decided that it was very important to get the right girl, we had girls ranging from real 14 to real 26. You know she's got to start off as a young girl of 14, and yet in the end has to develop an incredible maturity, if not in years, then in experience, so it was a terribly difficult part for anyone. We eventually whittled the choice down to eight and did a screen text. (The remainder of the casting, thanks to a good casting director, was less of a problem.)

Leoni Mellinger, the girl eventually chosen, was somebody that I had had in mind from very early on, but she had been working on *Sons and Lovers* for the BBC, and I had thought she wouldn't be available, but by the time we were finally ready to start filming she'd finished the BBC work. Emily was a particularly difficult part to play. As you know, she is supposed to change and develop in character throughout the story, but for various reasons it was necessary to film completely out of sequence, so the actress had to keep flitting from one stage of development to the next, which must have been incredibly difficult.

JT   How did you cast the children and the gangs and the other extras?

DG   The children from the orphanage and the underground children all came from Anna Sherr, who's a woman who runs amateur drama classes in Islington for local children. But she's become so successful that her children are always in demand for professional jobs. So she's had to become an agency as well. They're not kids who want to take up drama as a profession, it's not the sort of school where mums decide they want their children to go on the stage, and therefore send them there. They go because they enjoy it, it's like a youth club, so that was the obvious place to go for the children, a whole range of them, from very young, from 6 to 16, and all very keen.

JT   And what about the other crowds?

DG   The crowd scenes as such, that is the people passing

through, going past the flat where the narrator lives? Well, if you film anywhere near London it's an obligation, a Union obligation that is, to use crowd artists, crowd union members.

JT   You mean people who specialise in being a crowd?

DG   Yes. You have to dress them how you want them dressed and provide the props and everything. It's a vast expense, crowd scenes, we couldn't possibly have afforded that, so we had to go sixty miles outside London, beyond the range of the Union requirement – where real people can be used as 'extras'. I knew there were suitable crowds to be found in Norwich, because I had made *Requiem for a Village* in Suffolk, and I knew what sort of people would be available and how to contact them. They are people who come together every summer for fairs in that part of the country. A lot of them are travelling people, and I knew that it would be possible to get them together to be the crowds. And not only would be the people be there, but also they would more or less look right, and they could bring animals and chattles quite easily. It would be very difficult to get animals in London, and carts and wagons and things.

JT   But how could that be reconciled with the fact that it's all supposed to happen in the middle of the city?

DG   Well, I looked for a city in East Anglia which would have a suitable tower block, and eventually found a place in Norwich. In fact, the best place would probably have been Ipswich, but I would never have got permission to close the road – as you know it's supposed to be by a main road out of the city, but at a time when motor traffic has become obsolete – and this would have been impossible in Ipswich because the road was a trunk road. But in Norwich I found a tall apartment block very near the centre of Norwich, on a by-road out of the city, not the main road. And found that I could get permission to have it closed for a week.

JT   How did you get that general sense of complete dereliction as in the episodes where people gather news for instance? One gets this general sense of lots of forages being made to disused shops, although it's always described, as it were, off-stage in the book. How did you achieve that?

DG I think that was the most difficult. I don't think we succeeded very well in the look of the outside world – it's played down in the film more than I would have liked. It was partly the time of year, there only being a short number of daylight hours available, and, partly, having to make every place that we went completely free of cars, but at the same time very urban and in a state of total dereliction, with lots of litter and garbage and so on. It wasn't just moving traffic, it was also parked cars – imagine finding somewhere in London completely free of parked cars! We could park our own wrecks there. All the scenes were very brief, it wasn't as if one could go to a place and stay there for a couple of days and get it exactly as you wanted it, you might just be there for half a day and we'd have to make that area, which had to be as broad as possible to make it believable, make it look a mess. We mainly used paper, and there was a lot of wind about when we were filming, so it blew all over whichever borough it was. The borough had given us permission originally, but when we had finished they invariably said never again because they had been getting telephone calls and complaints from all over the place. We didn't have rubbish that would stay only in the location we wanted to film it in.

JT If we could concentrate for a moment on the problems of filming the outside world and then contrast that with the internal scenes, through the wall, and so on. How did you get across that sense that's very strongly present in the book that there are authorities there, but that they're absent and irrational, and somehow out of control, and which is reflected through the narrator herself trying to understand and assimilate what's going on in her own mind, but which in the novel is closely linked with problems of language.

DG I'm not really sure whether it's there or not in the film. I'm very disappointed if it's not, but it's only someone like you who could answer that when they see the film. I'm disappointed in the way I think it wasn't possible to do it properly – to undercut the codes of realism.

JT   But how would it have been done if you think it had been done properly? How would you translate that attempt to break with realism into film language?

DG   I think the film could have been much more fragmentary even than it is. It already is fragmentary, but it's very difficult to translate the essentially inferential relationship between the narrative voice and the reader that you get in the book into film which is inevitably much more specifically located and referring to particular scenes and places. I wanted the film to be much more impressionistic, but, unfortunately, that did not seem to be possible given the constraints we were working with. I would have liked the film to have been much more experimental, using montage and juxtapositioning of shots much more freely, to break with realism.

JT   Yes, because the way you have described it does make the film sound as though it's very much coded within particular conventions of film realism, even naturalism, so that people will recognise quite clearly what they see and relate it to aspects of experience they already know, about urban decay, and so on.

DG   Yes, in order to do what I would have ideally liked to have done, I would probably have had to have been more self-confident than I was. As it is, it is rather unusual for a normal feature film in the juxtapositioning of scenes of fantasy and reality, so it would have been another drastic step to split up in a more impressionistic way the scenes that are there. So I settled, for accepting that there were these strange juxtapositions all the way through and getting those to work, but within each scene it's very conventional.

JT   Yet there certainly is such a surrealist tradition in European cinema, isn't there? Do you think it's more difficult in the context of British cinema and working with American funding to work in this way, working within a particular market and within a particular set of constraints? Would one also need to be much more experienced and have much more kudos as a director, because obviously such a film would cost far more?

DG I think so, and it was really on the bare minimum of schedule, you really had a job to get everything done even straightforwardly, to do anything different would have been quite impossible in that schedule, it needs so much more thought as you go along, there's so much more involved really. I think it's almost impossible to make a film directly from a book – to do justice to the book. I should imagine that people who know *The Memoirs of a Survivor* well as a book may be disappointed in the film. I wonder whether there's much point in making a film of a book really, unless you have got something specific and different to say to make out of the text, to use it as a resource.

JT How did you achieve that sense of ambiguity between the fantasy being the narrator's own projections and her actually being seen to participate in the world that's seen through the wall in the film?

DG I think that works quite well, the bits through the wall, you actually see the narrator step through, there's very little voice-over narration there, except at the very beginning, it's not explained at all.

JT How is that shot in terms of camera angles? Is the spectator positioned in the same way as the narrator? Is it shot through her point of view? Or is she portrayed as a figure in the scene? In the book, certainly, because everything is structured by the narrator, one imagines her simply as a perceiver, as an unseen presence, rather than as a participant.

DG There are, of course, different aspects of through the wall, aren't there? The first one is the state you mention, which is in various states of disrepair, and she's walking along corridors and looking in rooms – well, inevitably she's seen walking around the corridors and looking in the rooms. Secondly, there are the Victorian scenes. The way I'd always scripted it is that one would just see a hand pushing open a door and from there on we don't see her in those scenes at all, just more or less her eye-view of what happens. I stuck to that really, except I did feel the necessity to see her standing at the door just watching at times.

JT   Yes, but you also get that very strong identification with the girl child don't you?

DG   Yes, well the emphasis is on little Emily in those scenes.

JT   How did you film the end?

DG   Well we left out the final moment of revelation that's in the book, although the climax of the film is a simplified version of it. After that, we have the scene where Emily and then Gerald and the children go through the wall, and finally the narrator turns and follows them. Then the wall closes up behind and the sunlight fades and it becomes an ordinary wall. And that's the end. The audience stays this side of the wall, which means that I'm not involved with that last page of the book at all, which is rather like the end of *2001*.

JT   What about the editing stage, what were the problems involved in the editing process, what had to be left out, for example?

DG   Actually, some got edited out during the shooting, when things began to get out of hand schedule-wise, and scenes just had to be dropped. The overly symbolic scene of the carpet is a case in point, it had to be left out, and could be because it was not essential to the narrative.

Emily in the provocative red dress is another such scene. But this *is* in the film. One scene I think we underplayed a bit is the one through the wall where the narrator goes into a room and finds it in order, then goes into another and then returns to find the first room in complete chaos and she is desperately trying to put it to rights. In the film it's really just her picking up things that have fallen down, whereas in the book, one feels that there's this real malevolent force creating, disrupting, the order which the narrator is desperately trying really to get to grips with – there's real squalor, there's dead bodies and offal and all sorts of things in there. We didn't get into all that, we were filming in a stately home, so we were limited in the mess we could make; partly in the time, because it was very expensive to film there; and also we had to be able to leave it exactly as we had found it – so all that got rather diluted. It is a pity.

JT What else?

DG I think the underground children are a bit disappointing probably, they work as a symbol, but they're not as realistic as perhaps they should have been, I'm not sure that they're convincing, but I don't think any of the real world is convincing, perhaps because it's too literal, and our resources weren't quite up to it. I don't know that we got all the stages and metamorphoses that Emily goes through, either – particularly in the middle area where adolescence is represented.

JT Finally, did you feel at all that having both of the women as such striking 'star' figures you were in a sense caught in familiar traps of the representation of women?

DG Well, considering how beautiful they are, I don't think it is too voyeuristic, no. Well, you would have to say more than I can, of course. I don't think it's as bad as it might have been in that respect. But then, neither Julie nor Leoni were concerned to present 'glamorous' images. They were too involved and interested in the story.

Select bibliography of Lessing criticism

Over the last ten years there has been a burgeoning of Lessing criticism, above all in the United States. This bibliography is extremely selective and is confined to English language criticism. For comprehensive coverage of primary and secondary sources, see Dee Seligman, *Doris Lessing: An Annotated Bibliography of Criticism*. Westport, Greenwood Press, 1980.

Books

Brewster, Dorothy, *Doris Lessing*, Twayne's English Authors Series, New York, Twayne, 1965.

Gindin, James, *Post War British Fiction; New Accents and Attitudes*, Berkeley, University of California Press, 1962.

Kaplan, Sydney Janet, *Feminine Consciousness in the Modern British Novel*, Champaign, University of Illinois Press, 1975.

Morris, Robert K., *Continuance and Change: The Contemporary British Novel Sequence* Carbondale, Southern Illinois University Press, 1972.

Rubenstein, Roberta, *The Novelistic Vision of Doris Lessing*, Champaign, University of Illinois Press, 1979.

Schlueter, Paul, *The Novels of Doris Lessing*, Carbondale, Southern Illinois University Press, 1973.

Showalter, Elaine, *A Literature of Their Own, British Women Novelists from Brontë to Lessing*, London, Virago, 1978.

Singleton, Mary Ann, *The City and the Veld: The Fiction of Doris Lessing*, Lewisburg, Bucknell University Press, 1977.

Spacks, Patricia Meyer, *Contemporary Women Novelists*, Englewood Cliffs, New Jersey, Prentice-Hall, 1977.

Thorpe, Michael, *Doris Lessing's Africa*. London, Evans, 1978.

Published essays and articles

Barnouw, Dagmar, 'Disorderly Company: from *The Golden Notebook* to *The Four Gated City*', in Annis Pratt and L. S. Dembo (eds), *Doris*

Lessing: Critical Studies, Madison, University of Wisconsin Press, 1974.
(Article first appeared in *Contemporary Literature*, 14, autumn 1973, pp.
148–64.)

Bazin, Nancy Topping, 'The Moment of Revelation in *Martha Quest* and
Comparable Moments by Two Modernists', *Modern Fiction Studies*,
26, spring 1980, pp. 87–98.

Berets, Ralph, 'A Jungian Interpretation of the Dream Sequence in Doris
Lessing's *The Summer Before the Dark*', *Modern Fiction Studies*, 26, spring
1980, pp. 117–29.

Bolling, Douglas, 'Structure and Theme in *Briefing for a Descent into Hell*',
in Pratt and Dembo, *Doris Lessing: Critical Studies*, pp. 147–53.

Butcher, Margaret K., ' "Two Forks of a Road". Divergence and
Convergence in the Short Stories of Doris Lessing', *Modern Fiction
Studies*, 26, spring 1980, pp. 55–61.

Carey, John L., 'Art and Reality in *The Golden Notebook*', in Pratt and
Dembo, *Doris Lessing: Critical Studies*, pp. 20–39.

Cohen, Mary, ' "Out of the Chaos a New Kind of Strength": Doris
Lessing's *The Golden Notebook*', in Arlyn Diamond and Lee Edwards
(eds), *The Authority of Experience. Essays in Feminist Criticism*, Amherst,
University of Massachussetts Press, 1977, pp. 178–93.

Draine, Betsy, 'Changing Frames: Doris Lessing's *Memoirs of a Survivor*',
Studies in the Novel, 11, spring 1979, pp. 51–62.

Draine, Betsy, 'Nostalgia and Irony: the Postmodern Order of
The Golden Notebook', *Modern Fiction Studies*, 26, spring 1980, pp.
31–48.

Duyfhuizen, Bernard, 'On the Writing of Future-History: Beginning the
Ending of Doris Lessing's *Memoirs of a Survivor*', *Modern Fiction Studies*,
26, spring 1980, pp. 147–52.

Eder, Doris L., 'Doris Lessing's *Briefing for a Descent into Hell*: the Writer's
Consciousness Confronts Apocalypse', *Modern British Literature*, 2,
spring 1977, pp. 98–115.

Genver, Elizabeth, 'Women Revolutionaries in the Novels of Nadine
Gordimer and Doris Lessing', *World Literature Written in English*, 17,
April 1978, pp. 38–50.

Hinz, Evelyn J., and John J. Tennissen, 'The Pieta as Icon in *The Golden
Notebook*', in Pratt and Dembo, *Doris Lessing: Critical Studies*, pp.
40–53.

Howe, Florence, 'A Conversation with Doris Lessing', in Pratt and
Dembo, *Doris Lessing: Critical Studies*, pp. 1–19.

Kaplan, Sydney Janet, 'The Limits of Consciousness in the Novels of
Doris Lessing', in Pratt and Dembo, *Doris Lessing: Critical Studies*, pp.
119–32.

Karl, Frederick, 'The Four-Gaited Beast of the Apocalypse: Doris
Lessing's *The Four-Gated City*', in Robert K. Morris (ed.), *Old Lines,
New Forces, Essays on the Contemporary British Novel 1960–1970*,
London, Associated University Press, 1976, pp. 181–99.

Lessing, Doris, 'On *The Golden Notebook*', *Partisan Review*, 40, winter
1973, pp. 14–30.

Magie, Michael, 'Doris Lessing and Romanticism', *College English*, 38, February 1977, pp. 531–52.

Marder, Herbert, 'The Paradox of Form in *The Golden Notebook*', *Modern Fiction Studies*, 26, spring 1980, pp. 49—54.

Morgan, Ellen, 'Alienation of the Woman Writer in *The Golden Notebook*', Pratt and Dembo, *Doris Lessing: Critical Studies*, pp. 54–63.

Pickering, Joan, 'Marxism and Madness: the Two Faces of Doris Lessing's Myth', *Modern Fiction Studies*, 26, spring 1980, pp. 17–30.

Porter, Nancy M., 'A Way of Looking at Doris Lessing', in N. Hoffman, C. Secor and A. Tinsley (eds), *Female Studies VI: Closer to the Ground*, New York, Feminist Press, 1972, pp. 123–39.

Pratt, Annis, 'Woman and Nature in Modern Fiction', *Contemporary Literature* 13, autumn 1972, pp. 476–90.

Rapping, Elayne A., 'Unfree Women: Feminism in Doris Lessing's novels', *Women's Studies*, 3, 1975, pp. 29–44.

Rushforth, Leonie, 'Doris Lessing. The Individual and its Community: a New Kind of Politics', *Bananas*, no. 14, spring 1979, pp. 36–8.

Scanlan, Margaret, 'Memory and Continuity in the Seris Novel: in Example of *Children of Violence*', *Modern Fiction Studies*, 26, spring 1980, pp. 75–85.

Spencer, Sharon, 'Femininity and the Woman Writer: Doris Lessing's *The Golden Notebook* and the *Diary* of Anais Nin', *Women's Studies*, 1, 1973, pp. 247–57.

Sprage, Claire, ' "Without Contraries Is No Progression.": Doris Lessing's *The Four-Gated City*', *Modern Fiction Studies*, 26, spring 1980, pp. 99–116.

Sukenick, Lynn, 'Reason and Feeling in Doris Lessing's Fiction', in Pratt and Dembo, *Doris Lessing: Critical Studies*, pp. 98–118.

Sullivan, Alvin, '*The Memoirs of a Survivor*: Lessing's Notes towards a Supreme Fiction', *Modern Fiction Studies*, 26, spring 1980, pp. 157–62.

Swingewood, Alan, 'Structure and ideology in the Novels of Doris Lessing', in Diana Laurenson (ed.), *The Sociology of Literature: Applied Studies*, University of Keele Press, 1978, pp. 38–54.

Vlastos, Marion, 'Doris Lessing and R. D. Laing: Psychopolitics and Prophesy', *PMLA*, 91, March 1976, pp. 245–58.

Zak, Michele W., '*The Grass is Singing*: a Little Novel about the Emotions', in Pratt and Dembo, *Doris Lessing: Critical Studies*, pp. 64–73.

Theses and dissertations

Bordner, Marsha Stanfield, 'The Woman as Artist in Twentieth Century Fiction', PhD, Ohio State University, 1979.

Brooks, Ellen W., 'Fragmentation and Integration: a Study of Doris Lessing's Fiction', dissertation, New York University, 1971.

Burkom, Selma, 'A Reconciliation of Opposites; a Study of the Works of Doris Lessing', dissertation, University of Minnesota, 1970.

Burniston, Steven, 'A Reading of Doris Lessing's *The Golden Notebook*', PhD, Centre for Contemporary Cultural Studies, University of Birmingham, 1979.

Cederstrom, Lorelai, 'From Marxism to Myth: a Developmental Study of the Novels of Doris Lessing', PhD, University of Manitoba, 1978.

Draine, Mary Elizabeth, 'Stages of Consciousness in Doris Lessing's Fiction', dissertation, Temple University, 1977.

Holmquist, Ingrid, 'From Society to Nature: a Study of Doris Lessing's *Children of Violence*', PhD, Univesity of Gotenborg, 1980.

Kildahl, Karen A., 'The Political and Apocalyptical Novels of Doris Lessing: a Critical Study of *Children of Violence*, *The Golden Notebook*, and *Briefing for a Descent into Hell*', PhD, University of Washington, 1974.

Kurilof, Peshe C., 'Doris Lessing: the Practice of Realism in the Novel', PhD, Bryn Mawr College, 1979.

Seligman, Claudia Dee, 'The Autobiographical Novels of Doris Lessing', dissertation, Tufts University, 1976.

Sharran, C. P., 'Aspects of Freedom in Southern African Fiction: a Study of the Works of Olive Schreiner, Sarah Millin, Doris Lessing and Nadine Gordimer', External PhD, University of London, 1979.

Sims, Susan K., 'Repetition and Evolution; an Examination of Themes and Structures in the Novels of Doris Lessing', PhD, University of Oregon, 1978.

Wichmann, Brigitte, 'From Sex-Role Identification towards Androgyny: a Study of the Major Works of Simone de Beauvoir, Doris Lessing and Christa Wolf', PhD, Purdue University, 1978.

Index

Aaronovitch, Sam, 31
Africa, 2, 17, 18, 22, 23, 36, 45, 59,
  78, 94, 97, 99, 100, 102, 103,
  112, 129, 130, 136, 145, 153,
  164, 219, 221, 223; African
  literature, 22, 24, 219; Lessing as
  'African' writer, 2, 3, 221
aid to Spain, 44
Allah, 167, 174, 179
allegory, 5, 14, 38, 164, 173, 195
America, United States of, 19, 27,
  31, 212; American film industry,
  230, 232, 233; 'American threat
  to British culture', see Arena;
  Americans, 54
Amis, Kingsley, 16, 33; 'Socialism
  and the Intellectuals', 16
Anderson, Lindsay, 35, 231; 'Get
  Out and Push', see also
  Declaration
Angry Young Men, the, 2, 16, 32,
  58, 62
anima, 200, 202
animus, 200, 202
apartheid, 2, 19; see also colour bar
Arberry, A. J., 166
archetype, 9, 21, 194, 195, 200,
  201, 202; archetypal, 198;
  archetypal fiction, 215–17
Arena, 27, 30; 'The American
  Threat to British Culture', 31;
  'Britain's Cultural Heritage', 31;
  'Essays on Socialist Realism and

the British Cultural Heritage',
  31
Artaud, A., 115
artist, 4, 9, 140, 209; position of,
  9–11, 15, 18, 23, 27–35
astrological symbolism, 202–4
Atman, 174
Attar, Farid ud-Din, 164;
  Parliament of the Birds, 164
Auden, W. H., 33, 48
Austen, Jane, 115, 116, 209, 216;
  Pride and Prejudice, 116
autobiography, 18, 63, 64, 78, 227;
  autobiographical writing, 14,
  18, 62–4, 77–129
Ayer, A. J., 185; Central Questions
  of Philosophy, 185

Babousse, Henri, 228; Hell, 228
Babylon, 230
Balzac, H. de, 17, 90, 95, 96, 126–7
Barker, A. L., 217
Barthes, R., 125
Bawden, Nina, 217
Beauvoir, Simone de, 8, 54–5,
  58–72, 105; All Said and Done,
  68; Force of Circumstance, 60, 62;
  The Mandarins, 54, 66–8;
  Memoirs of a Dutiful Daughter, 65,
  67; The Prime of Life, 60, 71; The
  Second Sex, 8, 54, 55, 58, 64, 66,
  105
Beckett, Samuel, 129

Belinsky, V. G., 4
Benjamin, Walter, 4
Bentley, Phyllis, 217
Benson, Stella, 217
Berger, John, 24, 26, 35, 129; *A Painter of Our Time*, 24
Beyond the Fragments, 56
Bible, 86, 180; Biblical, 180, 181; the Gospels, 180; Gospel of St John, 180; Gospel of St Luke, 180–2; biblical Martha, 180–2; biblical Mary, 180–2
Bildungsroman, 90, 92, 95, 165
black nationalism, 20
Blake, W., 21, 52
Book of Changes, The, 198
Bowen, Elizabeth, 215, 217
Braine, John, 26
Brecht, B., 4, 14
British critical establishment, 2, 3, 212, 214, 220, 221
Brontë, Anne, 209
Brontë, Charlotte, 6, 106, 209; *Jane Eyre*, 106; *Villette*, 106
Brontë, Emily, 209
Brooks, Jeremy, 1, 2, 4
Brophy, Brigid, 218
Buddhism, 169
Burney, Fanny, 209
Burns, R., 19
Byron, George Gordon, Lord, 19

Campaign for Nuclear Disarmament, 25, 34
Camus, A., 61, 117; *L'Etranger*, 117; *L'Homme Revolté*, 61
Carribean, 3
Caudwell, Christopher, 27
Chekov, A., 17
Christ, Carol P., 180; *Diving Deep and Surfacing*, 180
Christian, 166, 170, 176, 180, 181–3, 193; Christianity, 168, 176, 180; Christian symbolism, 181–3, 193
Cloud of Unknowing, The, 181, 184, 186

Cold War, 15, 16, 17, 34, 46–9, 59, 76, 83
Colette, 90
Collins, Cannon, 25
colonial, 2, 14, 17, 22, 23, 24, 26, 27, 44, 219–22; anti-colonial, 2, 26, 219–22; colonialism, 18–21, 219, 220, 224; the colonies, 19
colour bar, 19, 23, 219; *see also* apartheid; race, racism
communism, 10–13, 19, 20, 27, 45, 47, 48, 50; Communist Party of Great Britain, 20, 24–7, 32, 44–7, 49–50, 54, 55, 70; Lessing's relation to communism, 19–37, 219–21; communist tradition, 24–34, 43–56; Twentieth Congress of the Soviet Communst Party, 24, 44, 45; *see also*, Left; socialism
Comte, A., 127
Compton-Burnett, Ivy, 217
Conviction, 35
Cooper, Lettice, 217
culture, 15, 27, 31, 35, 102–3, 213; black African, 22, 24, 102; British literary, 206, 209, 219–23; British national, 27–8, 30, 31, 103, 218–19; dominant, 18–19, 22, 213–14, 220; mass, 31, 35; working-class, 31, 35; white settler, 19, 21–4, 102, 222; *see also* feminism

Daly, L., 47
Daily Worker, 44, 50
Daylight, 24; *see also World News*
Declaration, 16, 29, 35, 62; 'Get Out and Push', 35; 'The Small Personal Voice', 16, 17, 19, 35, 62; 'They Call it Cricket', 16
detective fiction, 213, 223
Dialectics of Liberation Conference, 178
Dick, Kay, 217
Dickens, Charles, 19, 89, 95; *Bleak House, Our Mutual Friend*, 89
Dostoevsky, F., 17

Drabble, Margaret, 56
dystopia, 224, 227; dystopian
  fiction, 222

Eliot, George, 91, 106, 115, 216;
  Daniel Deronda, 116;
  Middlemarch, 115–16; *The Mill on
  the Floss*, 106, 110, 116
Eliot, T. S., 33, 129
empire, 2; novels of empire
  tradition, 221; *see also* colonial
English, Isobel, 217
'Englishness', *see* British national
  culture
exile, 2, 20, 24, 59, 78, 103, 129,
  184, 206, 219, 221
Existentialism, 8, 31, 61, 69, 125,
  147

fable, 194, 195
fabulation, 6, 227
Fairburns, Zoe, 218, 223–4;
  Benefits, 218
fairy tale, 195
Federation of Northern and
  Southern Rhodesia and
  Nyasaland, 19
feminism, 9, 21, 50, 54, 55, 57–8,
  162, 177, 197, 207, 213, 223;
  Lessing's relation to, 9, 53–6,
  71–3, 104, 219; feminist
  criticism, 12, 207, 211, 213–14;
  feminist culture, 223–4
Flaubert, G., 122
*For a Lasting Peace and a People's
  Democracy*, 45
Fox, Ralph, 27–9; *The Novel and
  the People*, 27
Freeman, Gillian, 217
Friedan, Betty, 55; *The Feminine
  Mystique*, 55
Freud, S., 105, 125, 210; Freudian,
  52; Oedipus complex, 201

Gaskell, Elizabeth, 209
Gibbons, Stella, 218
God, 167, 174, 179, 182, 185, 187
God That Failed, The, 16, 40n, 48

Golding, William, 33; *Lord of the
  Flies*, 230
Gothic, 6, 223
Grassic, Gibbon, L., 27

Hammett, Dashiell, 62
Hall, Stuart, 33; 'Inside the Whale
  Again', 33
Hardy, Thomas, 6; *Jude the
  Obscure*, 91
Heinemann, Margot, 24
Hemingway, Ernest, 62
Hepburn, Ronald, 186
Hill, Christopher, 26
Hilton, Rodney, 26
Hindu ideas about karma, 193
Hobsbawm, Eric, 26
Holtby, Winifred, 216
Hoggart, Richard, 32
Howard, Elizabeth Jane, 217
Hungary, 19, 24, 46
Hyvrard, Jean, 115

insanity, 39, 59, 68–70, 85, 115,
  139, 145, 173–7; *see also*
  psychiatry
Irigaray, Luce, 104
Islam, 166, 168, 179; *see also* Sufi,
  Sufism

Jabès, 129
James, Henry, 111, 129
Jameson, Storm, 217
Jelinek, Estelle, 63–4
Johnson, Pamela Hansford, 217,
  218
Jones, Lewis, 27
Joyce, James, 7, 103, 106, 125, 129;
  Ulysses, 7
Jung, C. G., 22; Jungian, 21, 167,
  184; *see also* psychoanalysis;
  unconscious

Kafka, Franz, 125
Kavan, Anna, 217
Kermode, Frank, 182
Kettle, Arnold, 31–2
Khrushchev, 24, 44, 46

Koestler, A., 16, 33
Kristeva, Julia, 105, 133n

Labour Party, 16, 19, 34, 47;
    Labour movement, 19, 26;
    Southern Rhodesian Labour
    Party, 21
Lacan, Jacques, 105
Laing, R. D., 54, 69, 177–9, 187;
    The Divided Self, 177; 'The
    Obvious', 178
Lambert, J. W., 3, 4
Lawrence, D. H., 3, 6, 51, 52,
    'Lawrentian', 68, 79; *Fantasia of
    the Unconscious*, 33
Leavis, F. R. and Q. D., 30
Left, the, 13–14, 17, 25, 26, 32, 38,
    50; *see also* communism; New
    Left; socialism
Left Review, 44
Le Guin, Ursula, 191, 223
Lehmann, Rosamund, 215
Lessing, Doris: novels, *Briefing for
    a Descent into Hell*, 89, 115, 165;
    Canopus in Argos – Archives, 6,
    12, 182, 191, 209, 221, 224, 233;
    Children of Violence, 5–6, 26,
    75–130, 165, 221, 223; *Five*, 2,
    25; *The Four-Gated City*, 6, 70,
    76, 77, 80, 83–6, 89, 92, 93, 98,
    99, 110, 112–14, 118, 119, 121,
    128, 165, 169, 170, 172, 176–7,
    180–1, 183–6; *The Golden
    Notebook*, 1, 2, 4, 7–14, 21, 24,
    27, 33, 35, 37, 38, 42–56, 61–5,
    69–72, 85, 86, 96, 101, 103, 104,
    110, 124, 165, 177, 184, 209,
    218, 221; *The Grass is Singing*, 2,
    21, 59, 87, 88, 100, 124, 145, 219;
    Landlocked, 70, 76, 79, 82–3, 93,
    95, 101, 108–11, 117, 118, 120,
    122; *The Marriages Between
    Zones Three, Four and Five*, 13,
    191, 194–204; *Martha Quest*, 3,
    59, 76, 78, 81, 82, 87, 94, 99,
    112, 113, 115, 122; *The Memoirs
    of a Survivor*, 6, 13, 77, 97, 165,
    176, 180, 182–3, 185, 227, 230; *A
    Proper Marriage*, 4, 76, 79, 94,
    100, 101, 107, 111, 112, 119, 122;
    Retreat to Innocence, 24, 26; *A
    Ripple from the Storm*, 76, 77, 79,
    93–5, 99, 107, 112, 118; *Shikasta*,
    98, 111, 123–5, 191, 192, 194,
    225; plays, *Each in his own
    Wilderness*, 26; short stories, *A
    Man and Two Women* (volume),
    13, 135–63; *This Was the Old
    Chief's Country* (volume), 3, 219;
    'Between Men', 64, 146; 'The
    Day Stalin Died', 26; 'Each
    Other', 146–8, 151–2; 'England
    Versus England', 27, 154, 155;
    'How I Finally Lost my Heart',
    143, 157–8, 161; 'Note for a Case
    History', 149, 158–62; 'The Old
    Chief Mshlanga', 222; 'One off
    the Short List', 135, 136,
    138–43, 145, 147–50, 152; 'The
    Pig' ('The Trinket Box'), 104,
    109; 'The Story of Two Dogs',
    136, 139, 145, 162; 'The Sun
    between their Feet', 26, 101,
    136, 156; 'To Room Nineteen',
    156; 'Two Potters', 161;
    'Woman on a Roof', 143–5, 162;
    documentary writing, *Going
    Home*, 18–20, 22, 24, 77, 80–2,
    99, 110, 153, 221; *In Pursuit of the
    English*, 18, 27, 59, 77, 104, 221;
    essays, reviews and articles,
    'African Interiors', 22, 40; 'An
    Ancient Way to New Freedom',
    165, 167–70, 177, 180; 'Desert
    Child', 22, 40; 'In the World,
    Not of It', 165; 'Smart Set
    Socialists', 36–7; 'The Small
    Personal Voice', 16, 17, 19, 28,
    35, 62
Lévi-Strauss, C., 127
liberal humanism, 5, 6, 7, 9, 17, 25;
    see also radical liberalism;
    socialist humanism
Lindsay, Jack, 27–30, 31; *After the
    Thirties*, 27, 29, 30
London, 15, 83, 89, 92

Lukács, Georg, 4, 27, 28, 29

MacCabe, Colin, 116
Macaulay, Rose, 215, 217
mandala, 202
Mankowitz, W., 26
Mannin, Ethel, 217
Manning, Olivia, 217
Marquez, Dante Gabriel, 114, 127; *Hundred Years of Solitude*, 127, 128
Marx, 125; Marxism, 14, 16, 20, 25, 30, 32, 50, 62, 70, 127, 179, 184; Marxist criticism, 213
matriarchy, 201, 202; matriarchal, 196
Maurier, Daphne du, 218
Melly, George, 26
Memoirs of a Survivor, the making of the film, 227–40
meta-language, 116, 165
Meyer Spack, Patricia, 210
Mitchison, Naomi, 191, 217
modernism, 10, 92
Mohammed, 168
montage, 4, 229, 237
Morris, William, 4, 21, 27, 201
Mortimer, Penelope, 63, 217
Murdoch, Iris, 63, 218; *Under the Net*, 63
Musil, R., 103, 118
muting, theory of, 211
mystic, 167, 179, 181; mystical, 71, 77, 87, 91, 165, 172, 176, 177, 179, 182, 211; mysticism, 86, 165, 167, 170, 172, 179, 180, 183–6
myth, 6, 12, 18, 19, 194; mythic, 9, 12, 193; mythology, 21

Nato, 15; 'Natopolitan apathy', 33
Nerval, Gerard de, 115
New Left, 32, 34, 44, 47; New Left Clubs, 47; *see also* communist; Left; socialism
New Left Review, 25, 26, 35
New Reasoner 25–6, 35, 44,

47–8; 'State Patronage of the Arts', 35
New Statesman, 2, 22, 26, 36, 37; *see also* Lessing, essays, reviews and articles
nouveau roman, 62, 125

O'Brien, Edna, 58, 63
Orwell, George, 7, 16, 18, 32, 33, 37, 48
Osborne, John, 16, 26, 33, 37
Out of Apathy, 25, 48; 'Outside the Whale', 25, 48

parable, 162, 172, 204
patriarchy, 201, 202, 220; patriarchal relations, 213
Piercy, Marge, 223, 224
Pinter, Harold, 37
Poe, Edgar Allen, 115
Polish workers' uprising (1953), 24
Post, L. van Der, 22; *The Heart of the Hunter*, 22; *The Lost World of the Kalahari*, 22
Pound, Ezra, 129
Priestley, J. B., 25
Proust, Marcel, 62, 90, 93, 110, 125; *Un Amour du Swann*, 94; *Le Côtés des Guermantes*, 94; *La Prisonnier*, 94; *A la Recherche du temps perdu*, 90
psychiatry, 49, 59, 68–70, 166, 173–7; *see also* insanity; Laing
psychoanalysis, 27, 54, 69, 184, 185; Jungian psychoanalysis, 21–2, 184; *see also* Freud; Jung; unconscious
Pym, Barbara, 217

race, 21, 207, 209, 219; racism, 2, 18, 21, 40n, 59, 219; race consciousness, 21–4, 76, 153; *see also* apartheid; colour bar
radical liberalism, 19, 21, 76; *see also* liberal humanism
realism, 3, 7, 14, 26, 28, 29, 38, 62, 64, 122, 136, 185, 191, 194, 214, 217; classic realism, 17, 28,

125; critical realism, 5, 27;
Lessing's commitment to, 10,
17, 62; moral realism, 216–18;
nineteenth-century realism, 5,
22, 23, 38, 103; psychological
realism, 96; social realism, 222;
socialist realism, 10, 14, 27, 29,
31
Reasoner, The, 24–6
Renault, Mary, 218
revelation, 6, 183
Rhodesia, 20, 26, 76, 92, 100, 103;
Lessing as white Rhodesian
exile, 2, 19, 22–3, 59, 102, 207,
218–22; Southern Rhodesia, 15,
17, 20, 58, 219; *see also* Africa;
Lessing as 'African' writer;
culture, white settler; exile
Robbe-Grillet, Alain, 113; *La
Jalousie*, 62, 113
romance genre, 213–17; romantic
fiction, 157, 194, 195, 213,
215–16; Romantic tradition, 15,
21, 27; Romanticism, 52, 86
Royal Court Theatre, 27, 36
Rumi, 170, 176
Russ, Joanna, 223
Russell, Bertrand, 25
Russian Formalists, 4, 195

St John of the Cross, 175
Salisbury, 19, 20, 76, 83, 111
Samuel, Raphael, 44
Sarraute, Natalie, 62, 117
Sartre, Jean-Paul, 9, 14, 35, 61, 66,
68–70; *The Age of Reason*, 68;
Being and Nothingness, 66, 68;
Nausea, 94; *What is Literature?*,
14, 35
Saussure, F. de, 125
Saville, John, 24–5
Schreiner, Olive, 21, 102, 164,
173; 'The Hunter', 164, 173; *The
Story of an African Farm*, 164,
165, 168
science fiction, 191, 194, 213, 223
Scott, Walter, 95, 111, 128
Scrutiny, 30

Sedgwick, Peter, 44
sensibility, mode of, 214, 217
sexuality, 5, 8, 9, 50–4, 65–8, 72,
78, 106, 197
Shah, Idries, 166, 167, 169–70,
179, 180; *The Sufis*, 120; *The
Way of the Sufi*, 166–7
Sharp, Margery, 218
Shelley, P. B., 19, 21
Showalter, Elaine, 212, 214; *A
Literature of Their Own*, 213
Snow, C. P., 3
space fiction, 12, 191, 195
Spark, Muriel, 218
Spender, Stephen, 16, 33
socialism, 4, 10, 25, 30, 30–1, 35–7;
see also Left; New Left;
communism
socialist humanism, 25, 27, 29; *see
also* liberal humanism; radical
liberalism
socialist intellectuals, position of,
15, 26–9, 32, 35–7; *see also* artist,
position of
South Africa, 20, 102
Soviet Union, 20, 24, 46, 48
Stalin, 26, 45, 46; Stalinism, 15, 16,
17, 21, 24, 26, 48
Stendal, 17, 91, 96
stereotype, 65, 195, 199, 211
Stirling, Monica, 217
Sufi, 88, 118, 164–75, 180, 182;
Sufism, 165–74, 176, 178, 184,
185; teaching-story, 164, 165,
169, 171, 184
Suvin, Darko, 194

Tass (Soviet news agency), 19
Taylor, Elizabeth, 212, 217
Tel Quel, 125
Thompson, E. P., 24–6, 29, 33,
48–9; 'Outside the Whale', *see
Out of Apathy*
Tindall, Gillian, 63
Tippett, M., 26
Tolstoy. L. N., 17, 32, 91, 103,
106; *Anna Karenina*, 23;
Resurrection, 91

Toynbee, Philip, 26
Tribune, 26
Trickett, Rachel, 217
Turgenev, Ivan, 17

unconscious, 21, 22, 33, 68, 111,
167, 170, 200, 201, 204;
collective unconscious, 5, 21,
167, *see also* archetype; Jung
unconscious gender influence, 219
Universities and Left Review, 17, 25,
33, 35, 44; 'On the Uses of
Literacy', 35; 'Socialism and the
Intellectuals', 35
Upanishads, 175
Utopia, 197, 201, 224; Utopian
fiction, 223–4; Utopian
thought, 6, 27, 29, 198

Vambe, Lawrence, 20; *From
Rhodesia to Zimbabwe*, 20
Verité, La, 58

Wain, John, 33
Walters, Margaret, 58, 64
West, Alick, 27
West Rebecca, 217
Williams, Raymond, 32, 35, 37–8,
224; *The Long Revolution*, 37–8;
'Utopia and Science Fiction',
224
Wisdom, John, 185
Wittig, Monique, 223
Women's Movement, 5, 9, 52–3,
71, 104, 207, 219
women's writing, 207–24;
'feminine' writing, 103–11
Woolf, Virginia, 92, 99, 104, 106;
Between the Acts, 99
World News, 24, 27, 31

yin and yang, 198, 202

Zimbabwe, 20; *see also* Rhodesia,
Southern Rhodesia